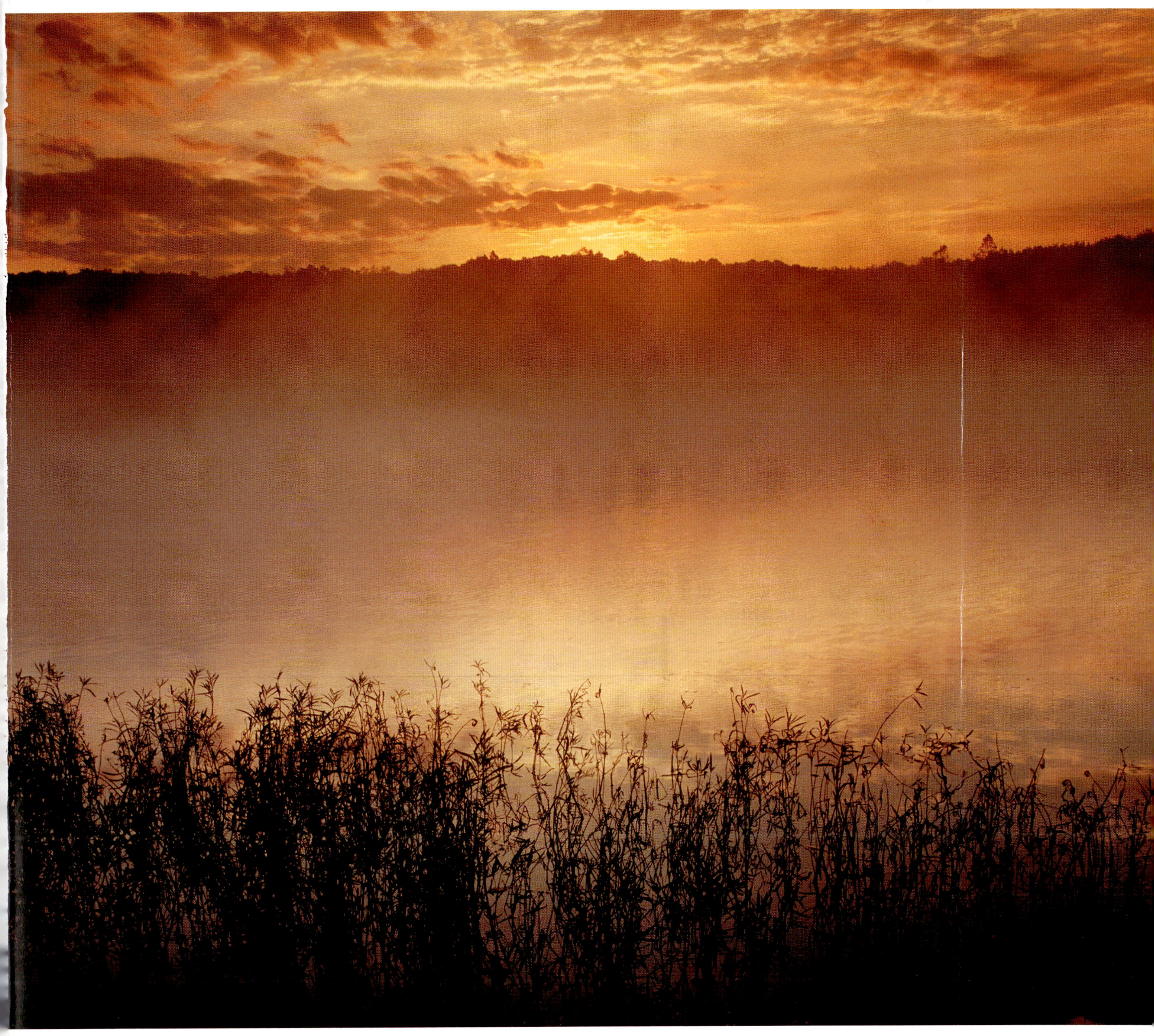

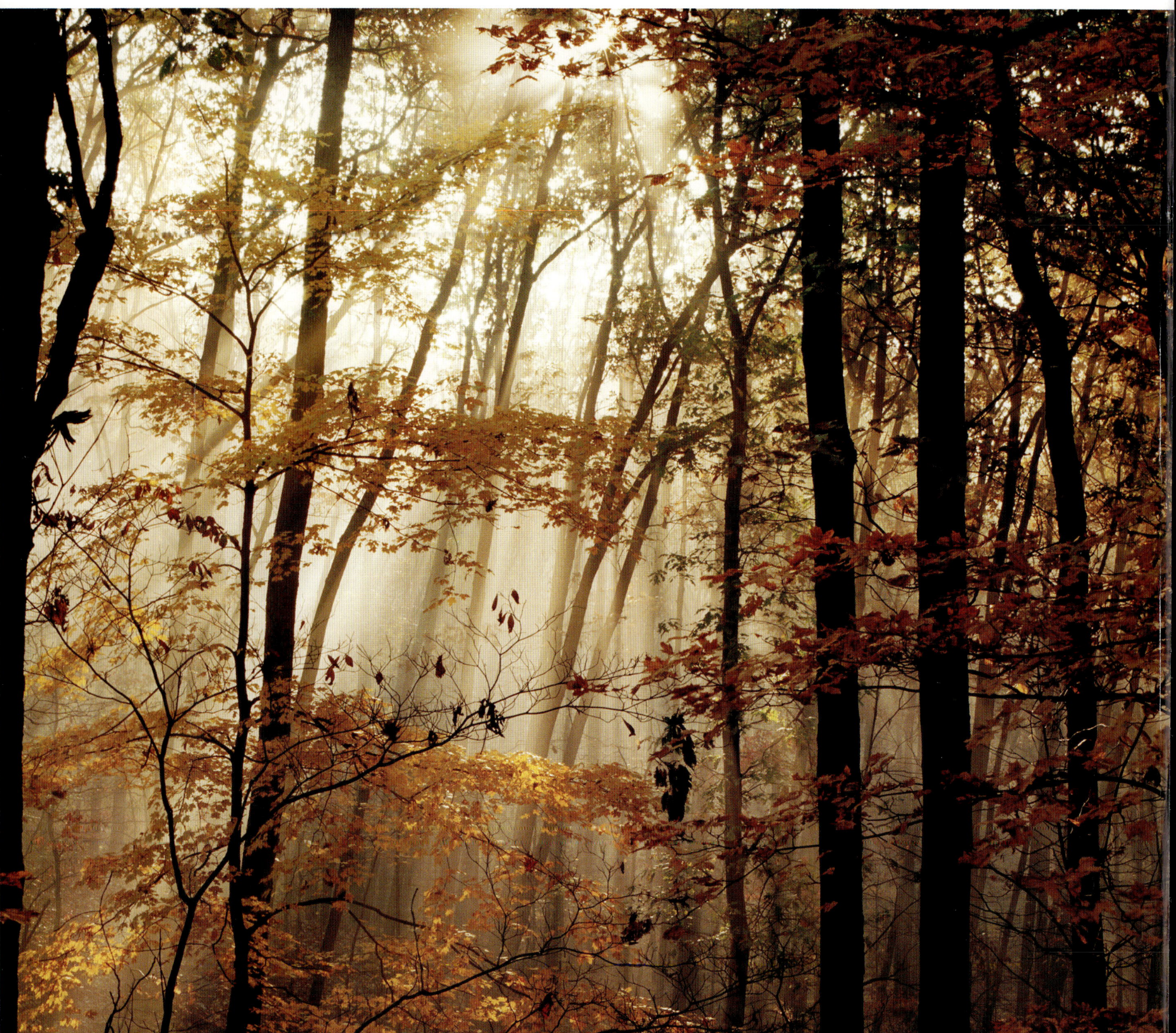

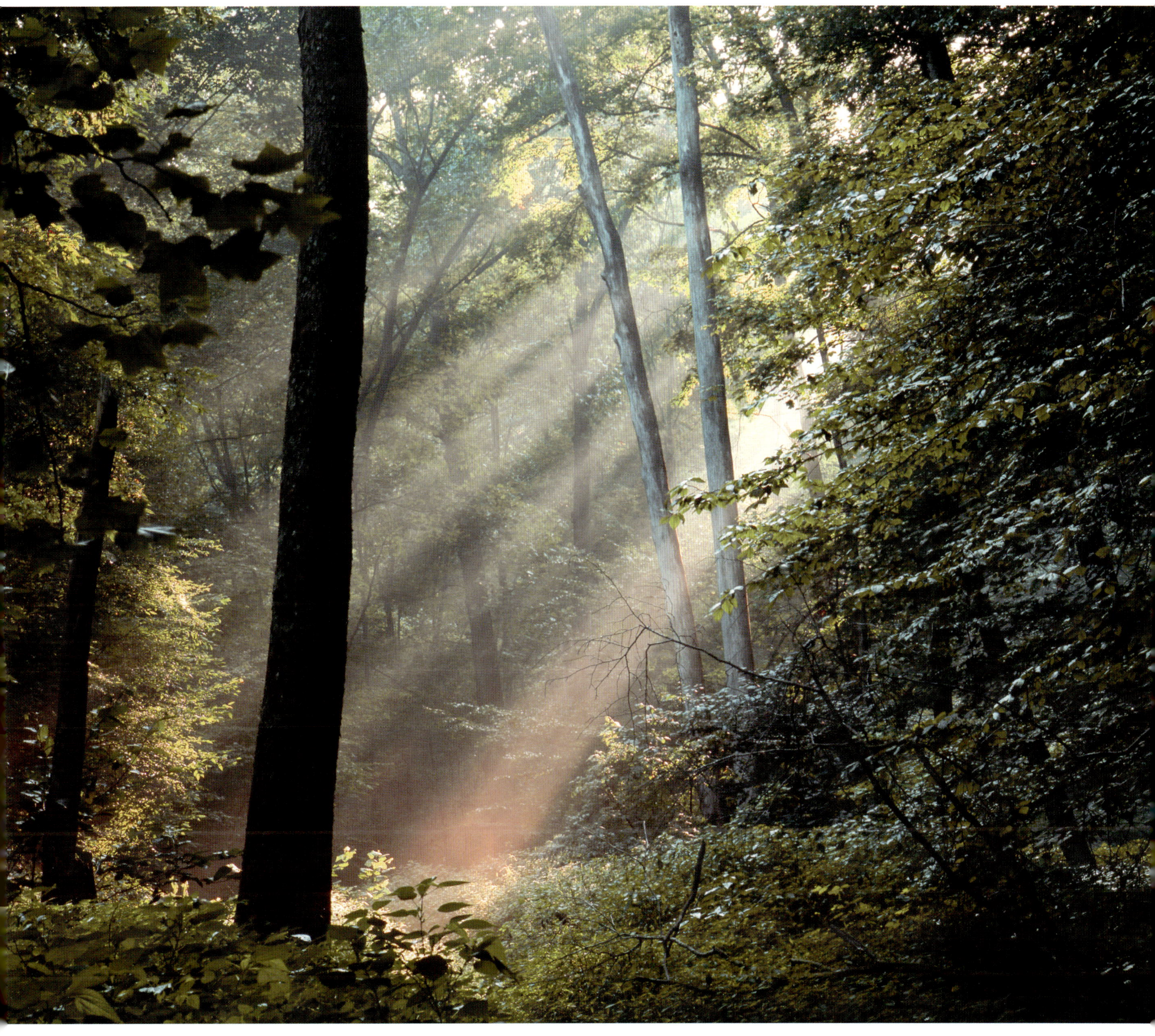

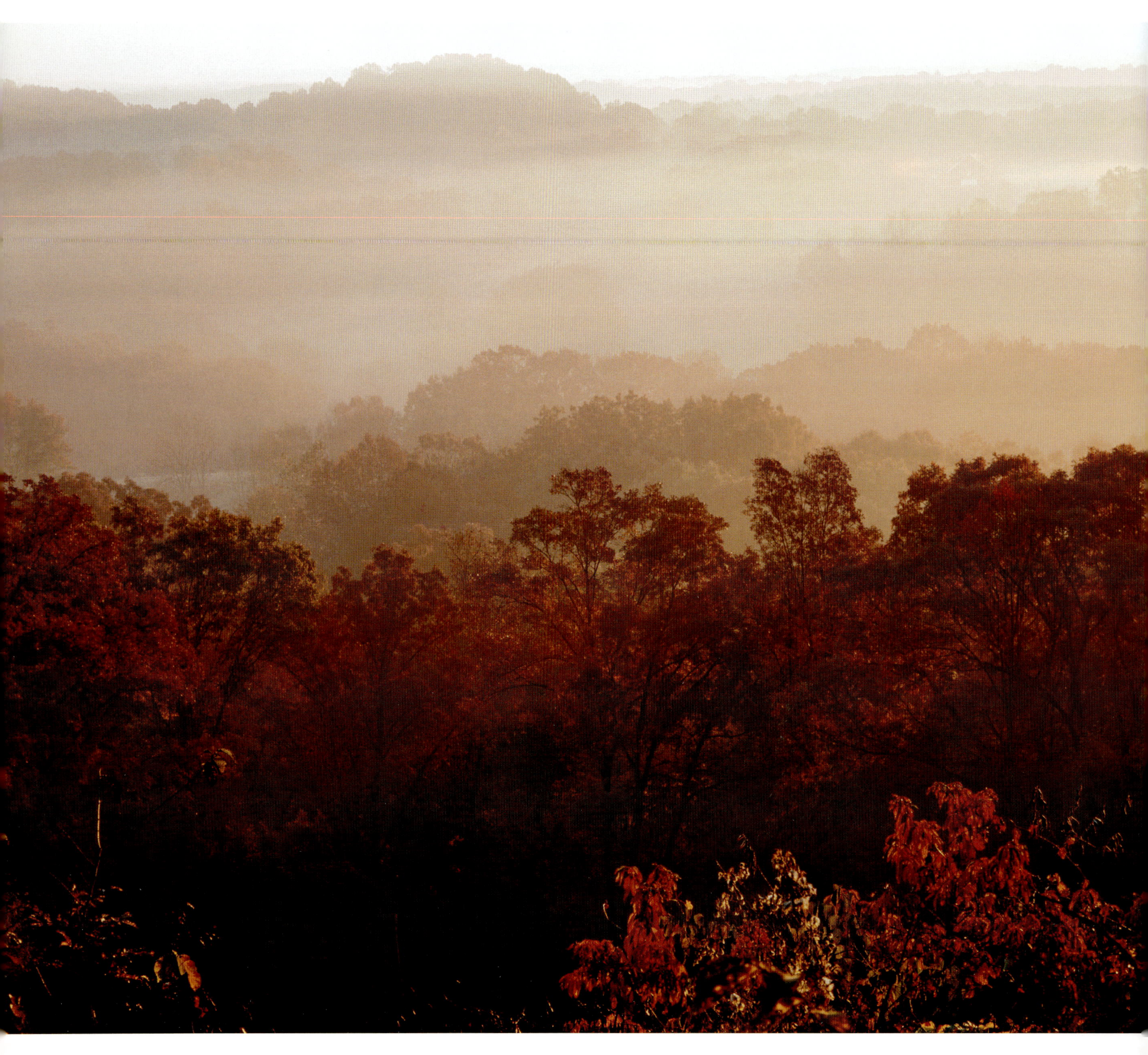

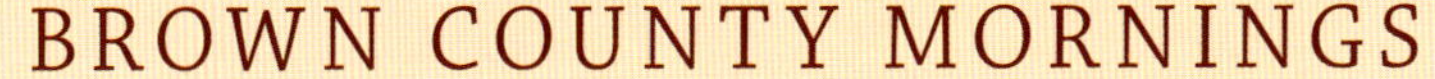

BROWN COUNTY MORNINGS

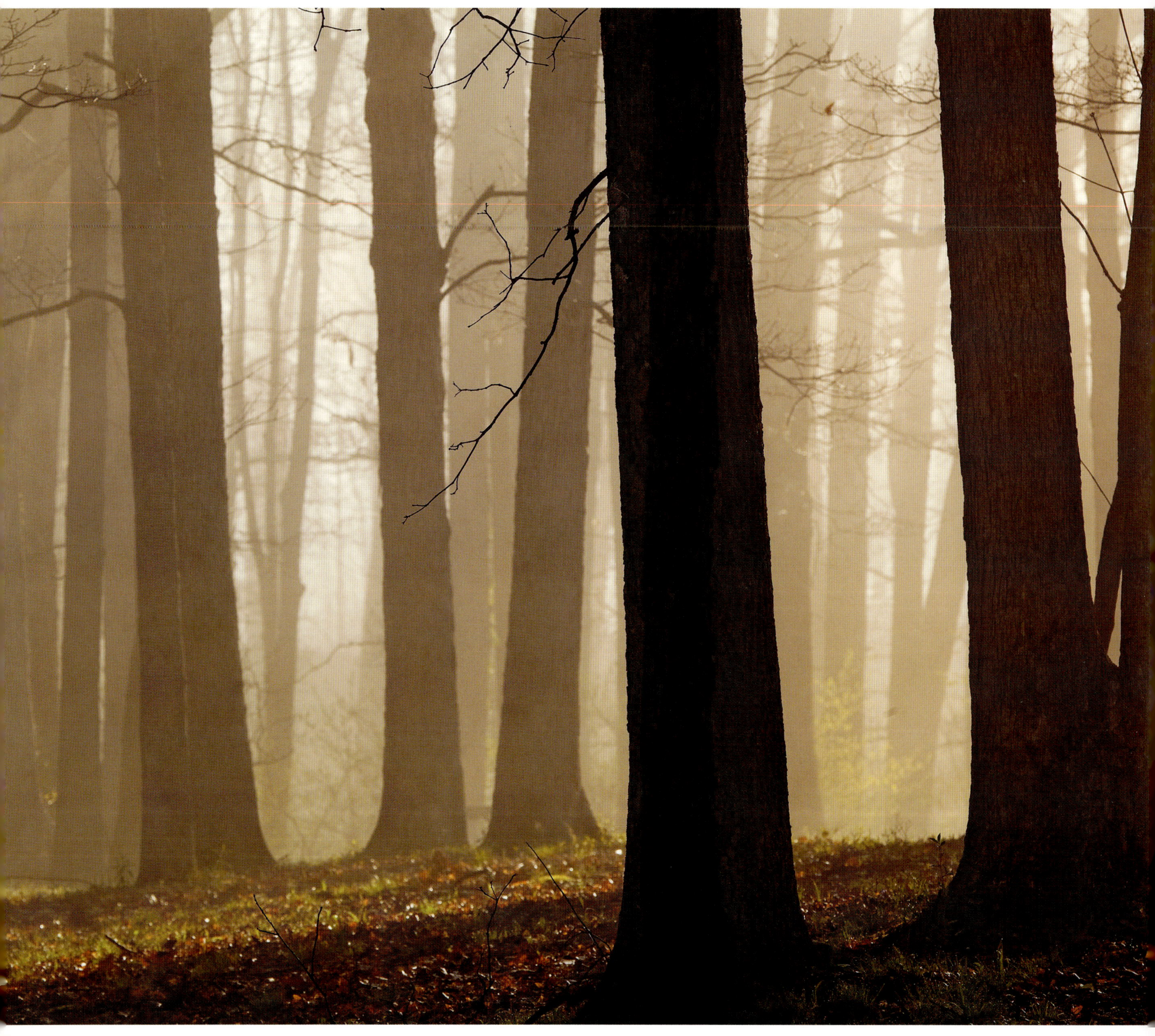

BROWN COUNTY MORNINGS

Gary Moore

GARY MOORE

Foreword by James P. Eagleman

QUARRY BOOKS *an imprint of* INDIANA UNIVERSITY PRESS *Bloomington & Indianapolis*

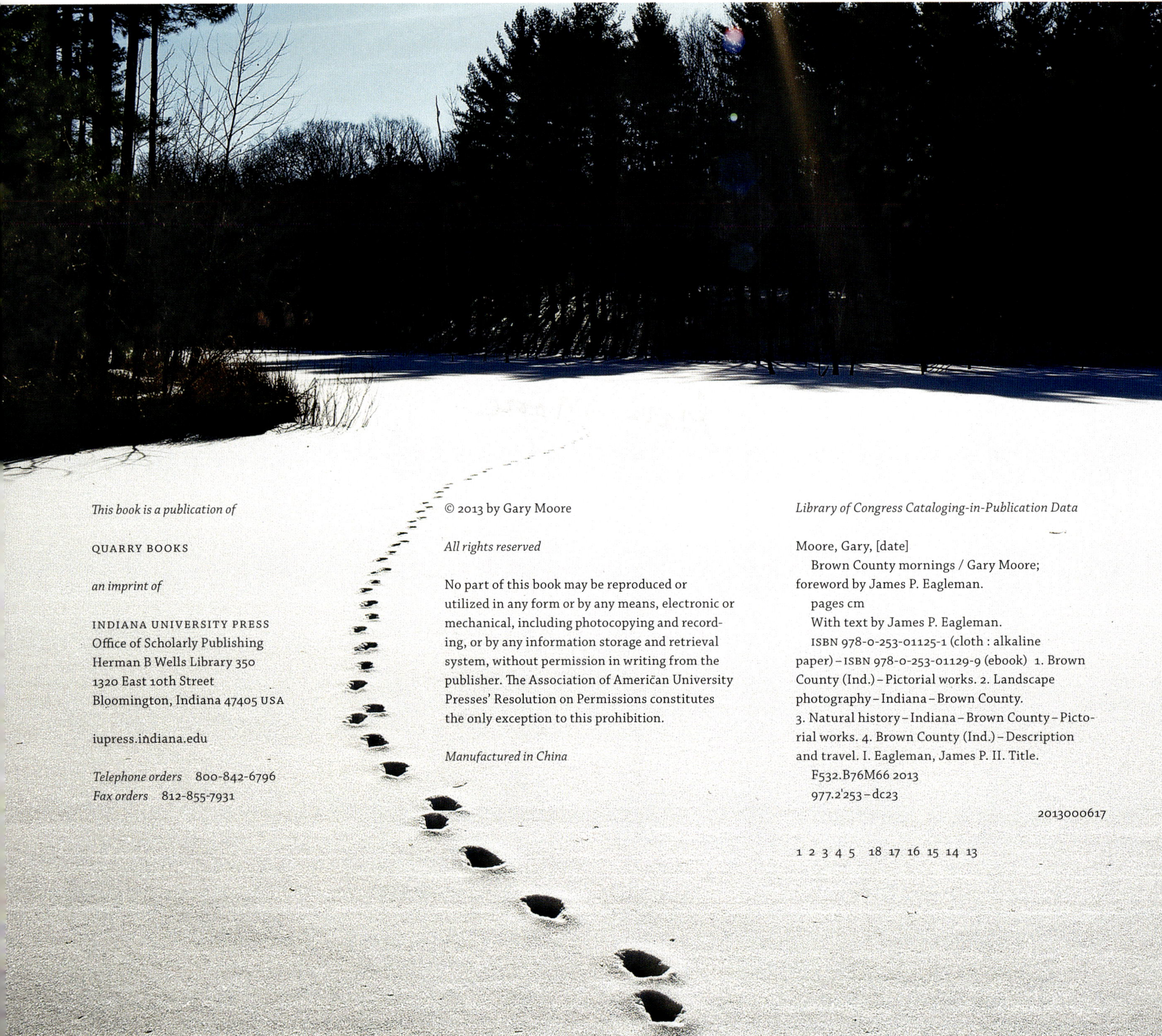

This book is a publication of

QUARRY BOOKS

an imprint of

INDIANA UNIVERSITY PRESS
Office of Scholarly Publishing
Herman B Wells Library 350
1320 East 10th Street
Bloomington, Indiana 47405 USA

iupress.indiana.edu

Telephone orders 800-842-6796
Fax orders 812-855-7931

Manufactured in China

Library of Congress Cataloging-in-Publication Data

Moore, Gary, [date]
Brown County mornings / Gary Moore; foreword by James P. Eagleman.
pages cm
With text by James P. Eagleman.
ISBN 978-0-253-01125-1 (cloth : alkaline paper) – ISBN 978-0-253-01129-9 (ebook) 1. Brown County (Ind.) – Pictorial works. 2. Landscape photography – Indiana – Brown County. 3. Natural history – Indiana – Brown County – Pictorial works. 4. Brown County (Ind.) – Description and travel. I. Eagleman, James P. II. Title.
F532.B76M66 2013
977.2'253 – dc23

2013000617

1 2 3 4 5 18 17 16 15 14 13

CONTENTS

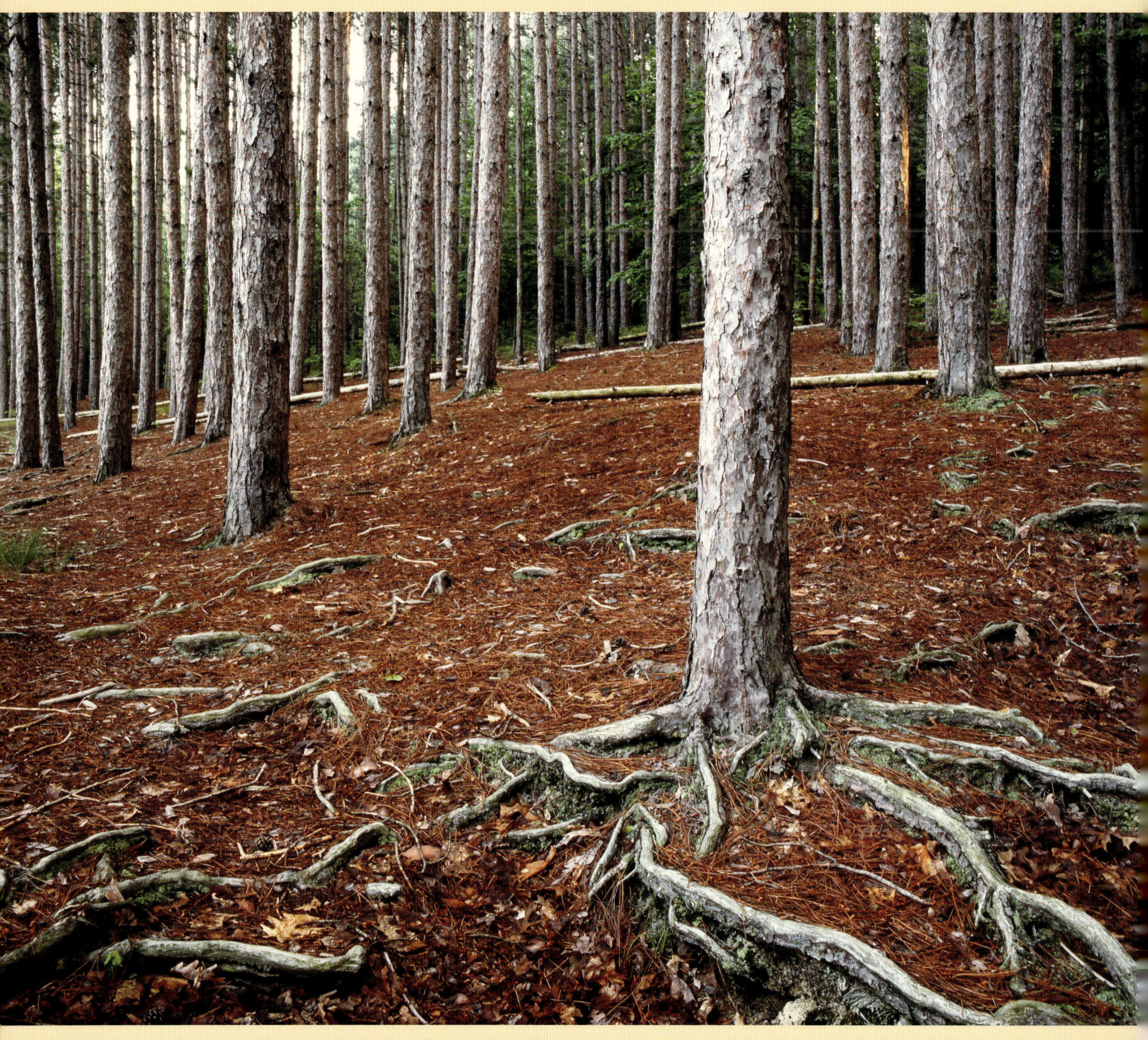

FOREWORD

James P. Eagleman,
Brown County State Park Naturalist

"UP AND AT 'EM!," MY GRAND-DAD, POP-POP, USED TO say. He'd do more work on our hilly, eastern Pennsylvania farm by mid-morning than his less-industrious neighbors, with his alarm clock being the big rooster. He told me he was up and gone when it was still dark, and wondered why it took me so long to get moving.

After an all-night snowstorm one winter, in an attempt to get me up, he'd say, "You'd like to see the trees, I bet."

I grew up reciting poems about trees and reading pioneer stories; visions of smooth-handled tools, rustic cabins, and wooden boats all captivated me. Hillside pines gave us climbing challenges, woodlots a place to play.

Moving to the prairies of east-central Illinois as a teen, I almost forgot what trees looked like. Flat lands with rich soil ("as black as your hat!") replaced pines and hardwoods and created table-top views. Grain elevators and outbuilding silhouettes, partially hidden by miles of corn, could be better seen from a highway overpass, the only elevated spot around.

Since then I realized I was missing a lot, and became a lover of trees.

Morning time is a given for any birder, nature lover, forest walker. True for any spectator, if you wish to beat the crowds, get the best seat, head out with no competition, you are up early. Capturing with camera demands this same mantra. Birders know early morning is best; ravenous after fasting all night, birds feed early and go about life largely undetected. Some mornings an early stroll around the lake or woodlot rewards with fleeting glimpses of animals rarely seen. And who hasn't marveled at the thick haze rising off a remote pond, or spider webs covered with dew?

If you enjoy southern Indiana, wish to recall a favorite hike, or generally like woodland scenes, you have in your hands a wonderful collection of some of Brown County's best. And life-long photographer and forest walker Gary Moore would just as soon have you tote a camera along; he believes that you never know what great picture is just ahead, around the bend.

Brown County's most picturesque woodlands, on both private and public land and photographed throughout the year, are assembled here. All scenes captured were taken before noon, some just after daylight. Gary has tried to keep man-made structures at a minimum in these photos, and only a few livestock are seen. We both ask, where better to represent Indiana's forestland than Brown County? Mention Brown County, Indiana, to any Hoosier and thoughts of forested, rolling hills, fall colors, and rugged ravines come to mind.

As a naturalist, I have talked with many visitors over the years. Questions and comments about trees are some of the most common. To help explain the county's vast, forested acreage, I often show a large image of the Hoosier state taken 400 miles in space. Even from this perspective, and seen on the Indiana map on the evening weather report, the green blob that is the Brown County forest is unmistakable. Biologists call it a "biologic sink," this green space that acts as a magnet to migrating birds and resident animals. As long as its forest canopy is maintained, a joint mission of a local chapter of The Nature Conservancy and the Indiana DNR, we will continue to enjoy its year-round beauty. All agree this beautiful, natural area is worth saving, with land conservation efforts already in place. But beyond the esthetic, it has other value as well.

Brown County is home to rare plants, reptiles, and mammals, some federally listed. Represented here is a large inventory of shrubs, wildflowers, and trees some say equal the diversity of rainforests. There are about 12 species of oak, 3 hickory, 4 dogwood, 3 ash, along with 2 beech, persimmon, red cedar, 4 maple, hackberry, basswood, 2 aspens, several willows, sassafras, river birch, 2 locusts, black cherry, sycamore, 2 elms, black gum, walnut, mulberry, sumac, tulip, etc. with an accompanying herbal layer. The Oak-Hickory and Beech-Maple complex as described by botanists, with hardwood oaks generally occupying the ridge-tops and beech and maple on the slopes, produce some of the best and world-renowned quality hardwoods. Veneer, solid wood furniture, and flooring from Indiana counties continue to be recognized as unsurpassed for durability and beauty.

A walk through any of Brown County's woods, even to the casual observer, might reveal what's happened here. After enjoying a view from any of the several park vistas, I've remarked to visitors that there's probably not a tree within view that's much over 100 years of age. The same is true throughout the county. Luckily for us tree lovers, a few Indiana state parks exhibit stands of old-growth forest, with Turkey Run's forest – the state's largest stand of virgin timber – reaching 600+ years. But Brown County's young forest may surprise people: views of 10 to 15 miles of uninterrupted forest and its internationally-known reputation make it seem ageless.

Having undergone much use and abuse by earlier Hoosiers, many already farming here by the mid-1800s, tremendous quantities of timber were cut off these steep hills. Before a market developed for timber at sawmills along Hoosier streams and rivers, Brown County trees were simply cut and hauled into the bottoms. Workers dragged timber into log heaps that were piled and burned, unattended for weeks. Turning vast forestland into farms might've seemed impossible, especially today when the Brown County forest stretches as far as the eye can see, but they still did it. Removal and eventual exposure of thin soils to wind and rains produced agricultural failure. Once the timber was gone, erosion set in and the land lay in ruin. Unproductive farms were deserted and residents moved on.

Abandoned, then left to recover, brushy fields soon converted to woodlots – first pioneer species like sassafras

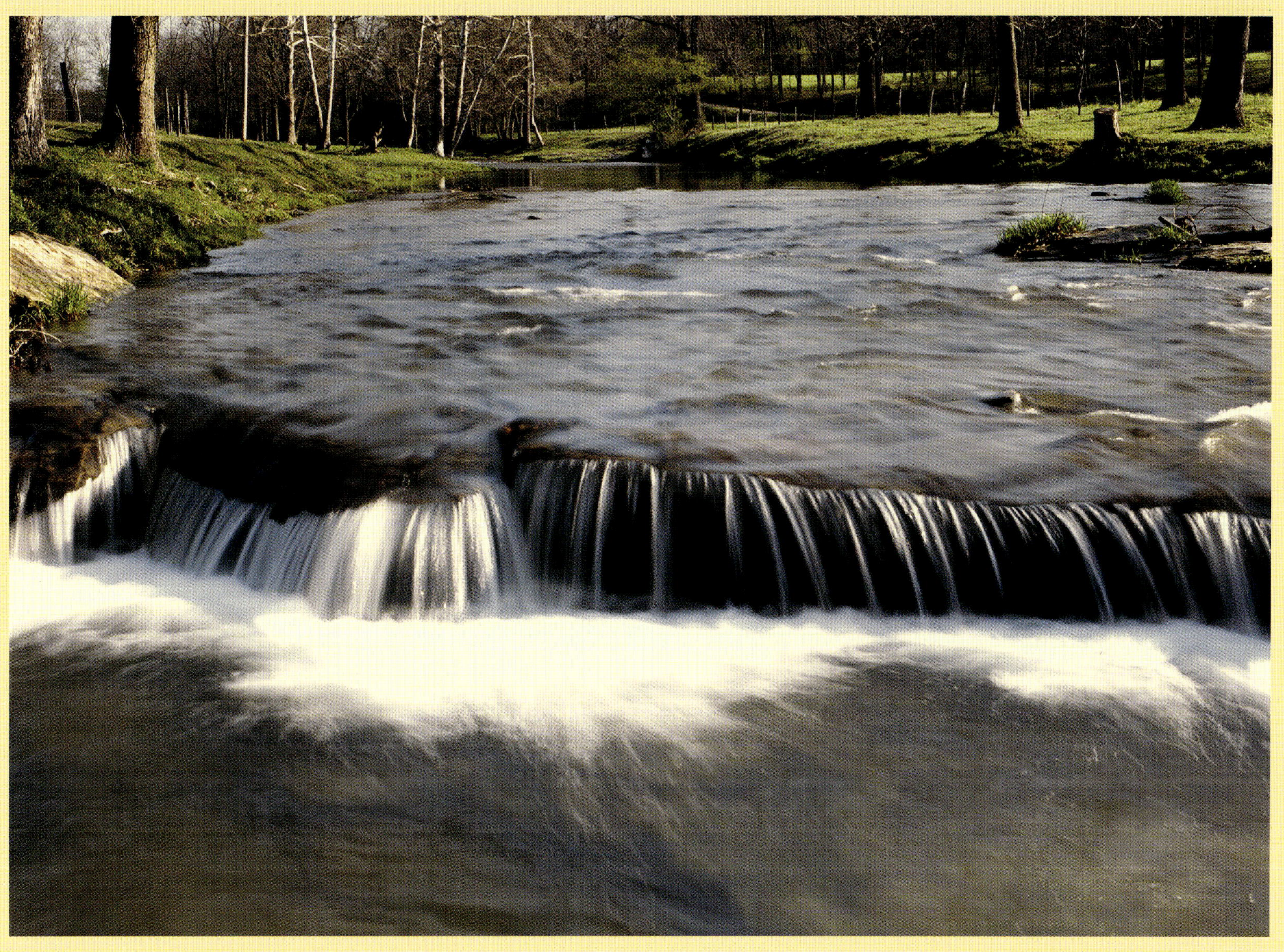

Private Property. *April.*

and sumac, then later, maple and tulip. A young forest like Brown County's can't be thought of as insignificant; it has more nooks and crannies, more ecologic niches that can be exploited by a myriad of creatures – surprisingly more and in greater number than a mature woods.

While on a walk, our attention is drawn into the understory, or maybe overhead. Birds, a hawk, or vulture distract us and cause us to stop. Later while peering into leafy layers – a chaotic mass of limbs, stems, and twigs – we become mesmerized. It's hypnotic to watch leaves and limbs swing and sway. In a high wind, how can they bend to such extremes and not break? Then calmly, sunlight flecks seem to lay on each leaf, shadowing and overlapping. The life processes for a tree are continual during warm weather, but growth in height and circumference only occurs within a 40-day period each spring. Summer is for maintenance, and in late summer leaf drop prepares trees for cold.

We tend to ignore what miraculous thing is happening at our feet. Subterranean burrows in this forested habitat cross over each other; runways made by shrews, mice, and chipmunks that stop and start not only allow travel lanes but aerate the ground. Intermixed with tiny rootlets of trees and shrubs with gradually diminishing roots are soil microbes, fungi, insects, and bacteria that transform decayed leaf litter. This organic material combines into life-supporting soil. Trees use this to sustain life, and along with water, sunlight, and carbon dioxide, make food via the "little factories" we call leaves. The end result is a classic example of recycling at work: the gas we exhale is used by trees. In exchange, they give us oxygen, a by-product of photosynthesis. Can there be a more basic example of a vital relationship between us and the plant world?

When it came time to build, and with a family of big boys, a cabin of Brown County tulip logs seemed the right choice. Tulip poplar cabins built here in the 1800s are still lived-in, sound and resilient to termites. As a conservationist, I knew mature logs harvested by a local sawmill would eventually provide room for more trees to grow. Tops and unused portions started a woodpile that we still use to feed the woodstoves. Hardwood floors stretched over oak floor joists and rafters of beech give a feeling of permanency.

Gary has told me it is the mornings that bring on the best in color, lighting, and awareness. As a first-rate photographer, he knows this. Suggesting that we all get up early and get out, he enjoys much more of the day that previously had been "wasted" while sleeping. And I know this is true; when out with hikers at that early time, they confess they've missed much.

To many park visitors and local people, dialogue about trees, plants, fruits, garden produce, and landscaping is continual, perhaps more here than in other places. While trees may have been taken for granted in early Brown County days and thought of as a hindrance, or more a liability than an asset, fortunately we've changed. Literally "in the way" of what early people had come to do, we now place great value on trees. And why not? They increase worth of private property, improve heating and cooling of our homes, and create privacy and security. They provide homes for insects, birds, nesting sites, and wildlife dens. Trees are planted and watered as one of the first things new home owners do. We take pictures by them, gauge a youngster's growth, and seek shade under them. Like an old friend, we confide and enjoy their company.

To a Brown County homeowner, trees are a trademark, a family site, a legacy.

Gary's mission and mine are similar; we both wish to encourage people to get out and see the beauty of this place. With awareness comes appreciation, then protection and wise use. We both see the benefits and wish to share them, inform others, and encourage their exploration.

It's nothing new or earth-shaking. Set the alarm! Take the camera.

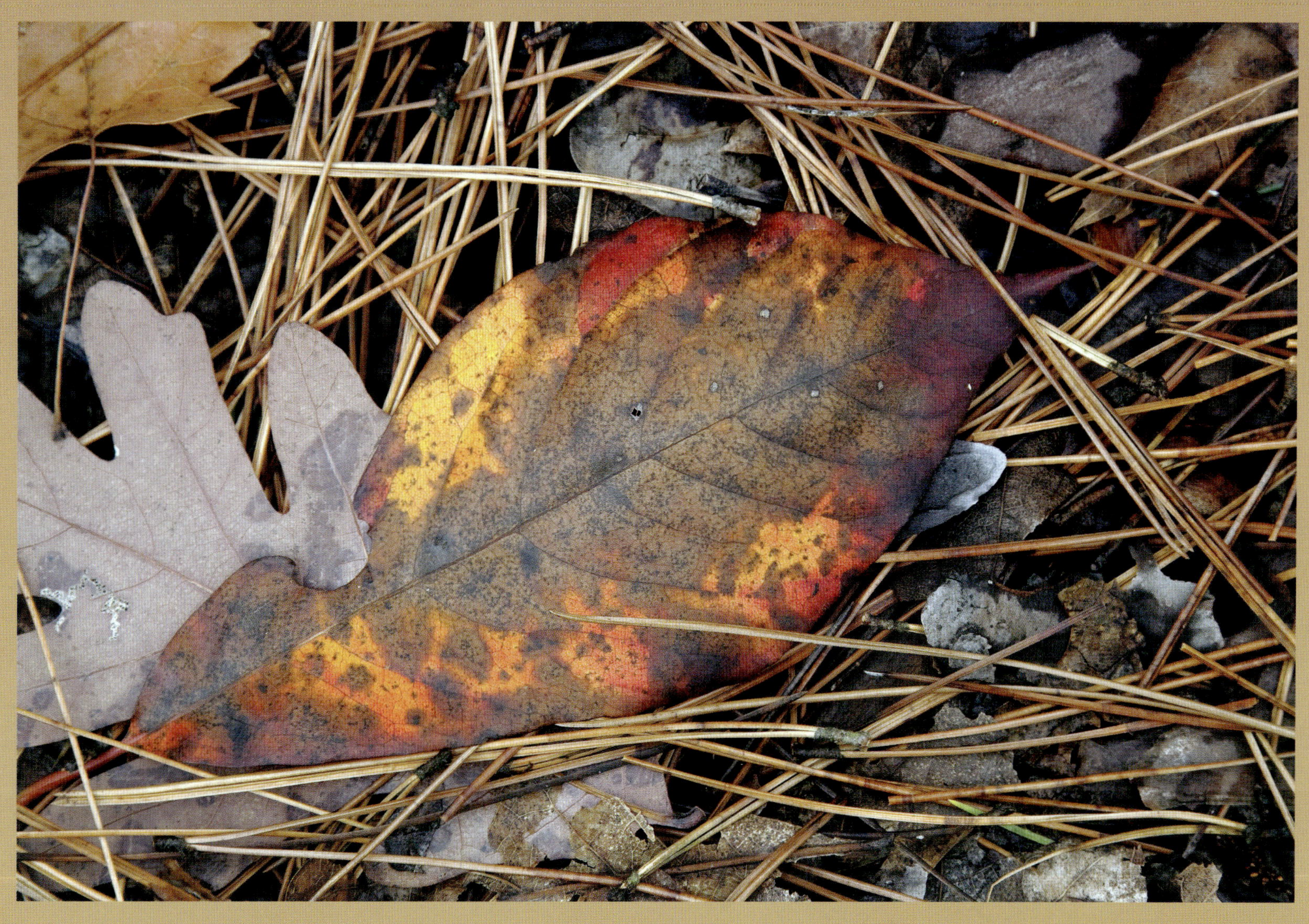

Brown County State Park. *October.*

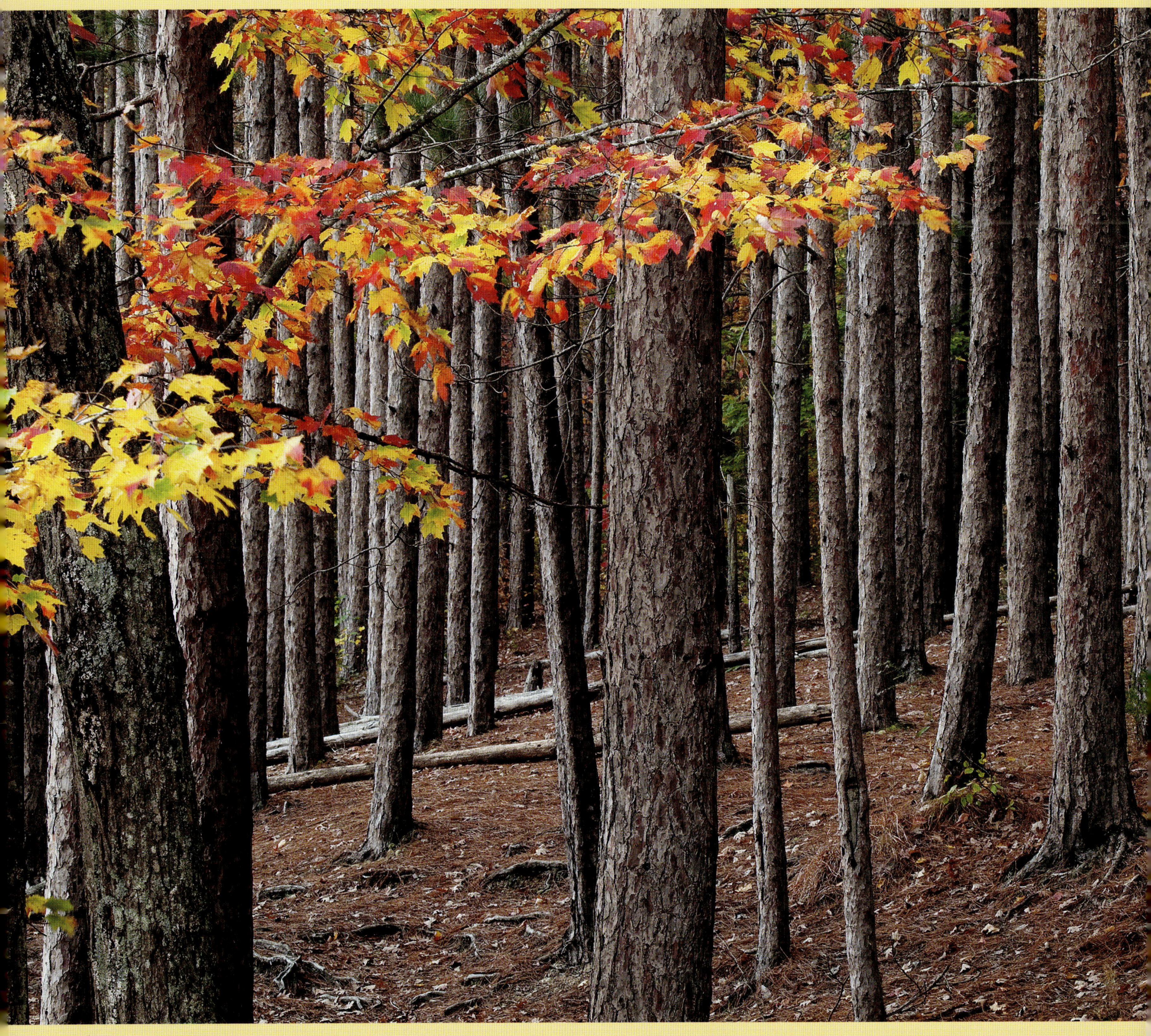

ACKNOWLEDGMENTS

I WISH TO THANK THOSE WHO HAVE HELPED ME IN so many ways to see the dream of this book being published. It began when I realized wedding photography was not for me! I decided my camera would be good to pursue my interest in landscape photography. From the outset I focused on Brown County because I believed many opportunities were there. More beauty is there than I ever imagined! My wife, Lynn, has been a great encouragement in allowing me the freedom to spend time scouting and shooting in Brown County. She graciously, and even sacrificially, allowed many things to be put on hold over the years. I've found she has a keen sense of what makes a landscape photograph a good one. Also, sons David and Daniel were invested in my dream. David and I often compared notes on places we found as favorites in the county. Through him, I was introduced to an obscure area I had not seen before. Daniel was patient as he and I waited for the light to do its wonder on a scene one morning. His technical knowledge has been invaluable as he helped me through some matters foreign to me.

Brown County State Park's Naturalist Jim Eagleman wrote a wonderfully appropriate introduction drawing on his knowledge of trees, forests, and the great outdoors. Thanks for his insight and speedy work!

Of course, I'm indebted to Indiana University Press Regional Books Editor Linda Oblack for seeing the possibility of my work becoming a beautiful book. She and her assistant, Sarah Jacobi, never seemed to tire of my questions as the work unfolded. Thanks to all at Indiana University Press for their diligent work to make it happen.

I very much appreciate the work of the Indiana Department of Resources and the Hoosier National Forest for their never-ending effort to keep their properties ready for the enjoyment of the public. Because of their work, city folk have wonderful places to get back to nature! Each of us should do our part to preserve that precious resource for future generations.

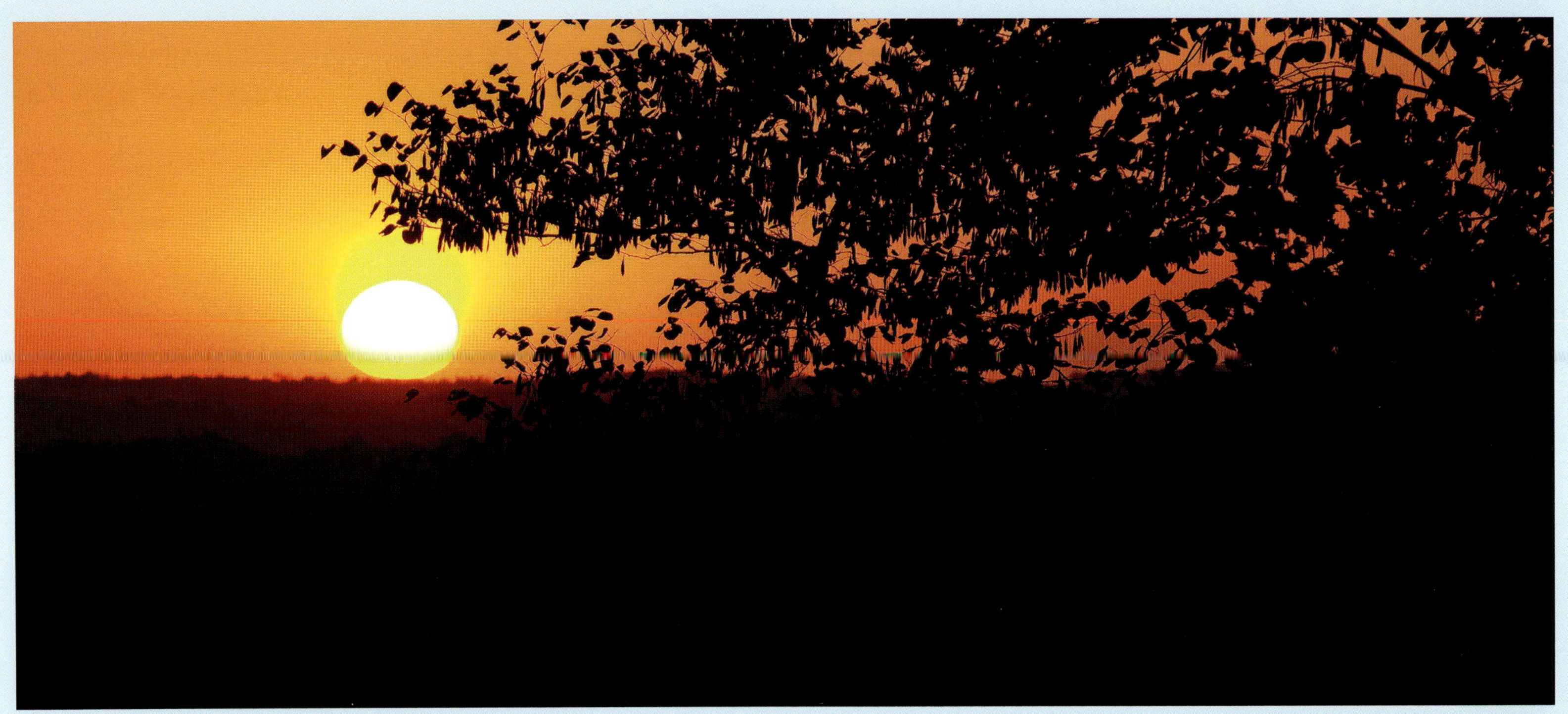

Brown County State Park. *October.*

Many private property owners have been receptive after seeing this stranger (myself) approach to ask for permission to scout their beautiful land for picture opportunities. I never know what is over the hill! Brown County landowners understandably guard their privacy, and I'm grateful for those who have allowed me to invade their space.

I could not have done this without God, and I thank Him for the vision he has given me. I believe He gives each of us a gift to be used and enjoyed. To that end, Brown County, Indiana, is my destination!

Yellowwood State Forest. *October.*

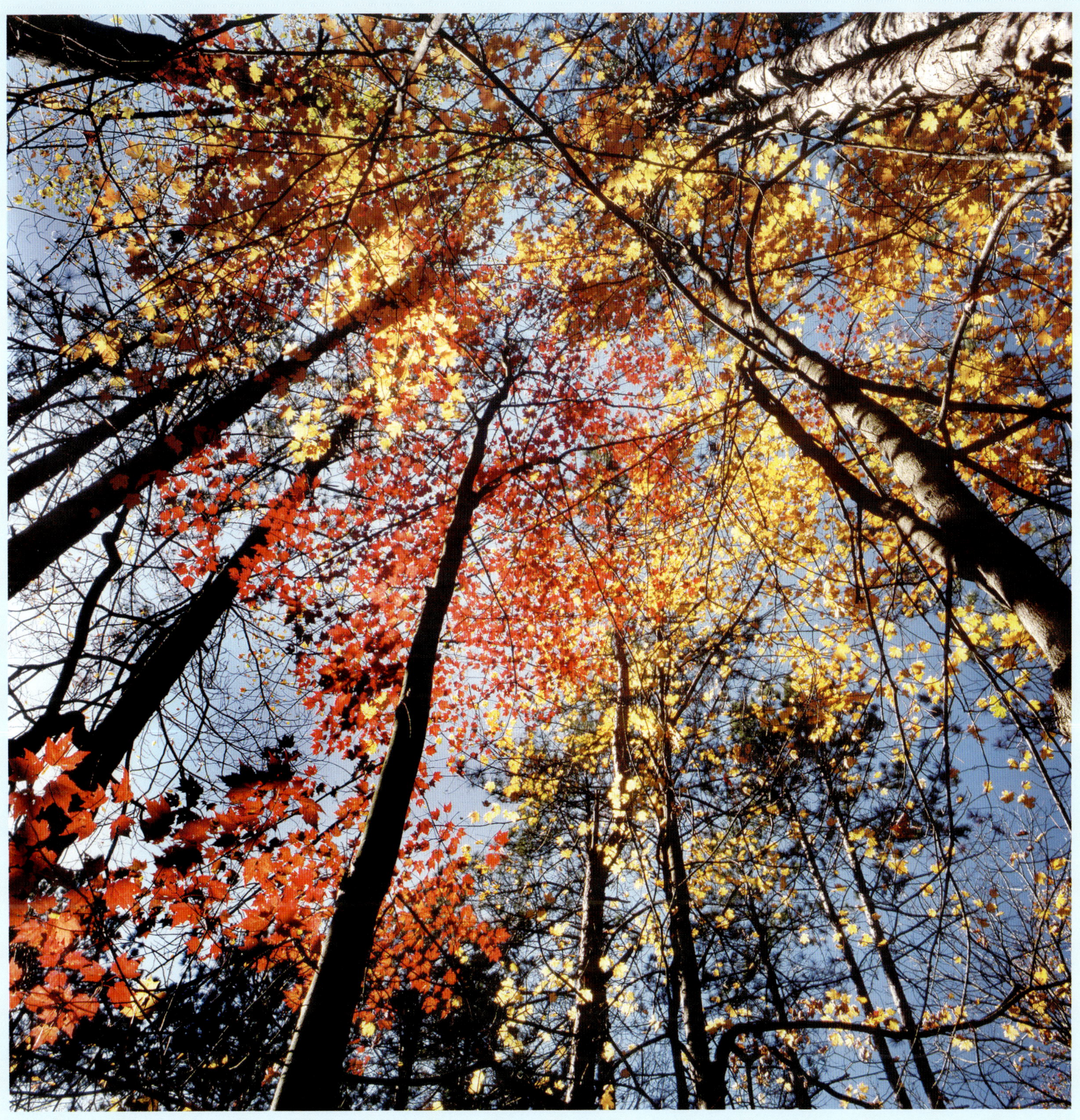

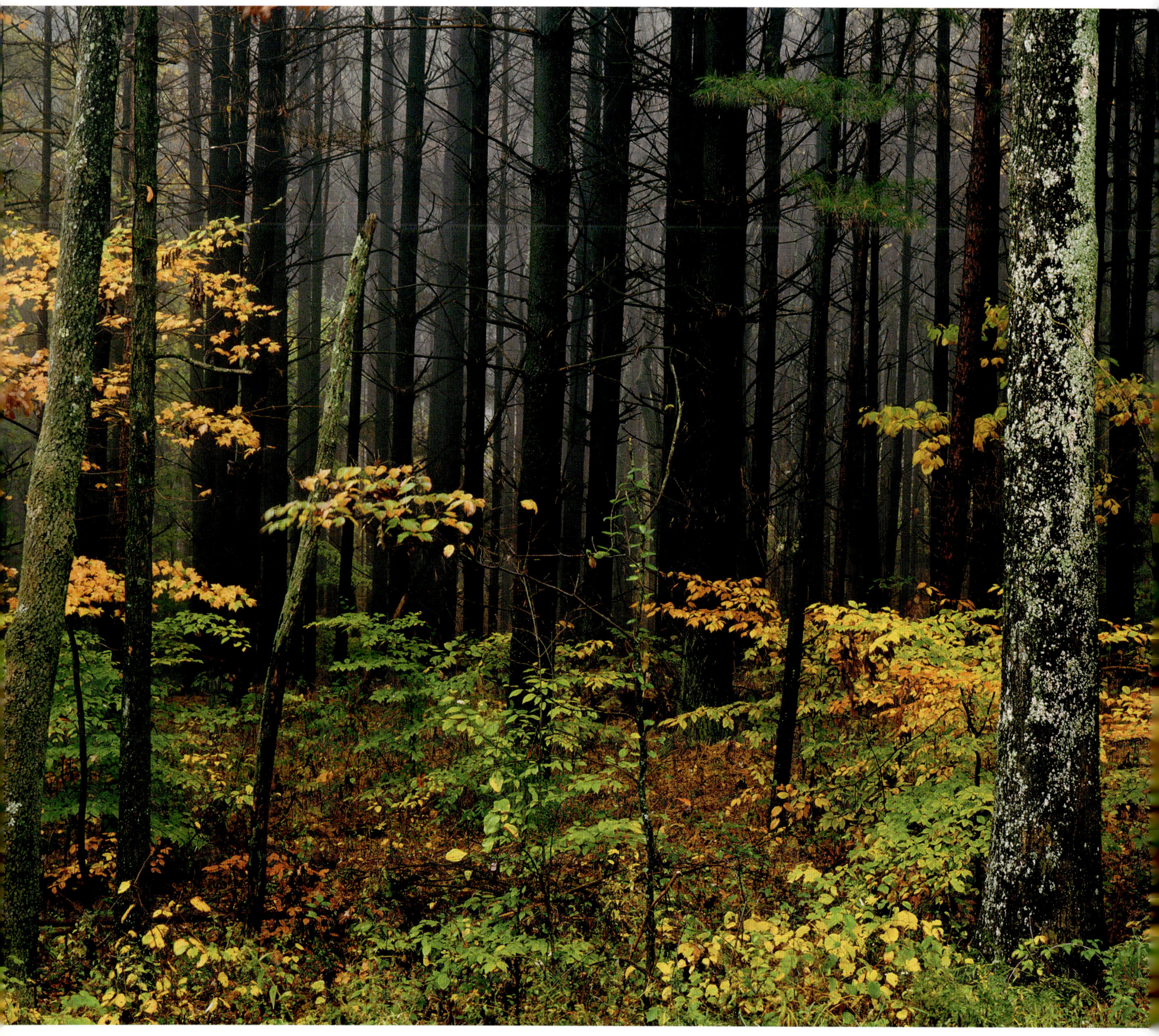

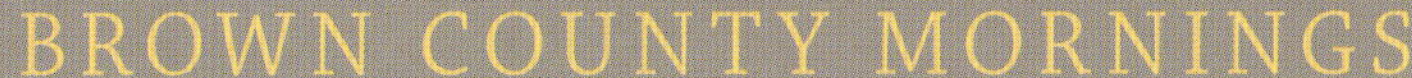

BROWN COUNTY MORNINGS

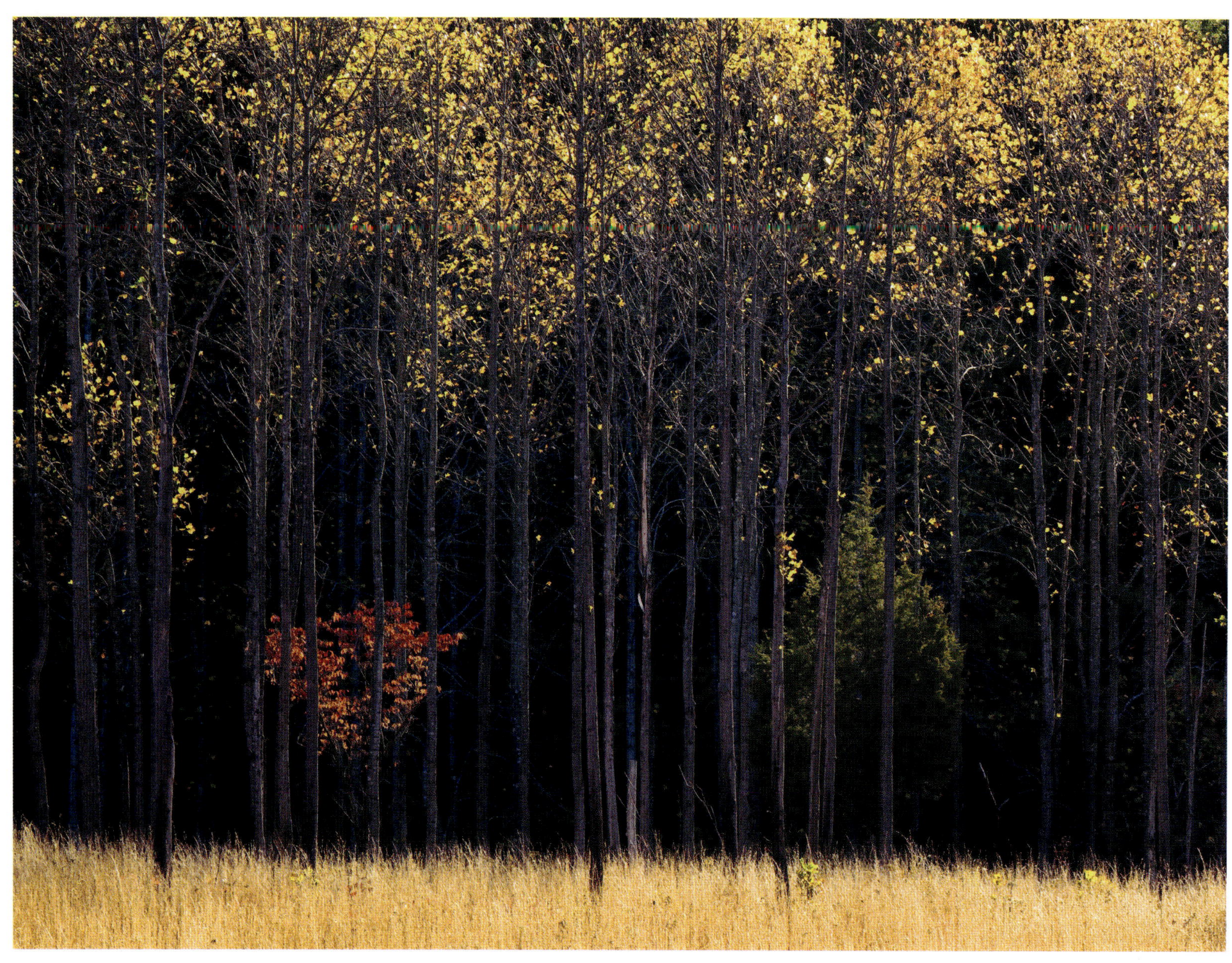

Hoosier National Forest. *October.*

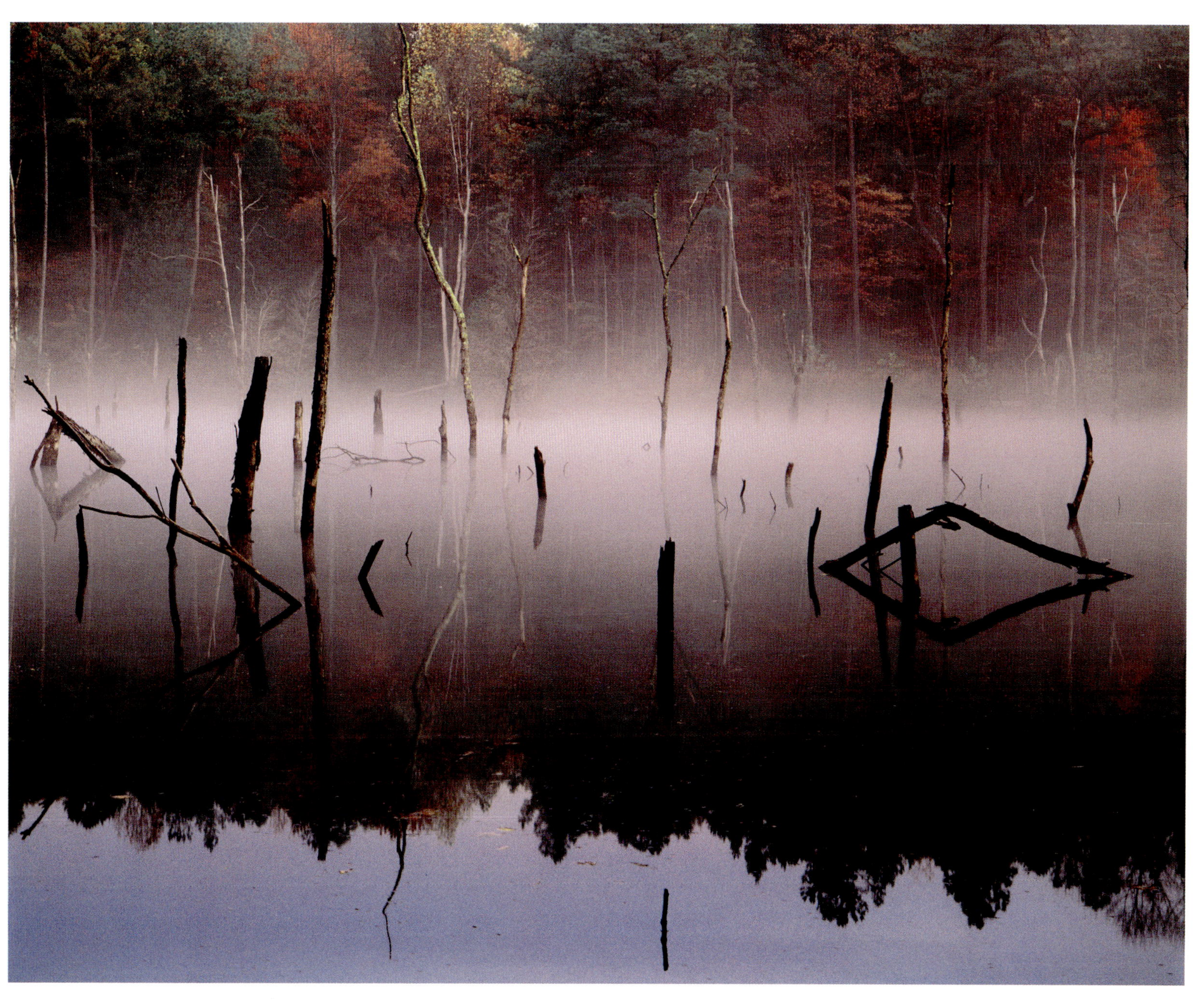

Sundance Lake in Hoosier National Forest. *October.*

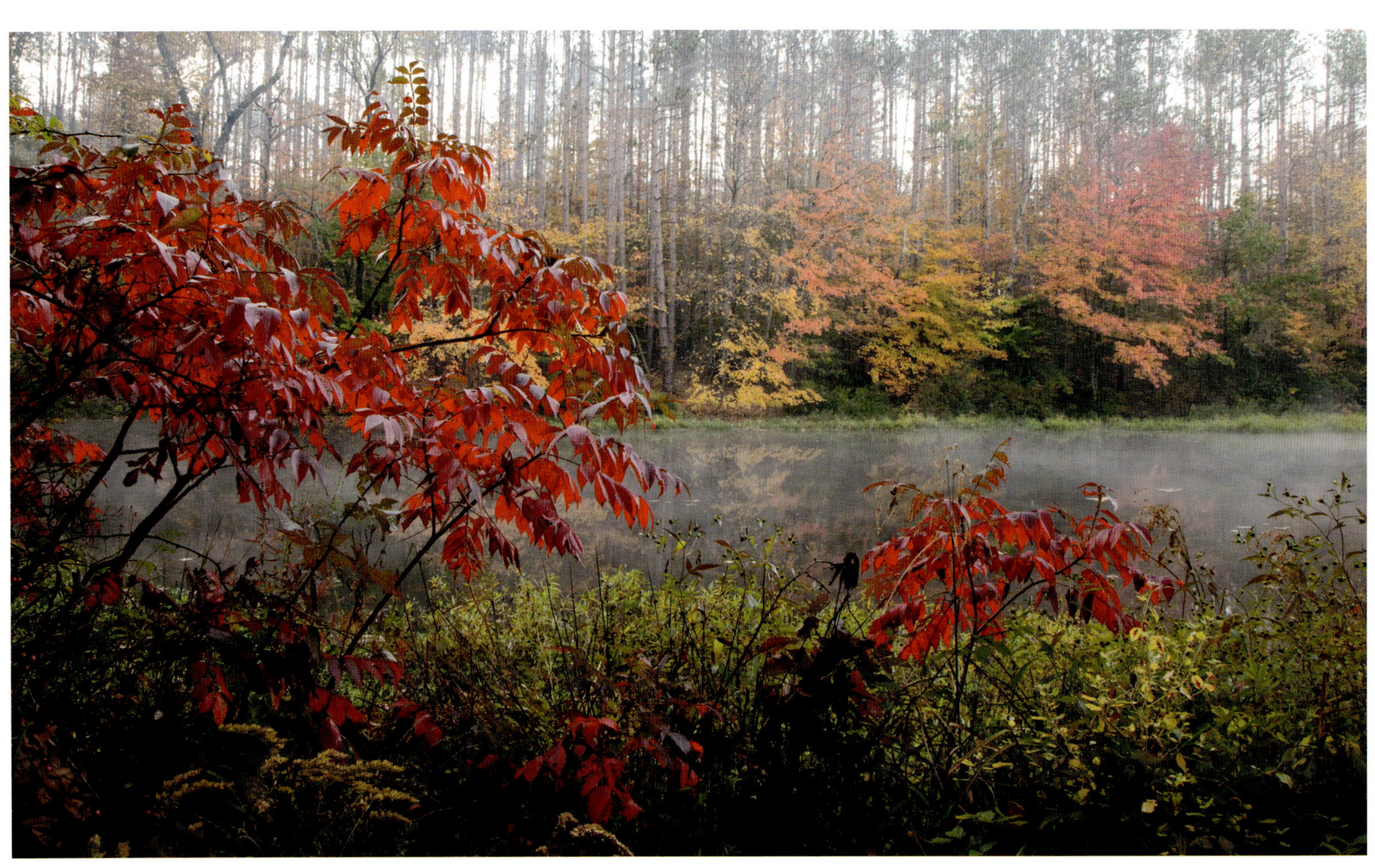

Yellowwood Lake in Yellowwood State Forest. *October.*

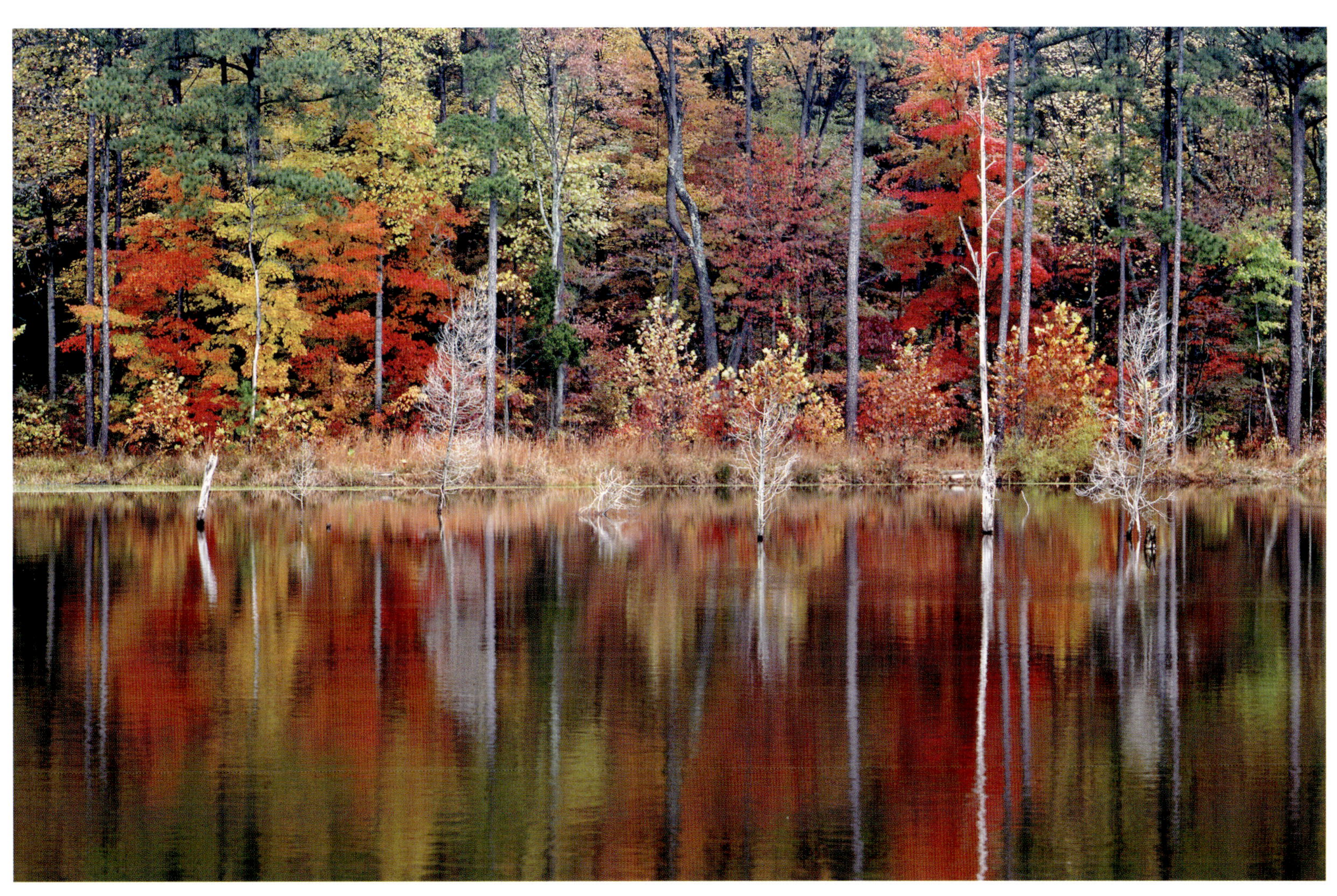

Sundance Lake in Hoosier National Forest. *October.*

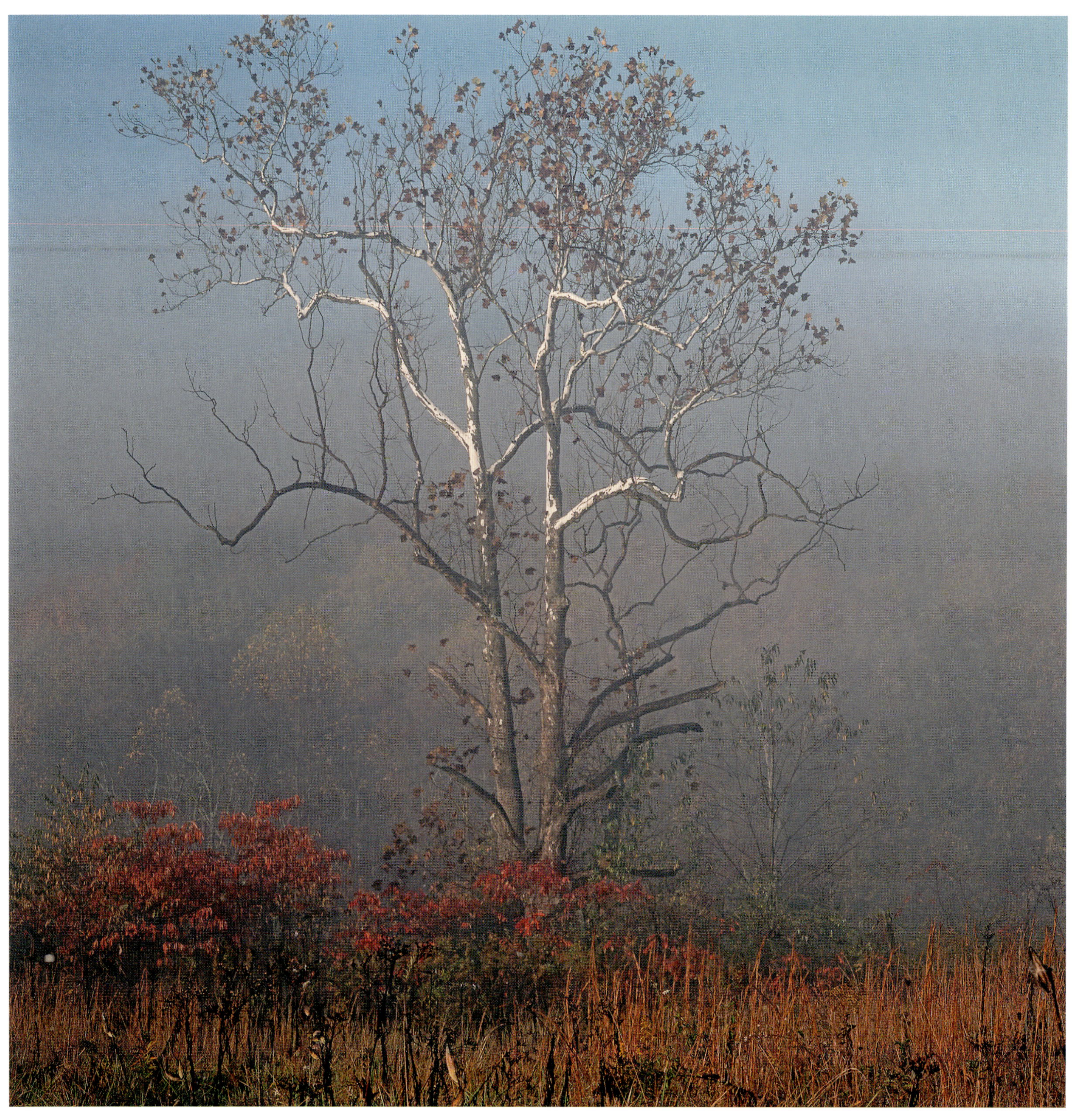

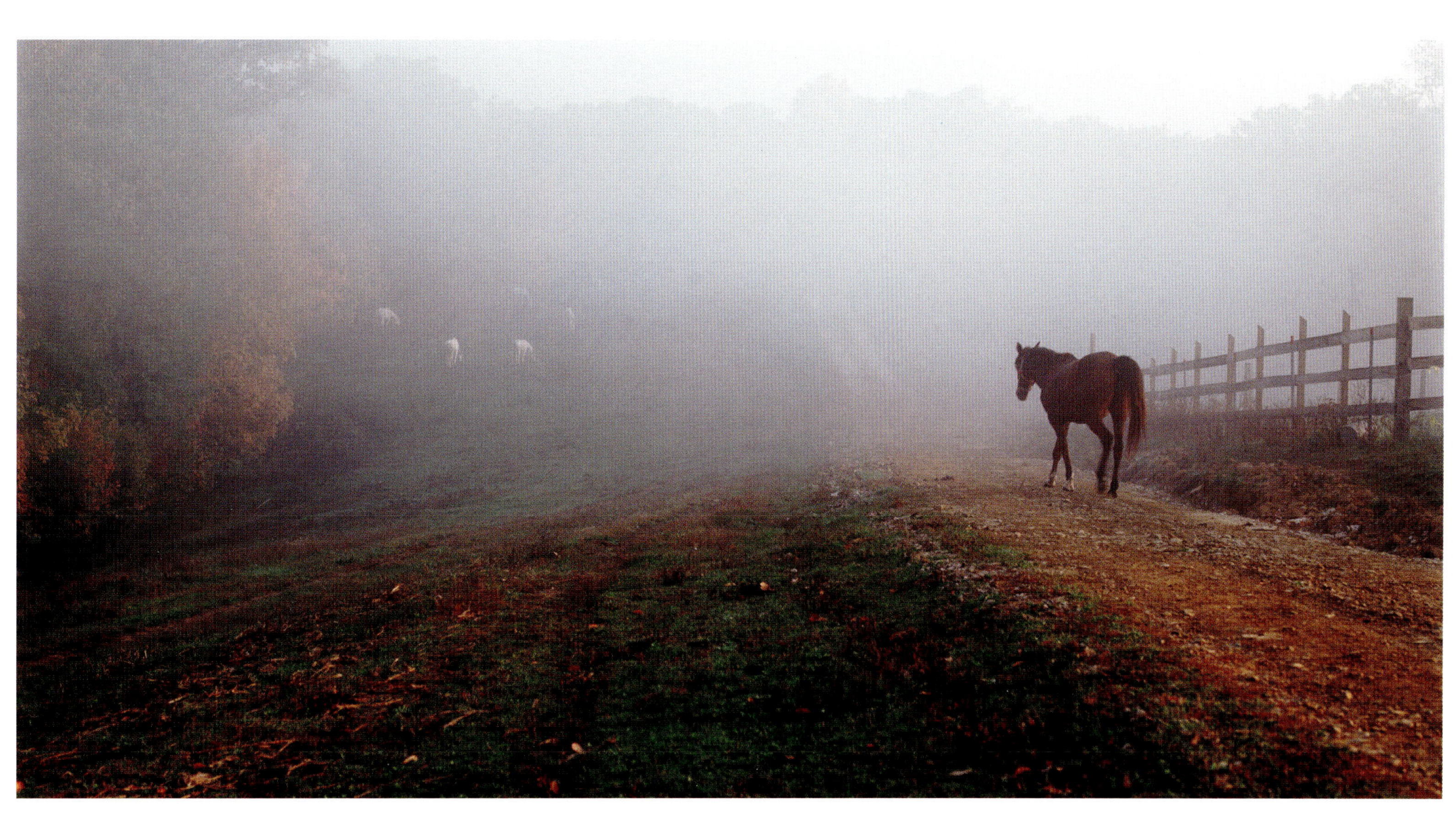

Private Property. *October.*

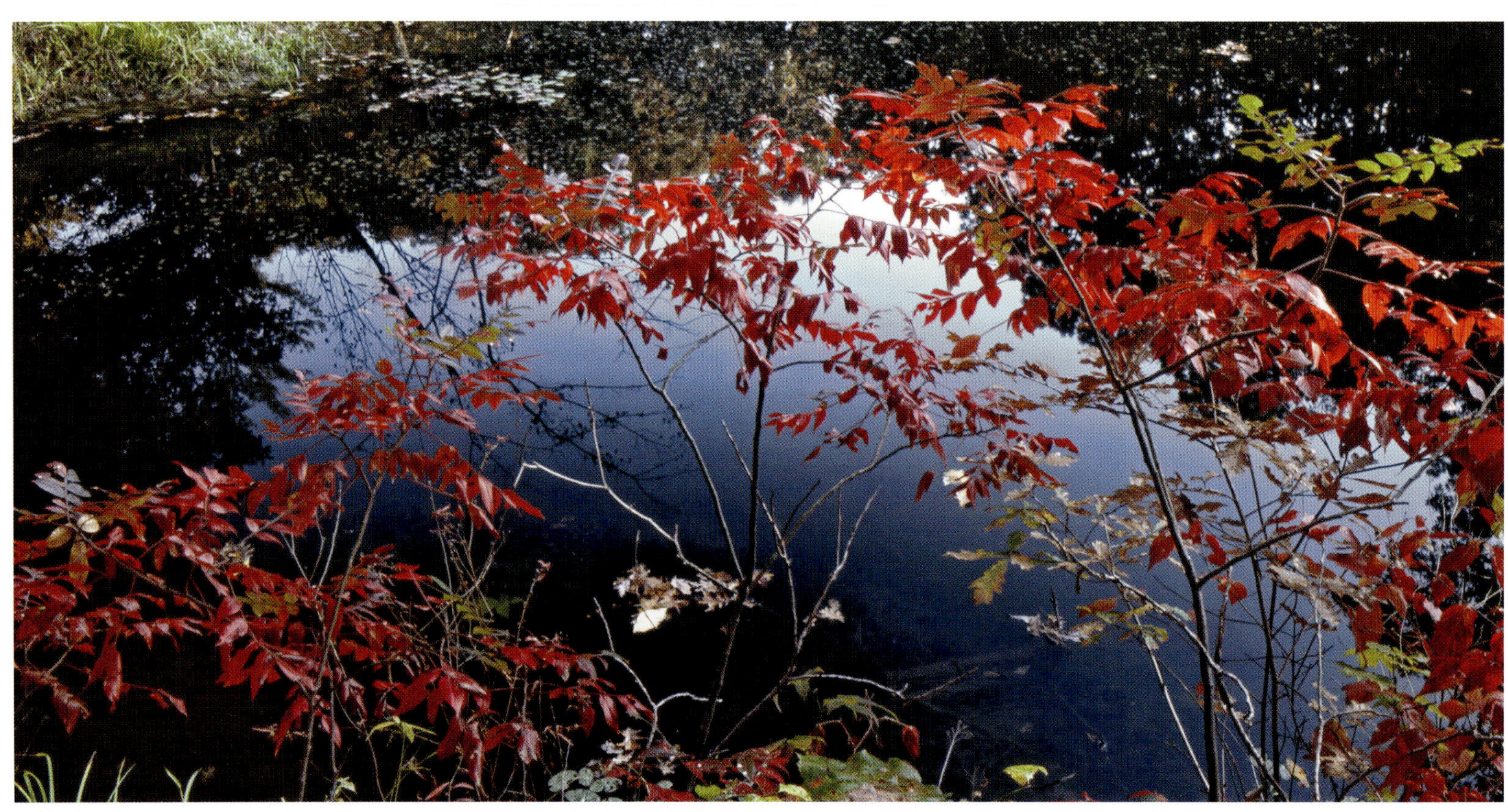

Private Property. *October.*

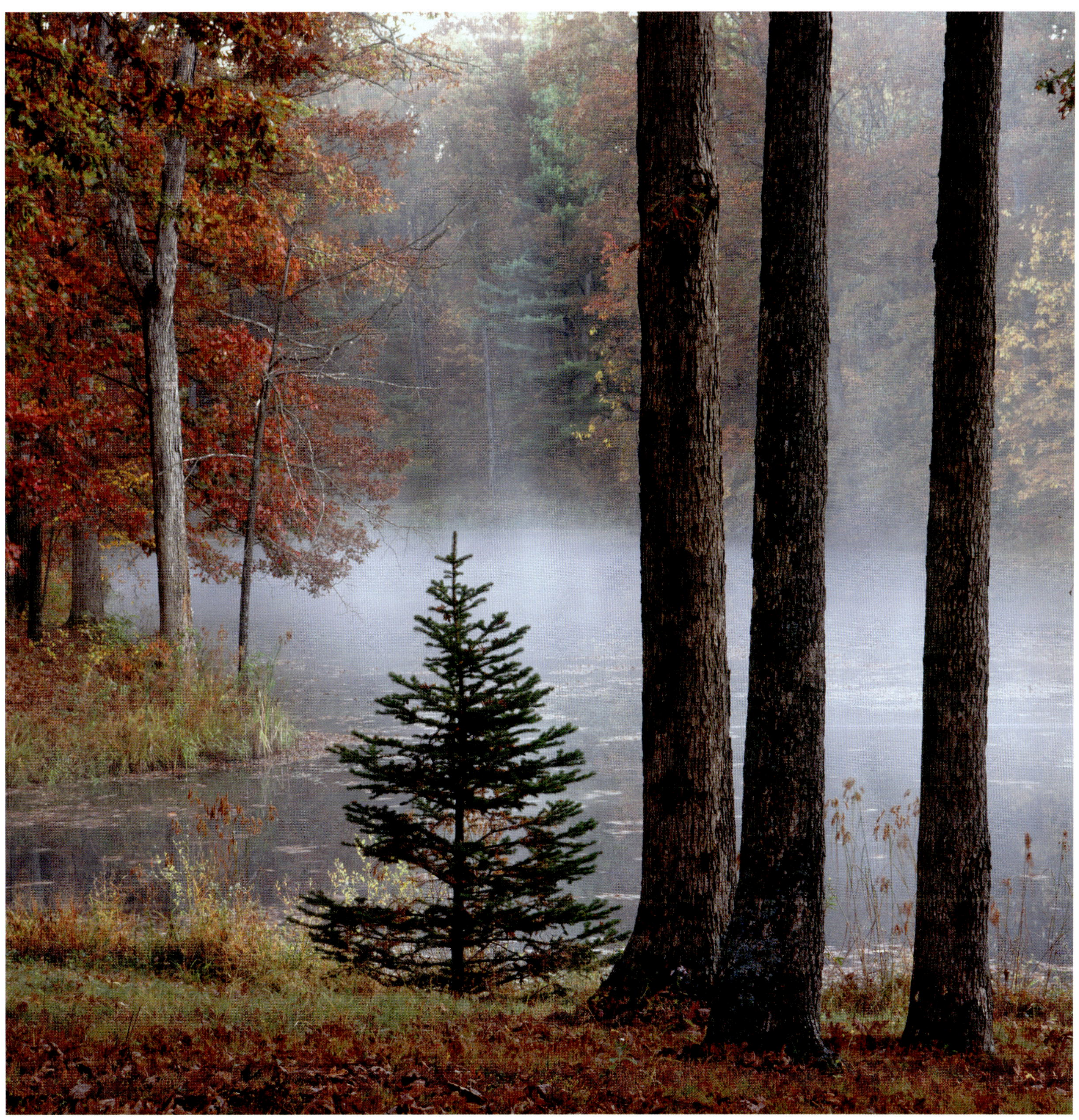

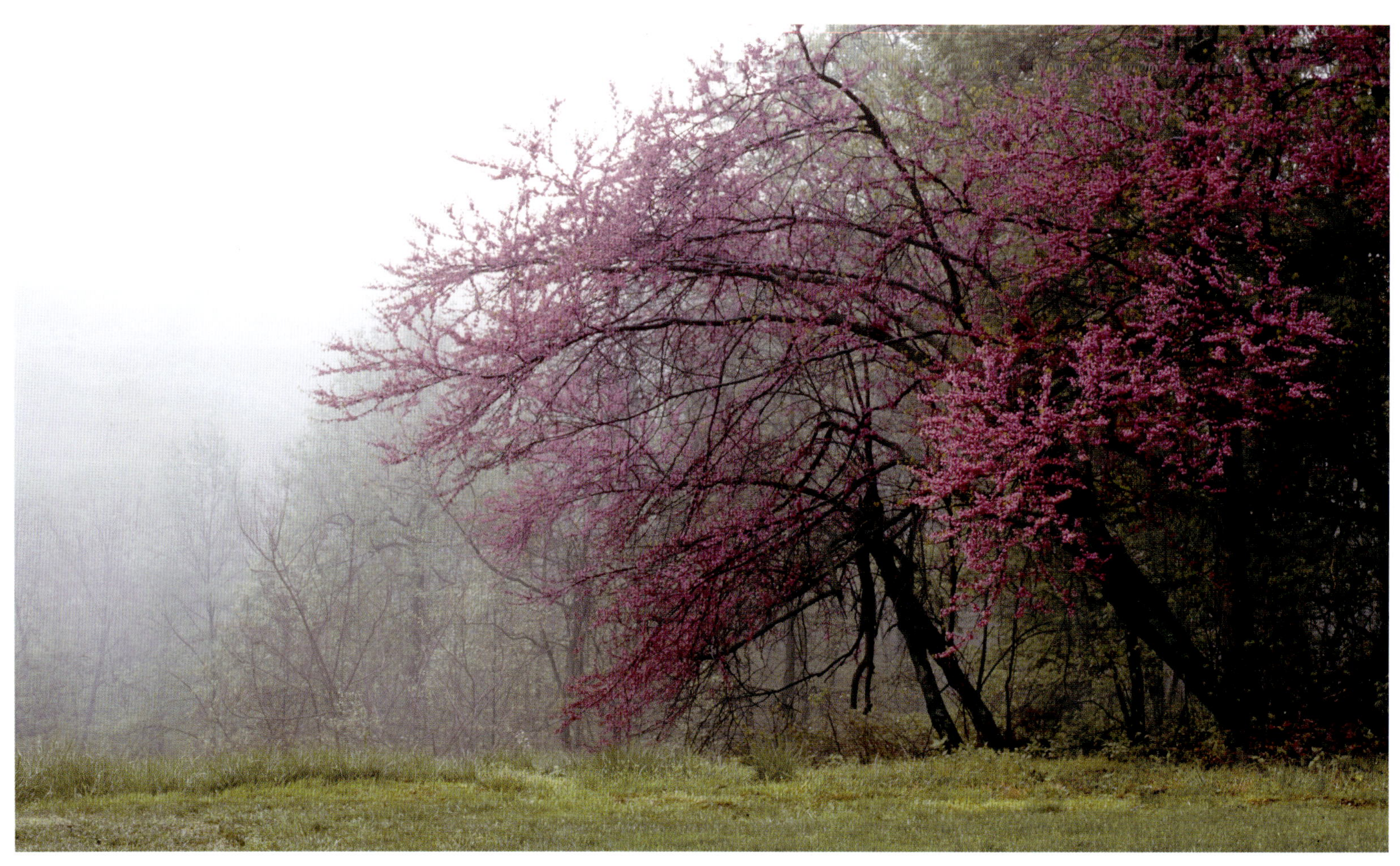

Brown County State Park. *April.*

Private Property. *October.*

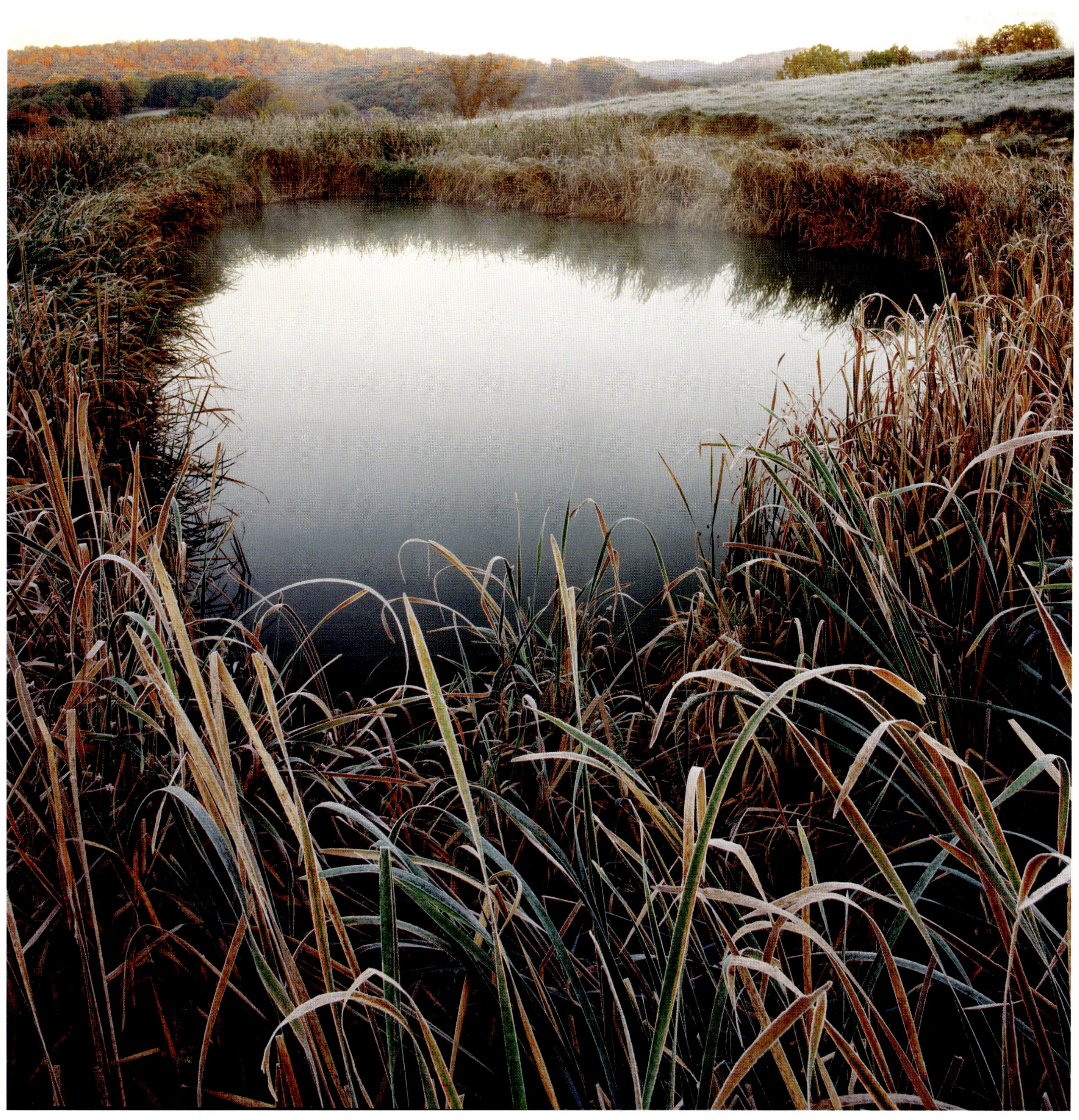

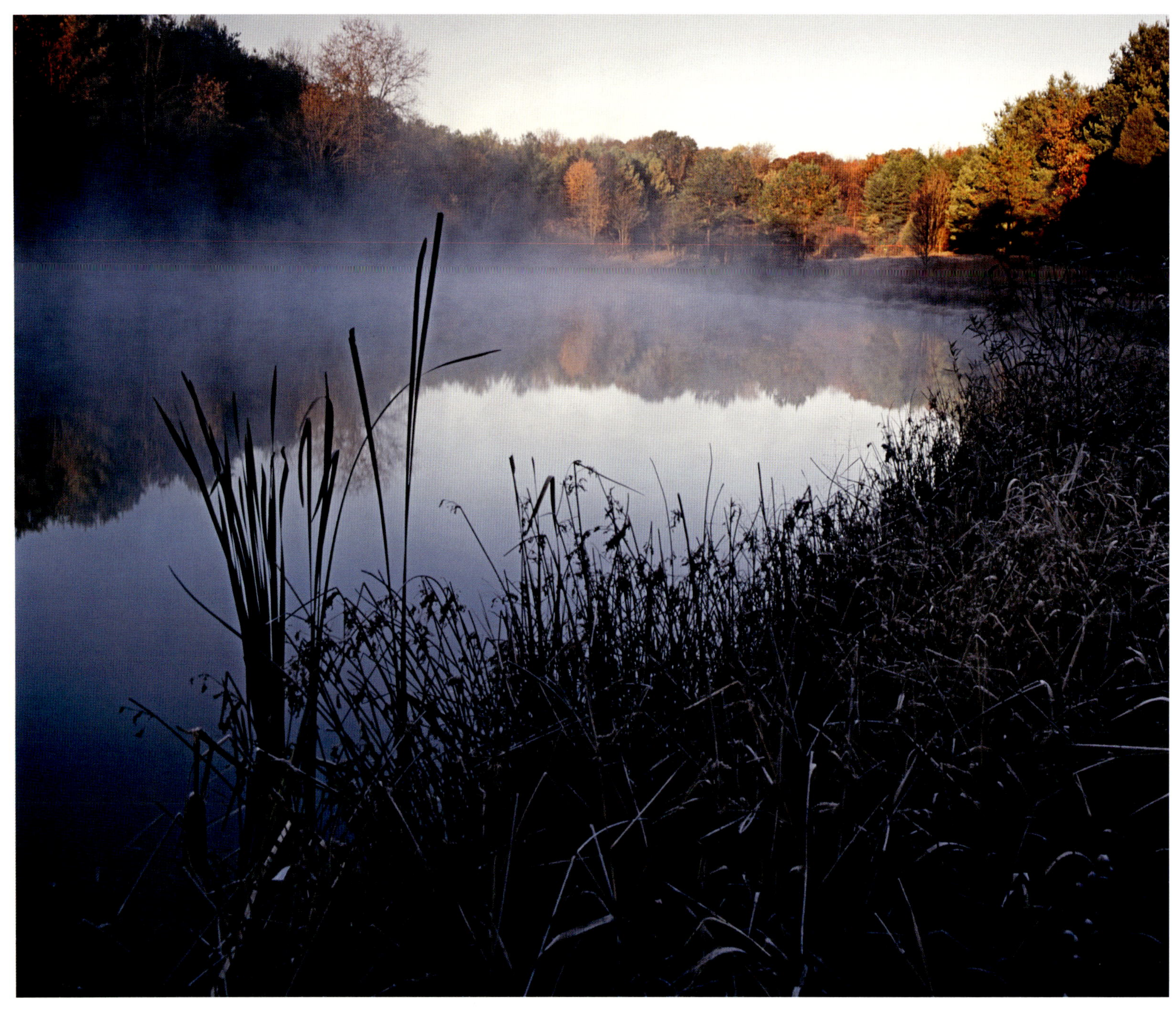

Scott Pond in Hoosier National Forest. *October.*

Hoosier National Forest. *October.*

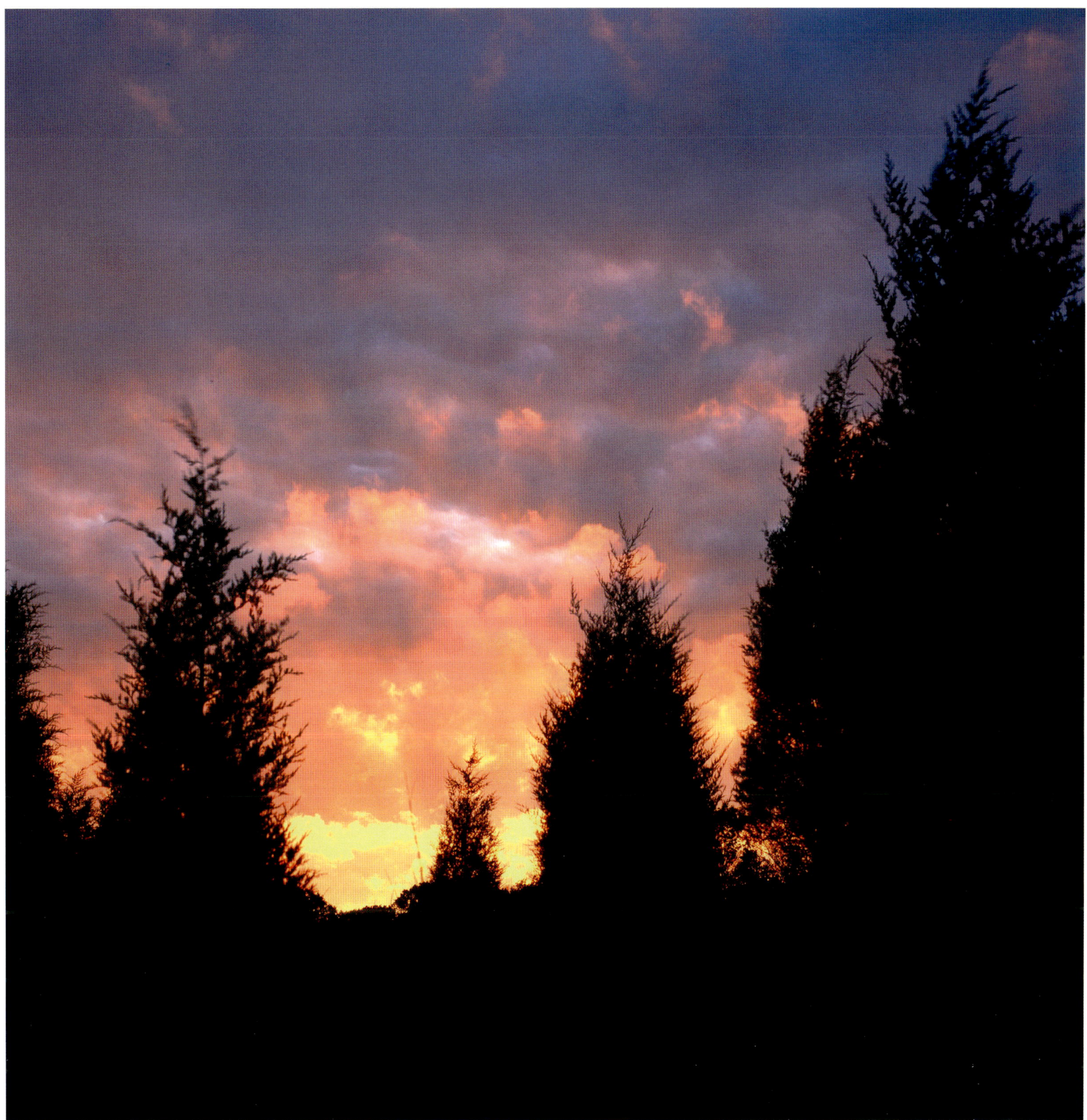

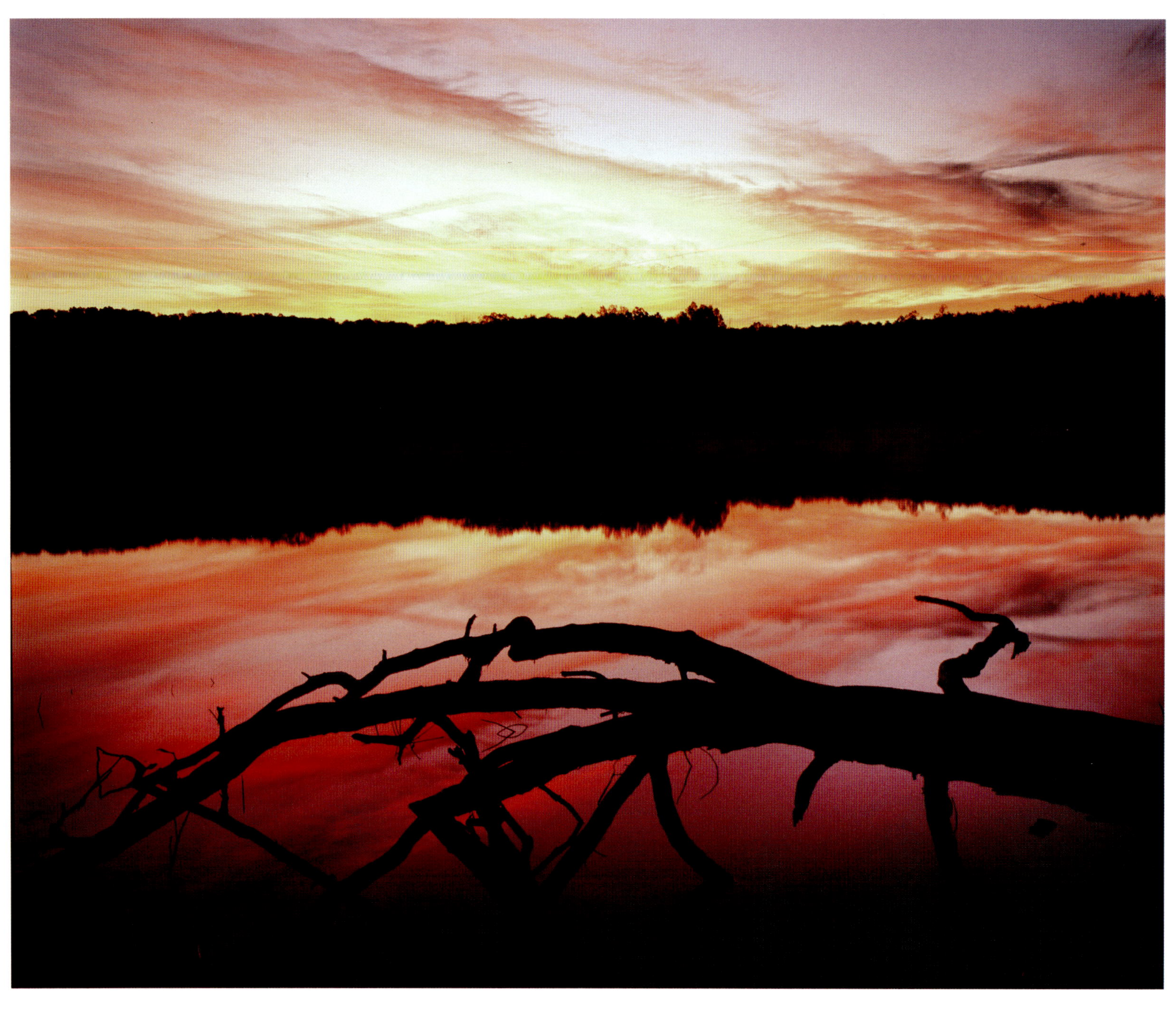

Yellowwood Lake in Yellowwood State Forest. *October.*

Hoosier National Forest. *October.*

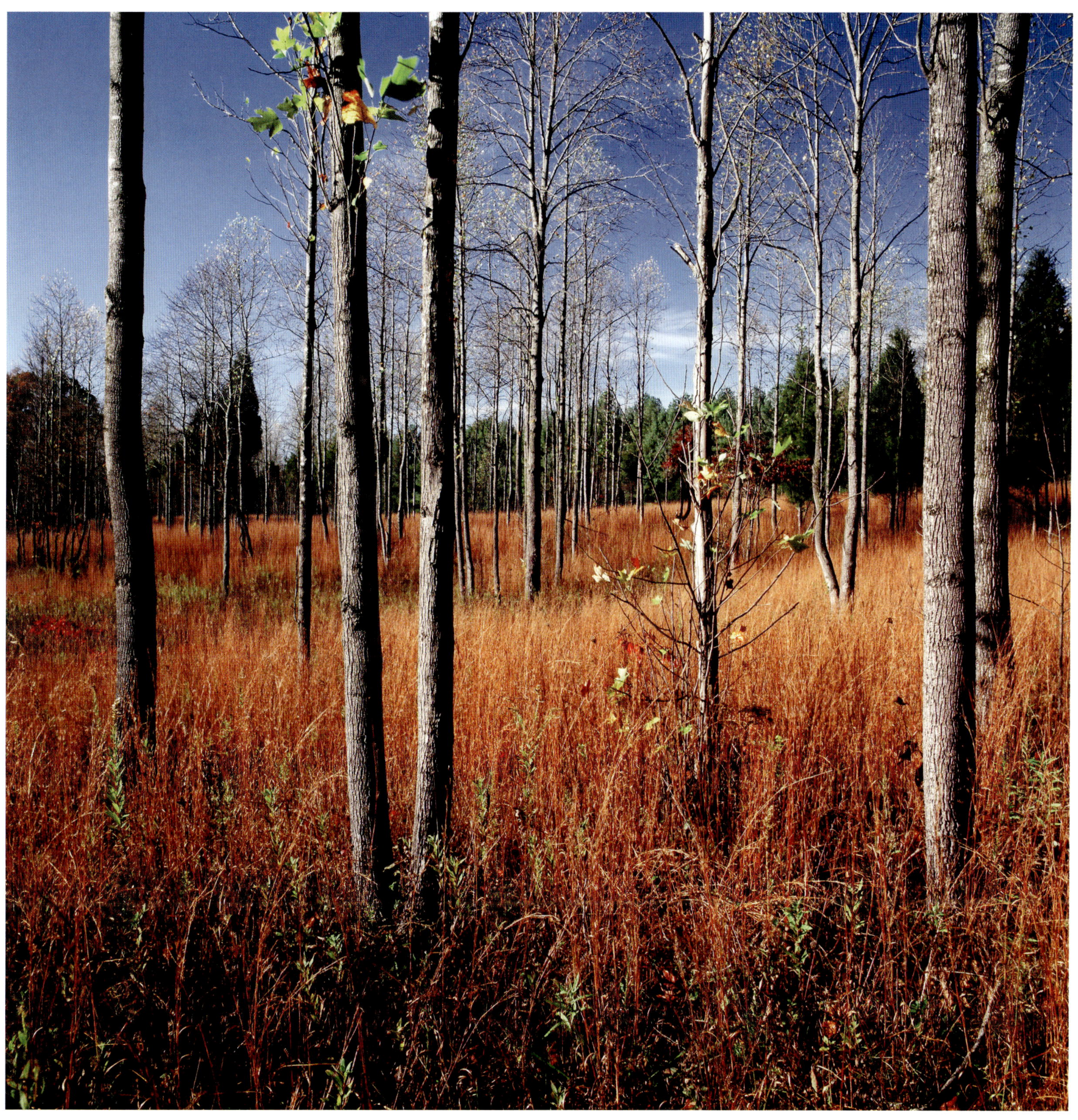

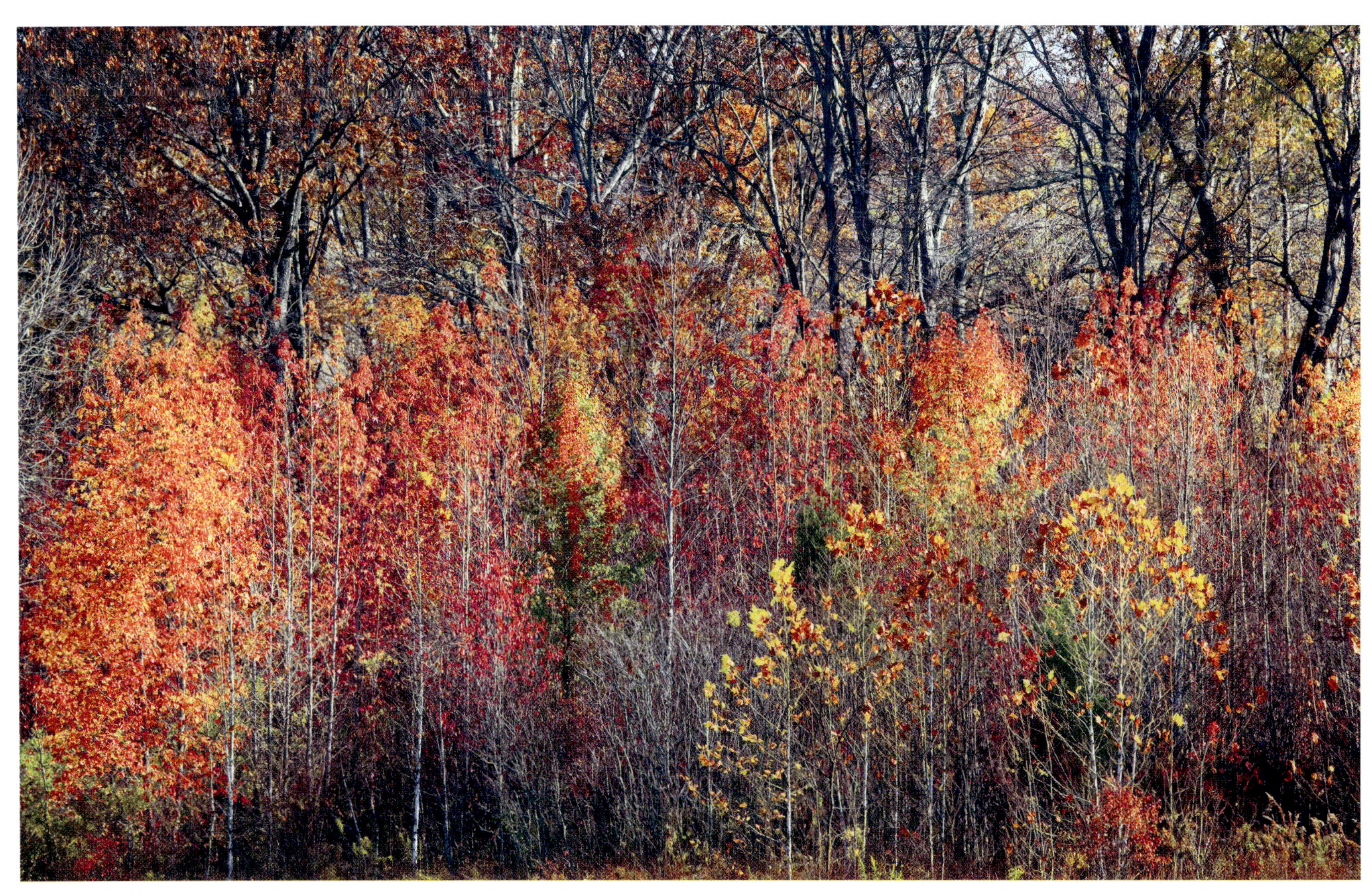

Brown County State Park. *October.*

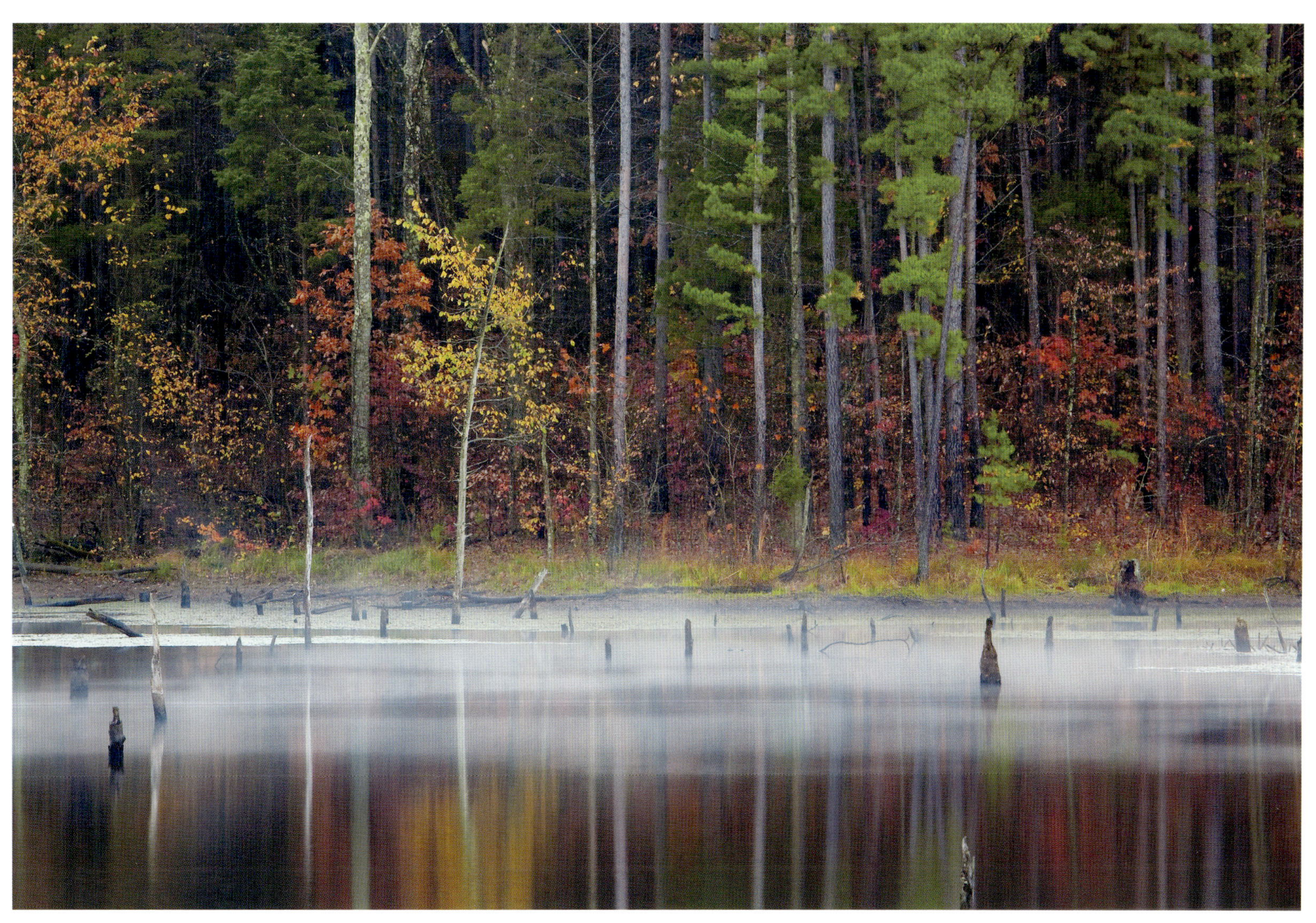

Sundance Lake in Hoosier National Forest. *October.*

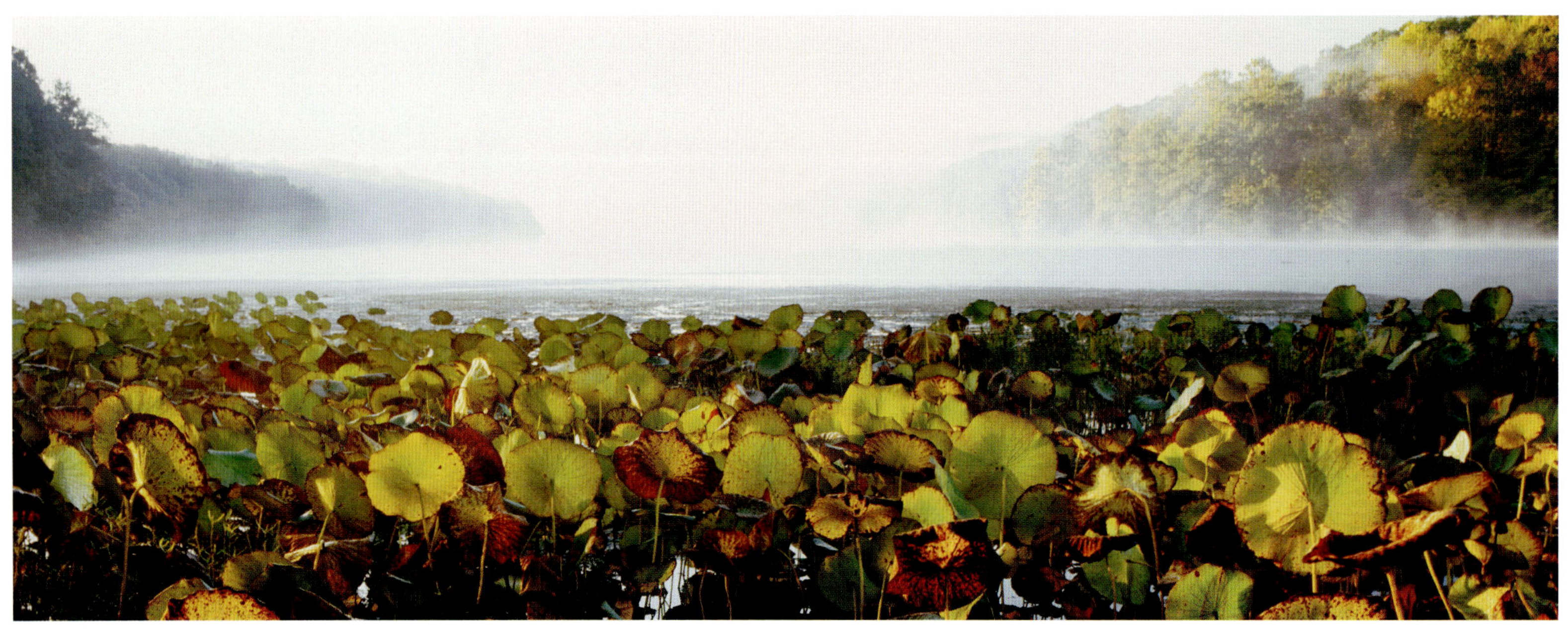

Yellowwood Lake in Yellowwood State Forest. *Summer.*

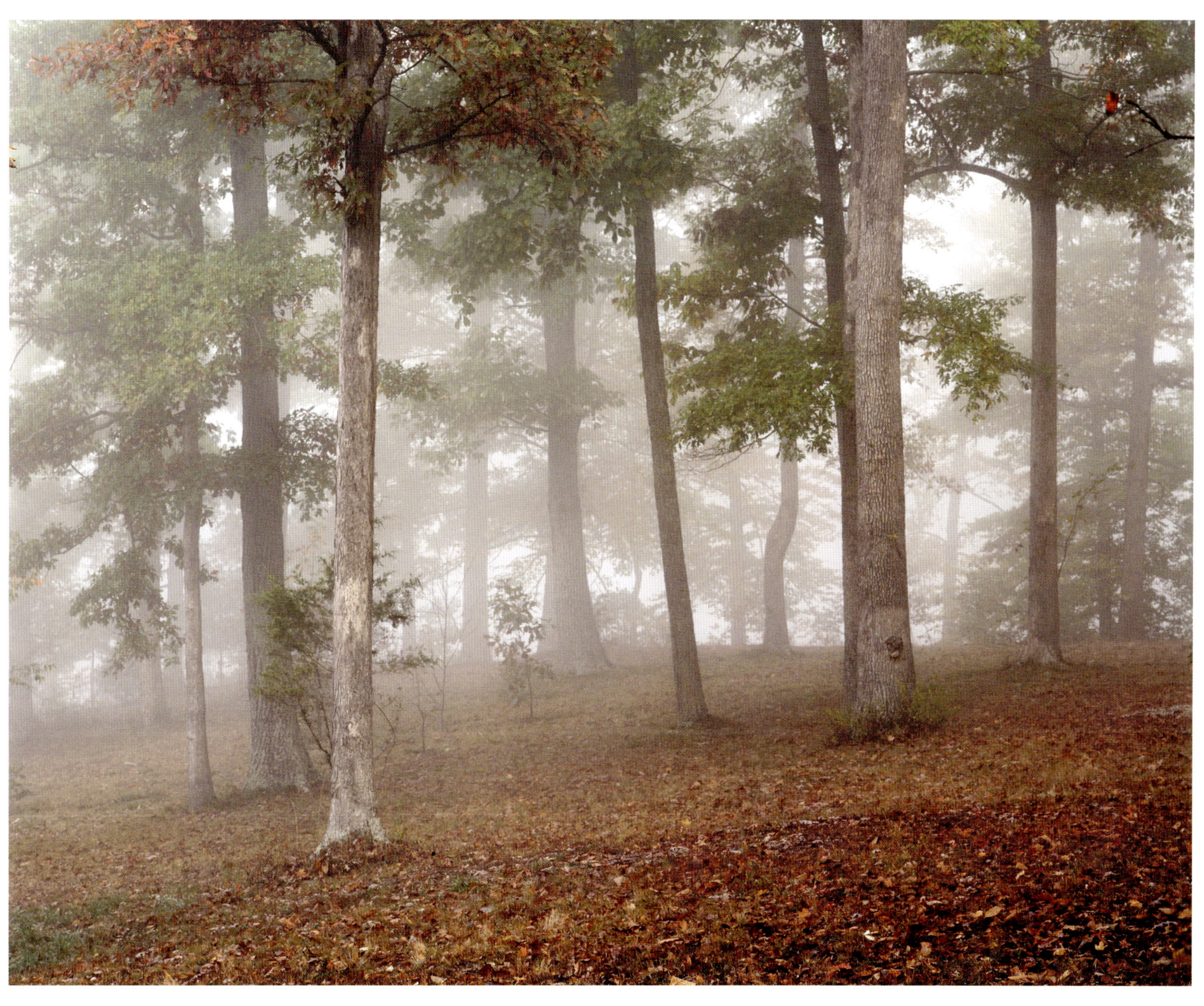

Yellowwood State Forest. *October.*

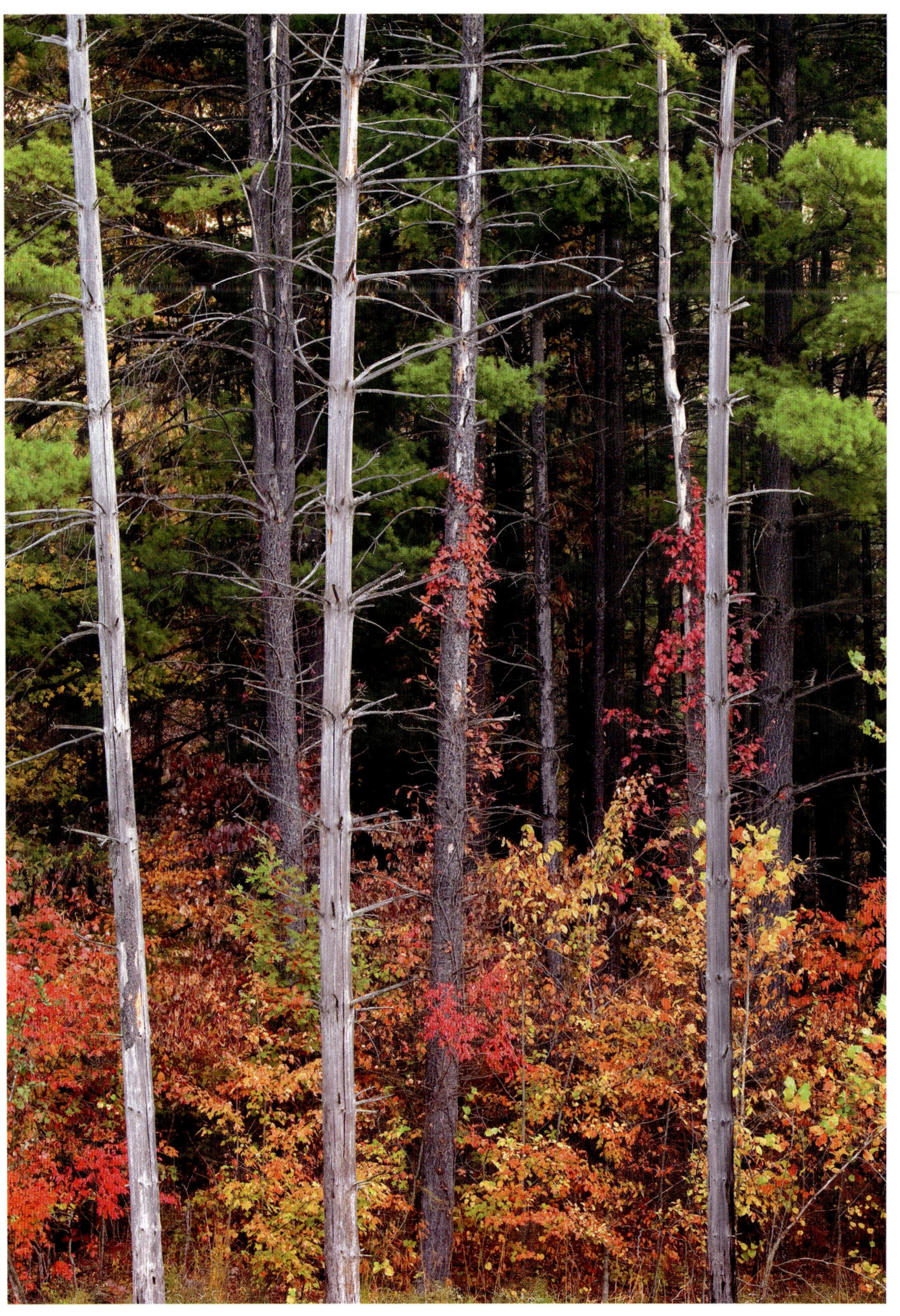

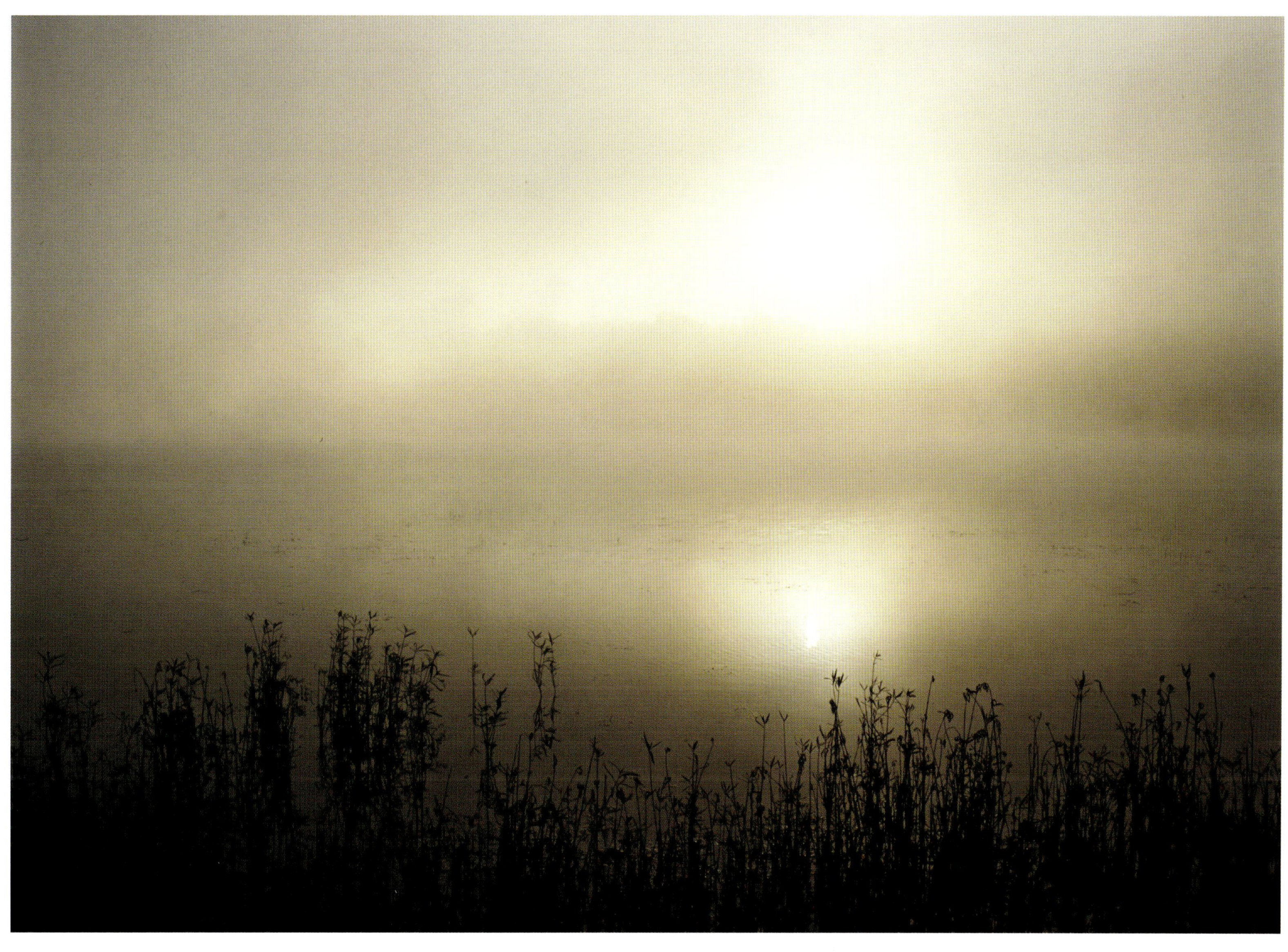

Hoosier National Forest. *October.*

Yellowwood Lake in Yellowwood State Forest. *October.*

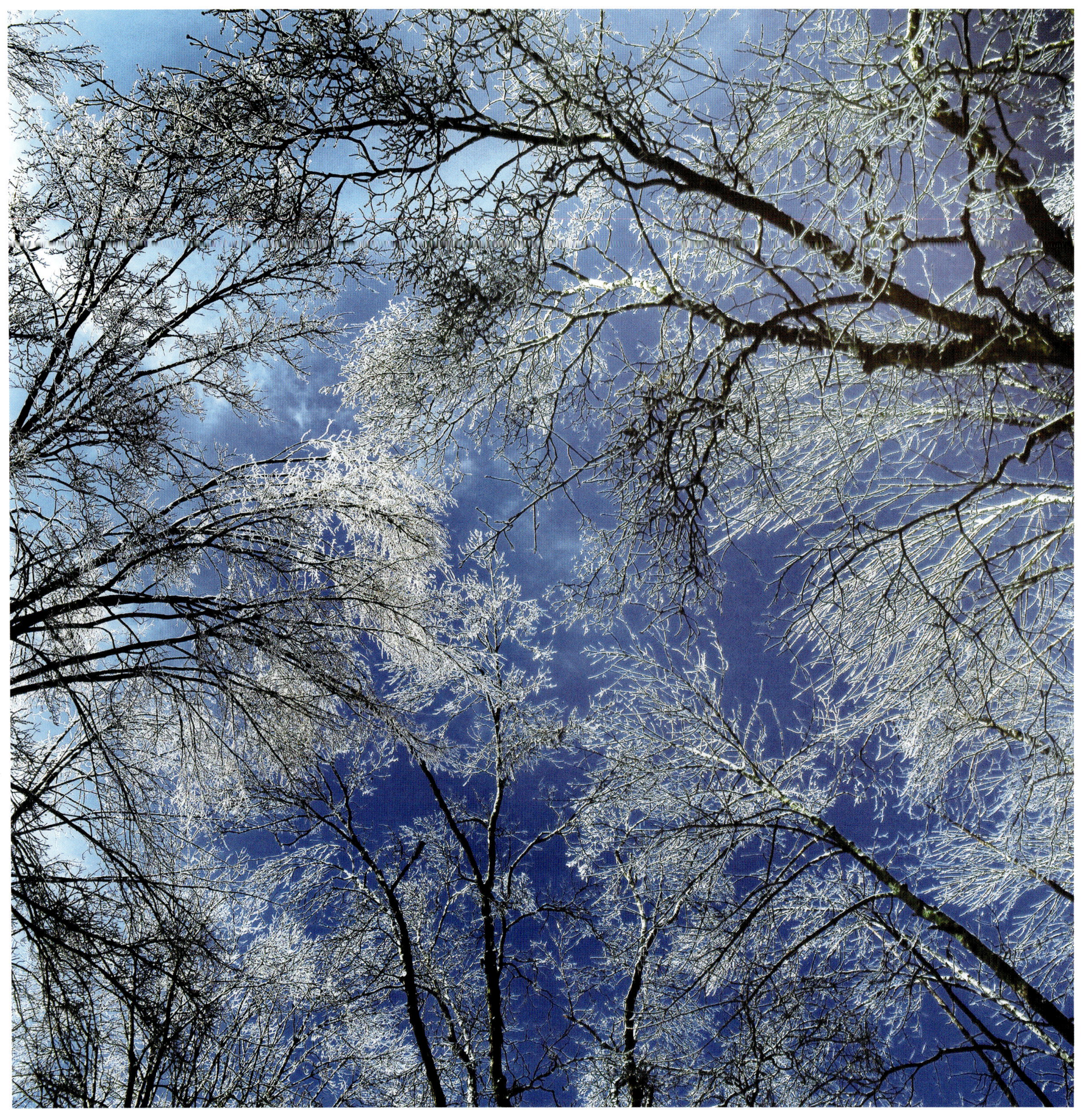

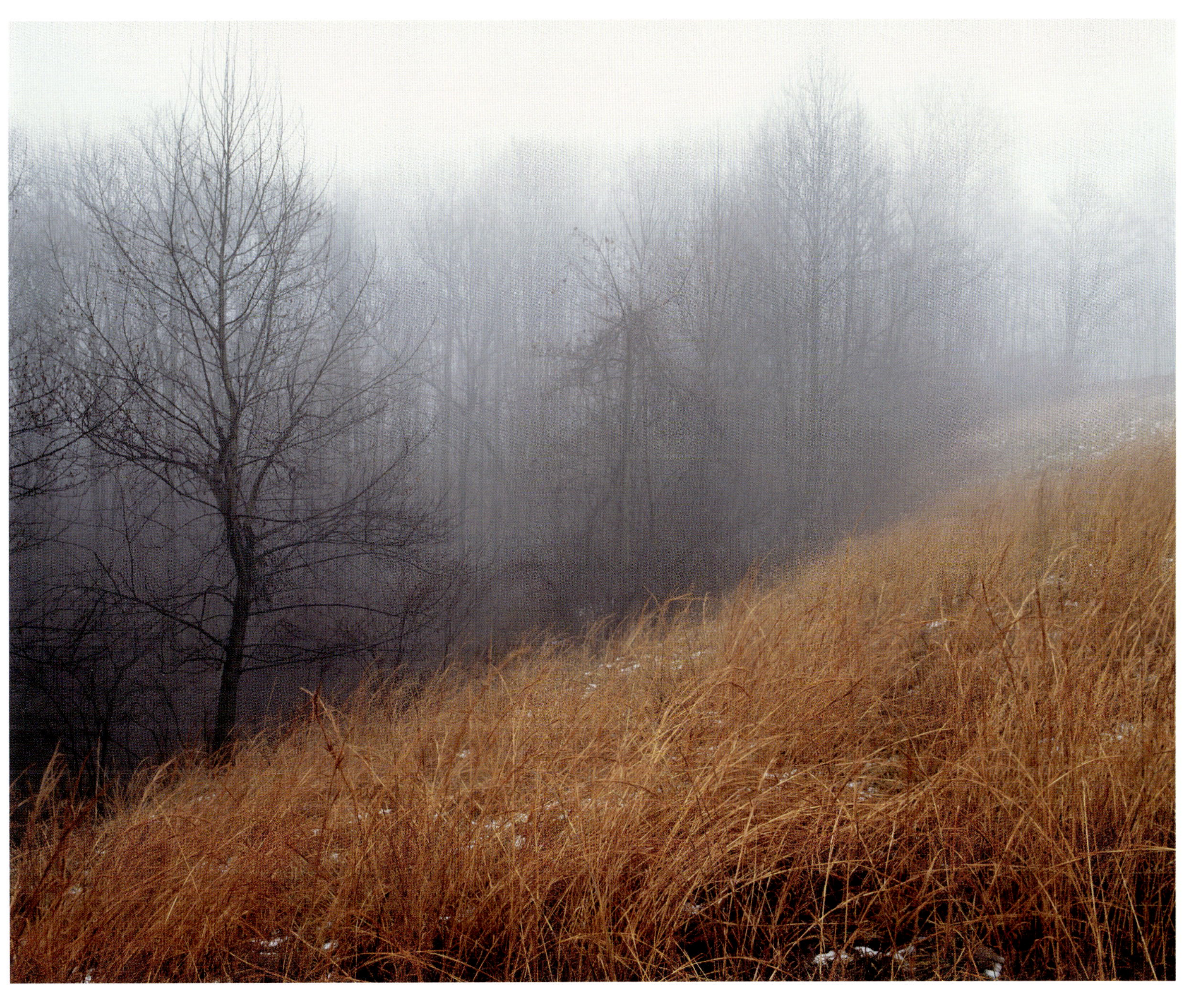

Brown County State Park. *January.*

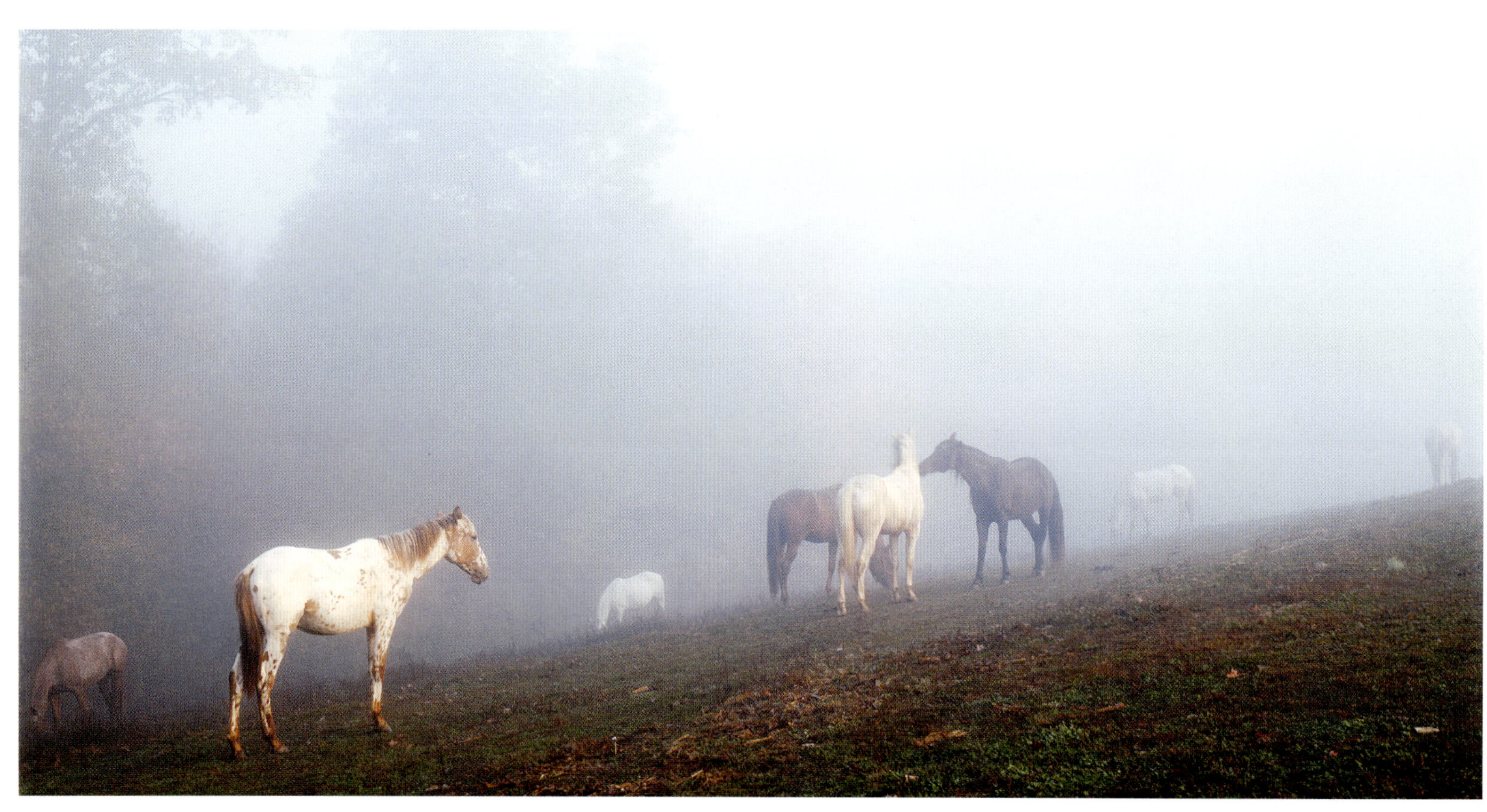

Private Property. *October.*

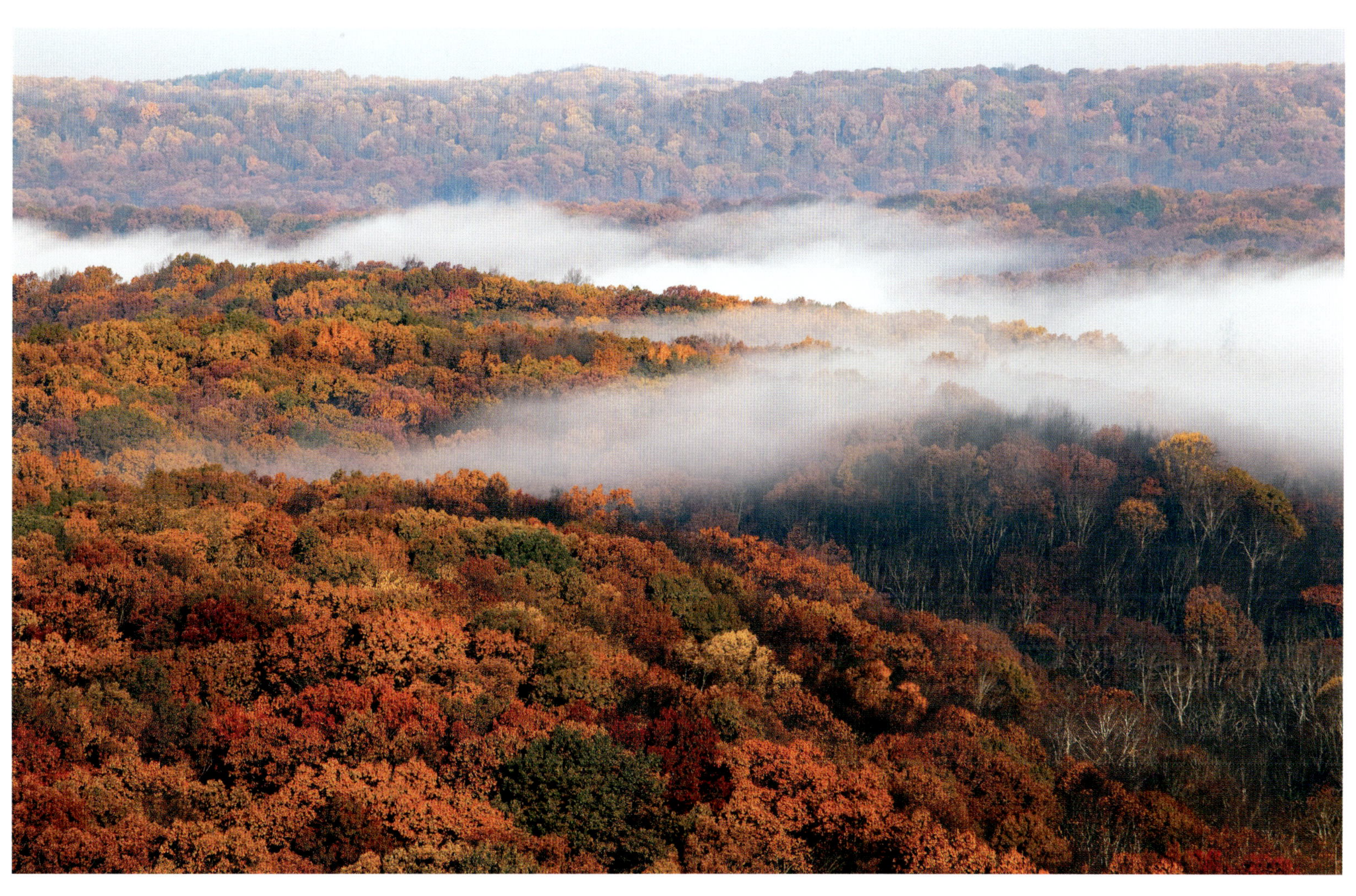

Brown County State Park. *October.*

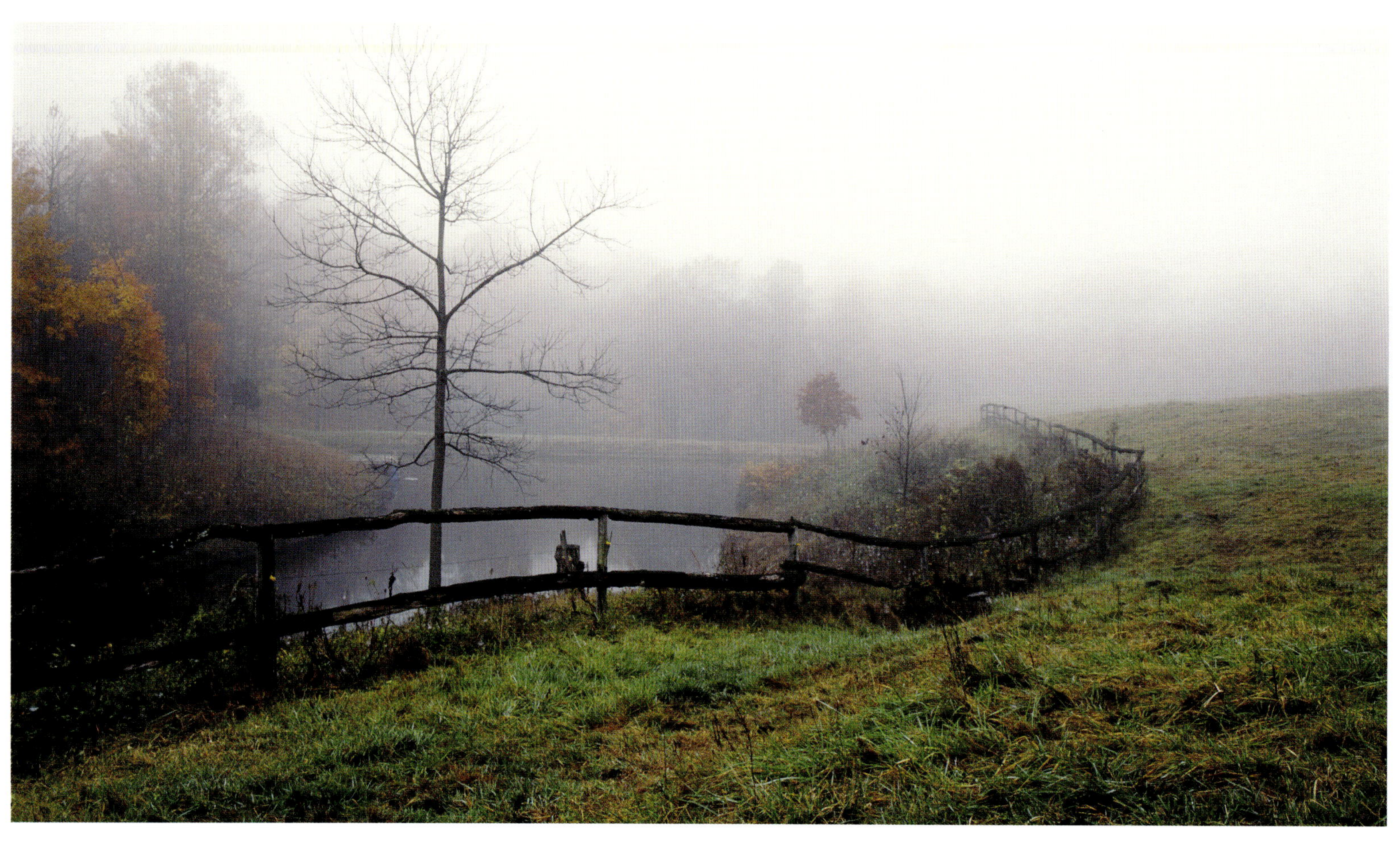

Private Property. *Fall.*

Brown County State Park. *Summer.*

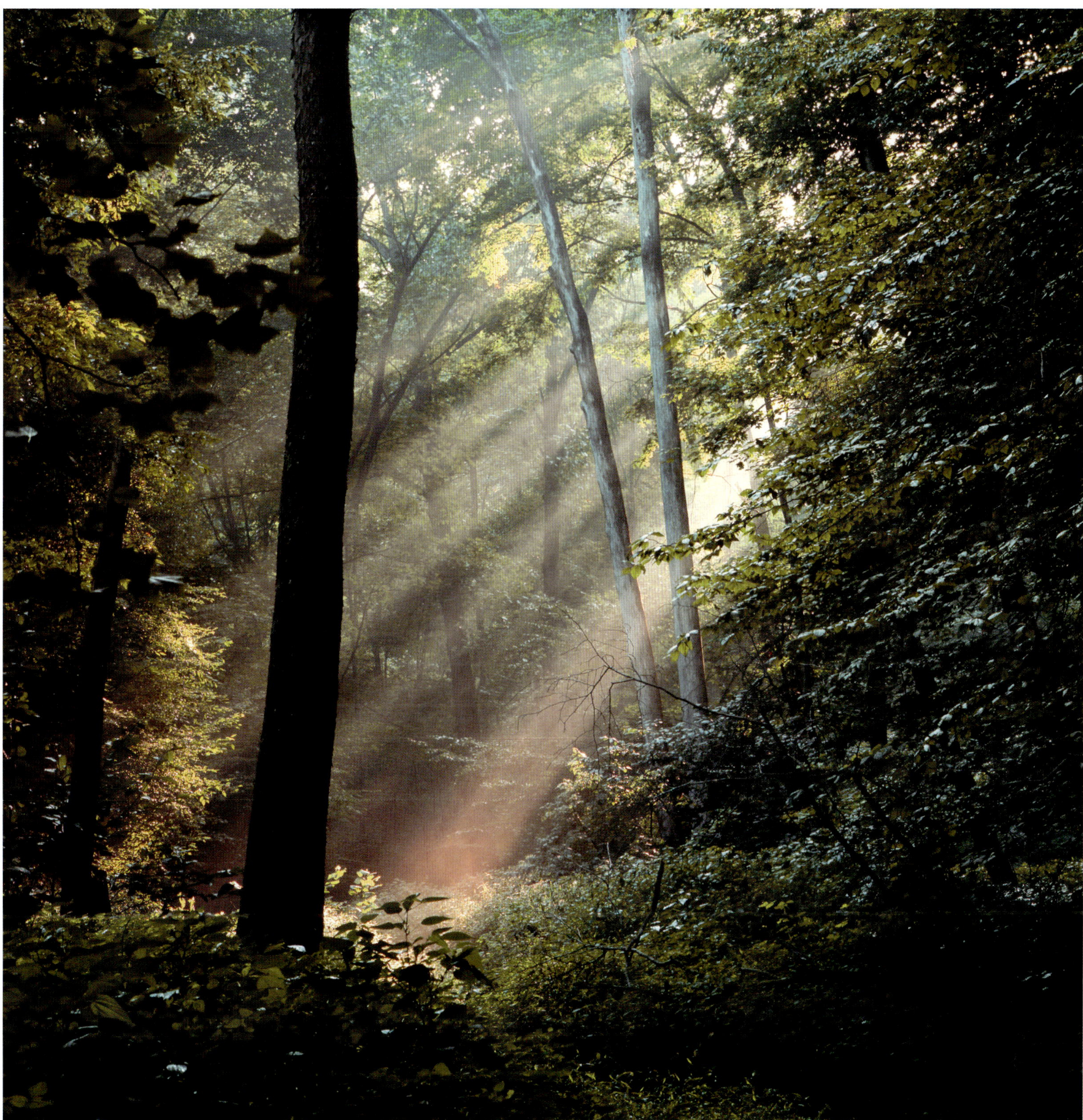

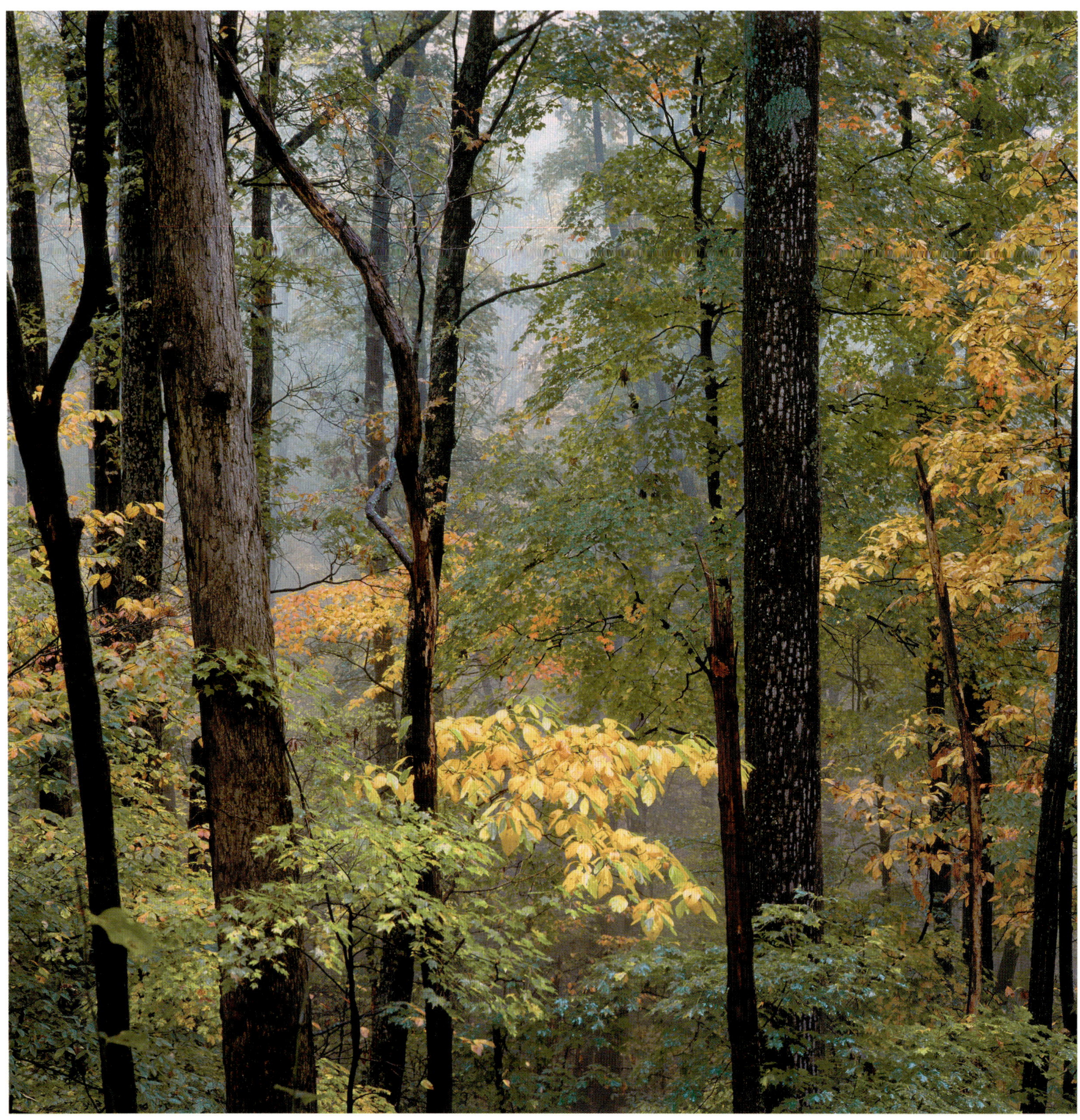

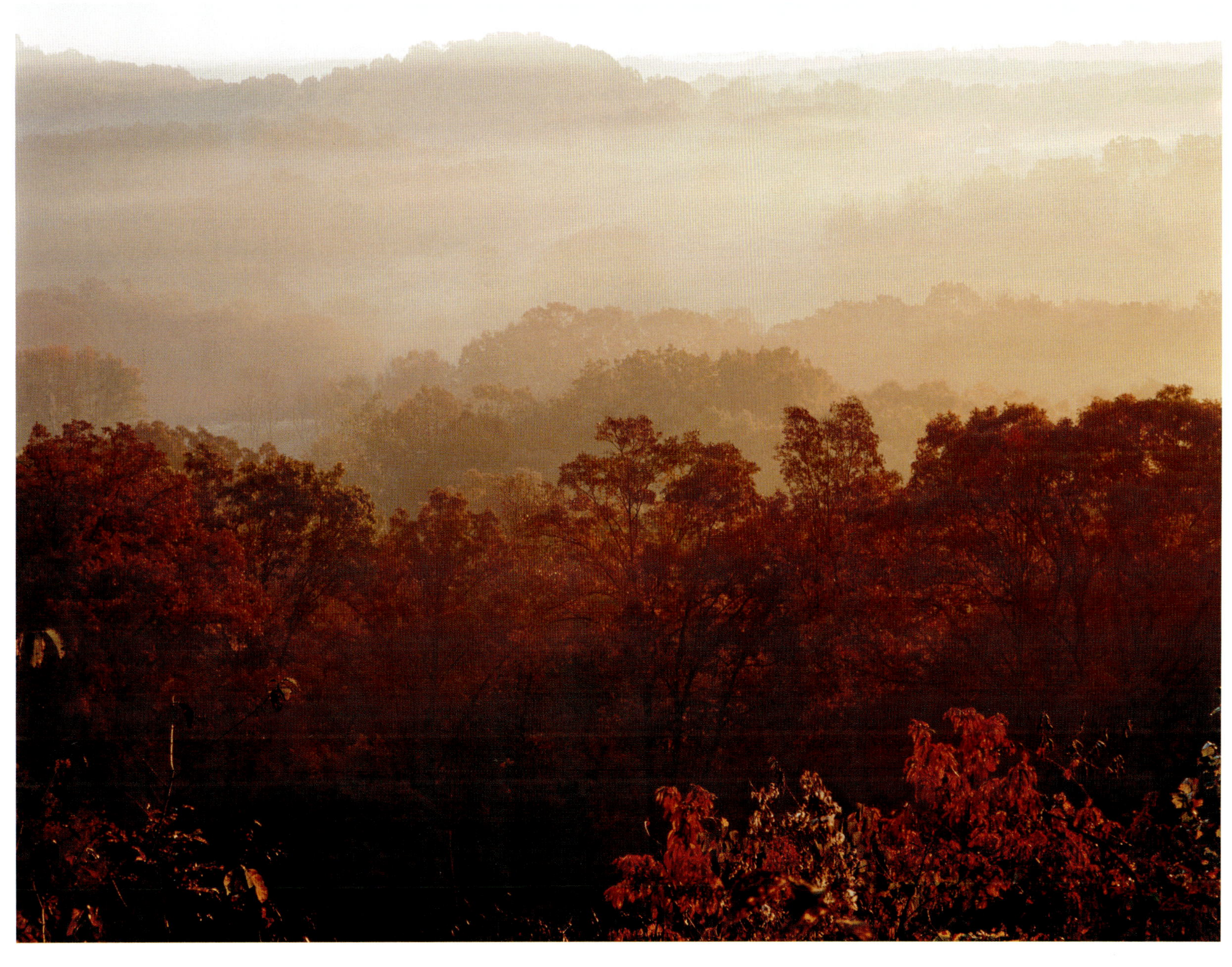

Brown County State Park. Private Property. *October.*

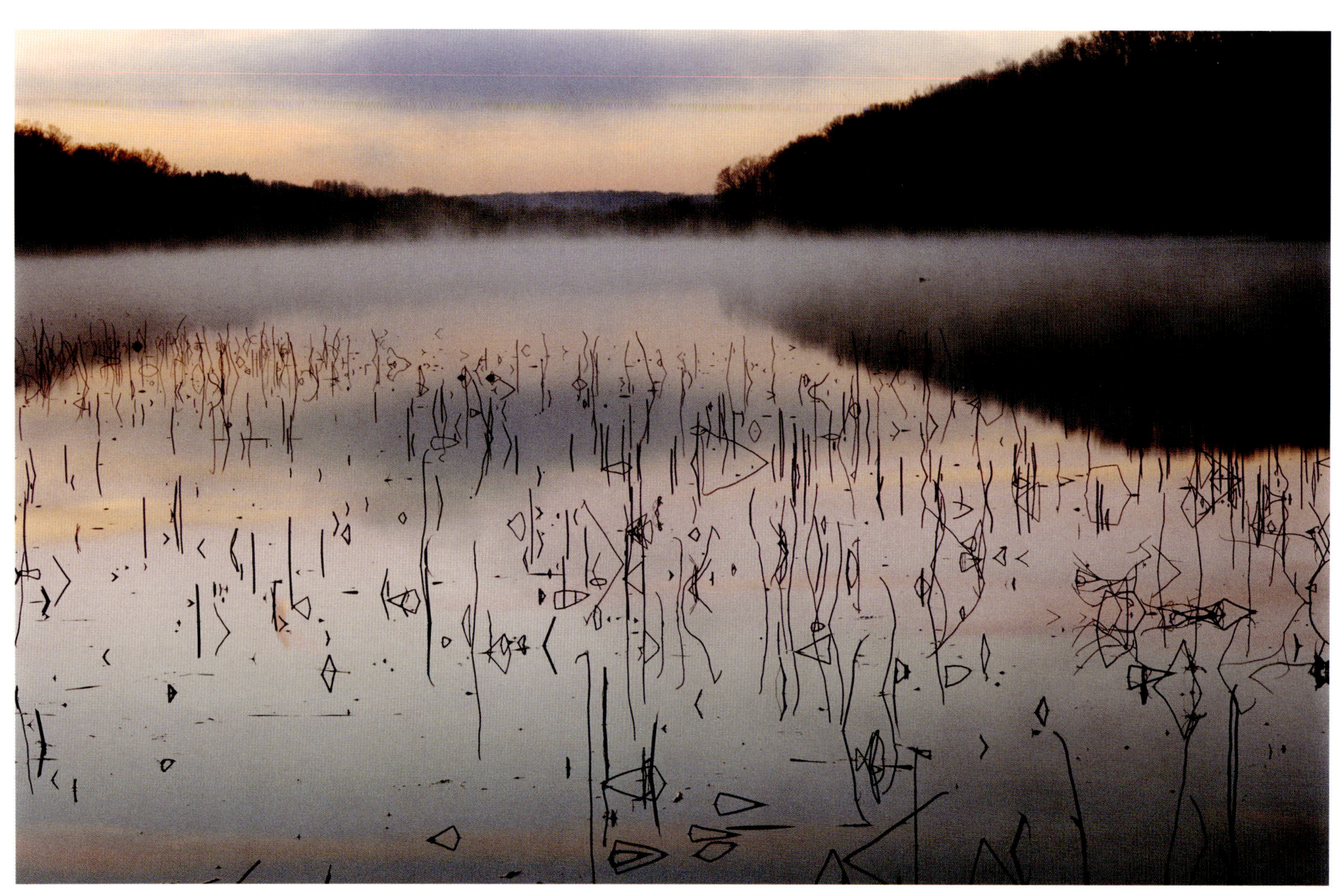

Yellowwood Lake in Yellowwood State Forest. *Winter.*

Brown County State Park. *October.*

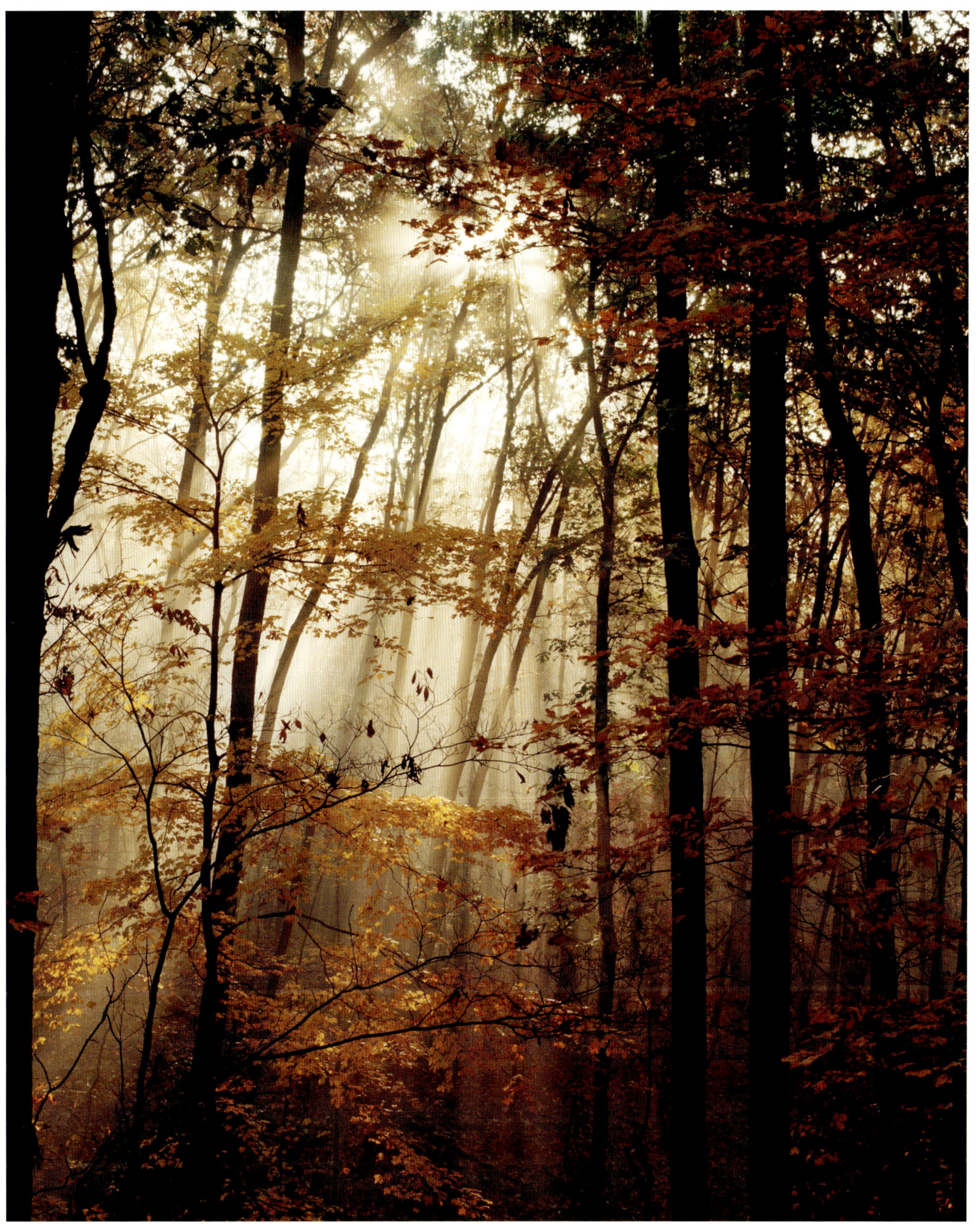

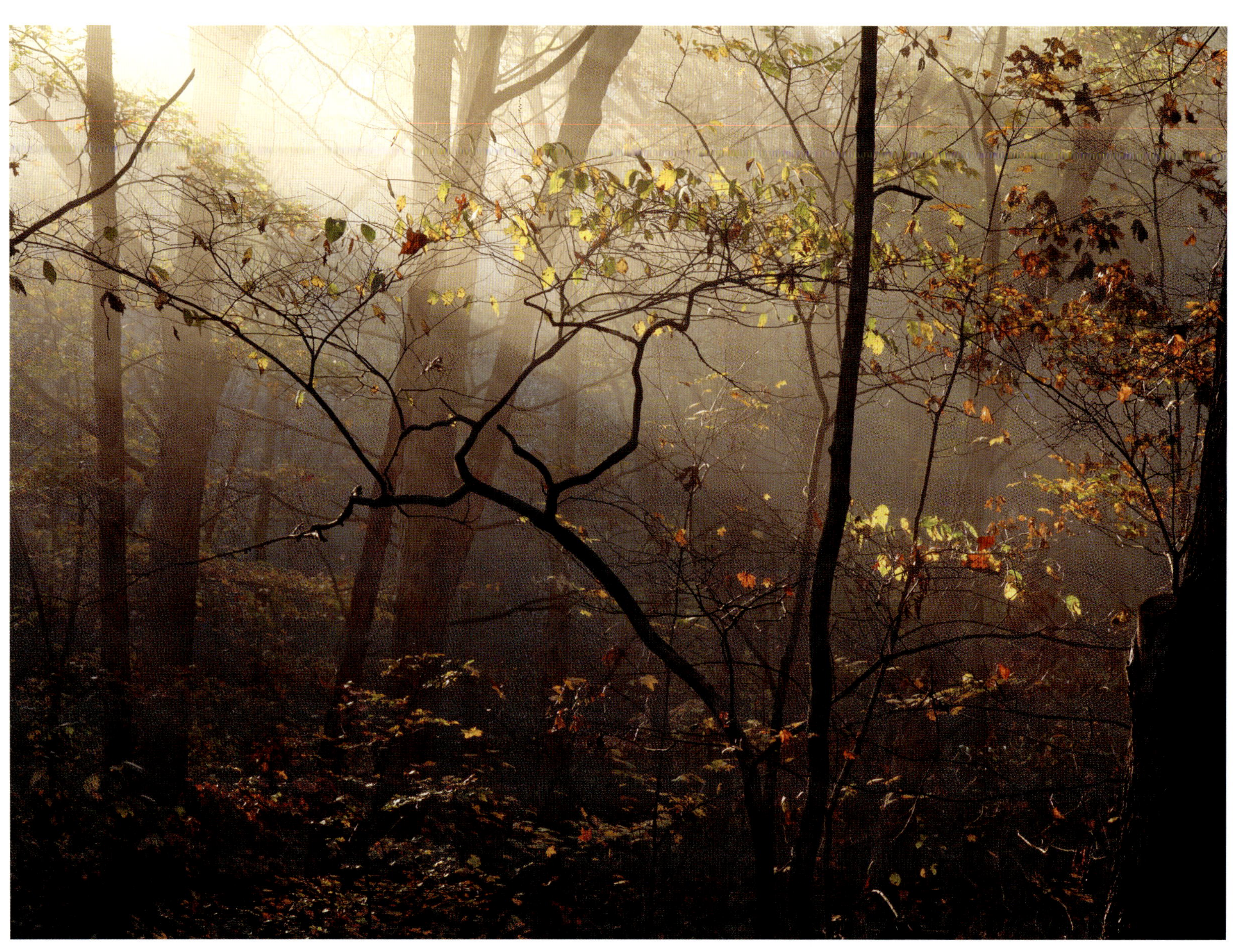

Brown County State Park. *October.*

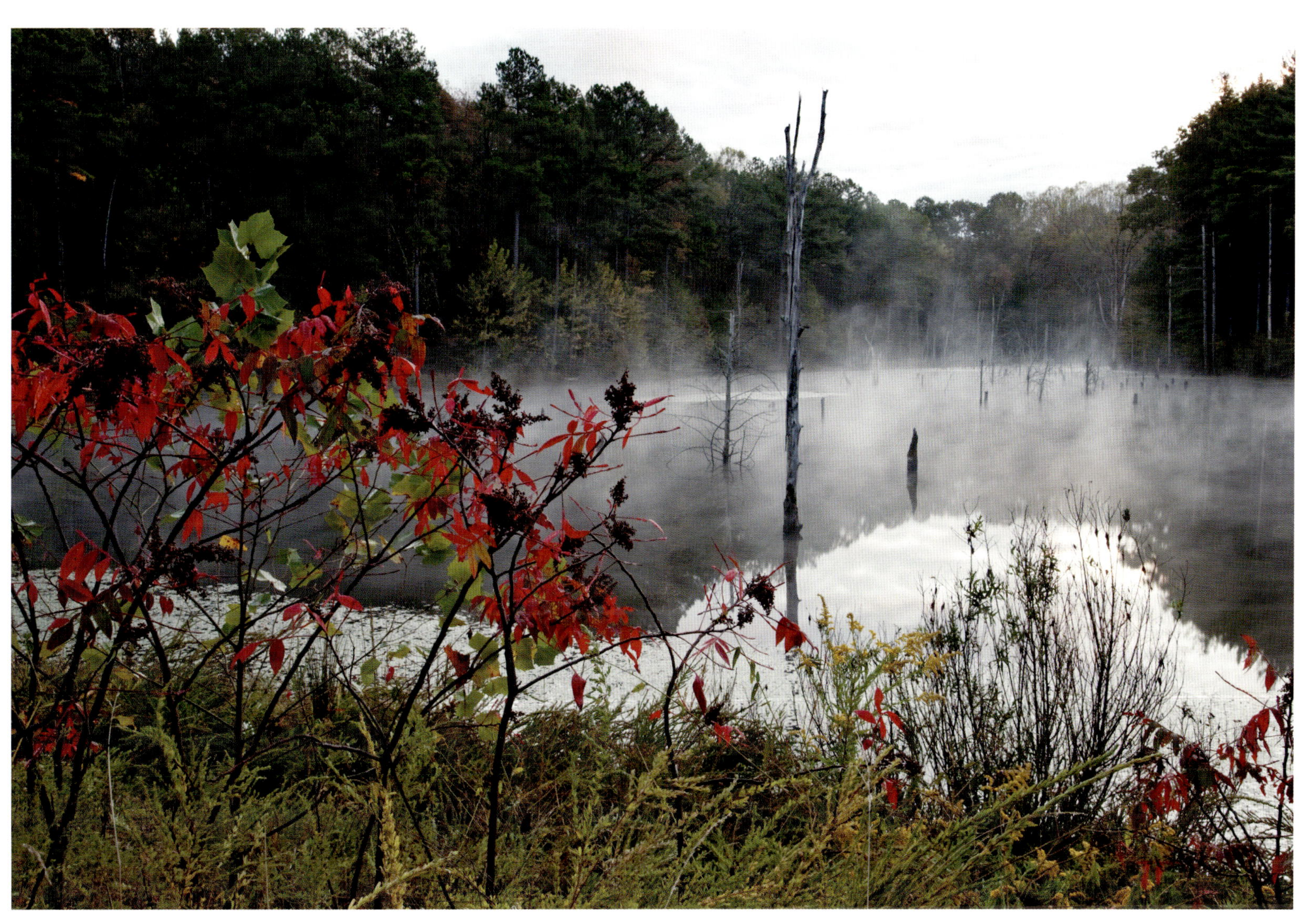

Sundance Lake in Hoosier National Forest. *October.*

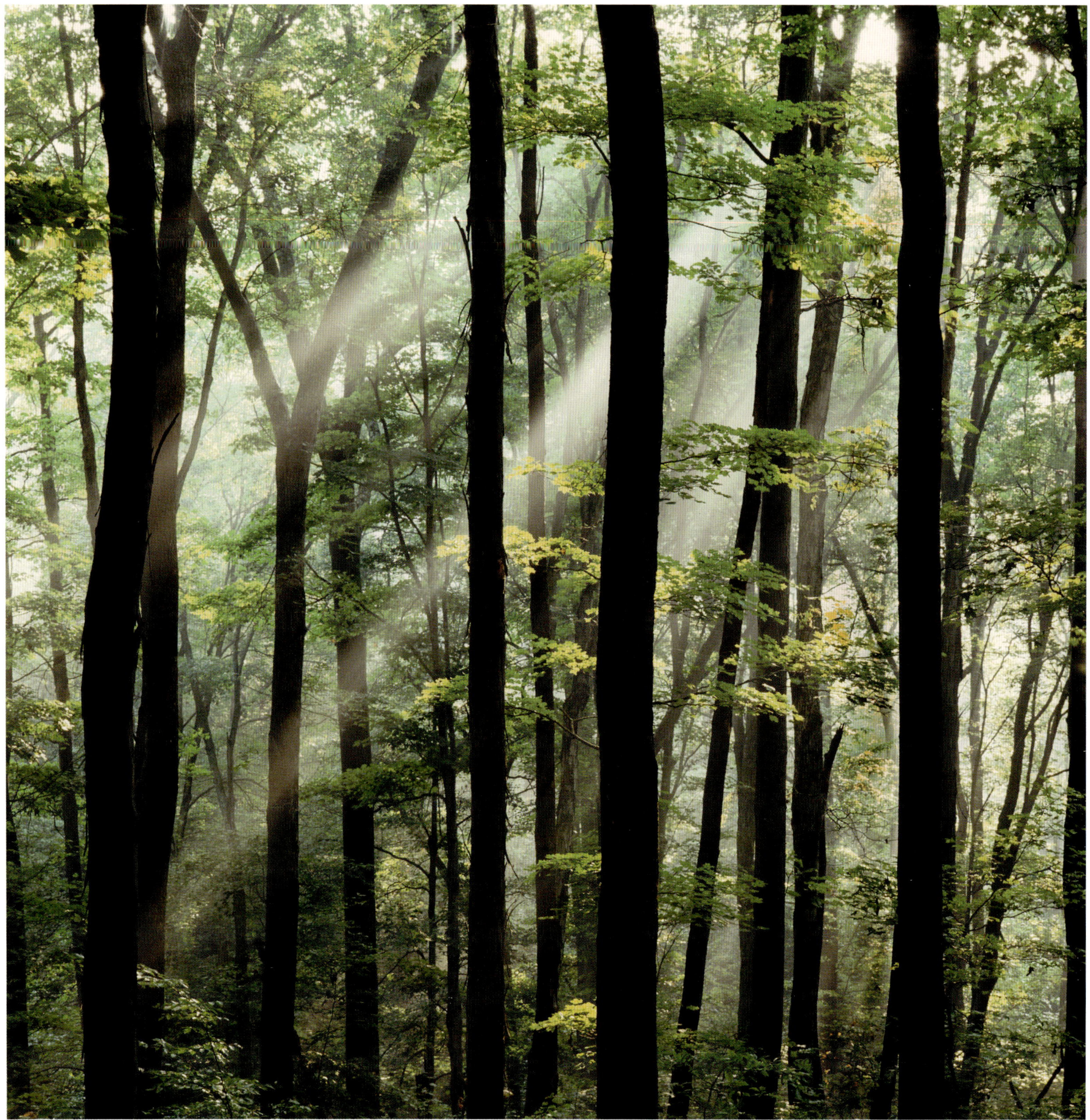

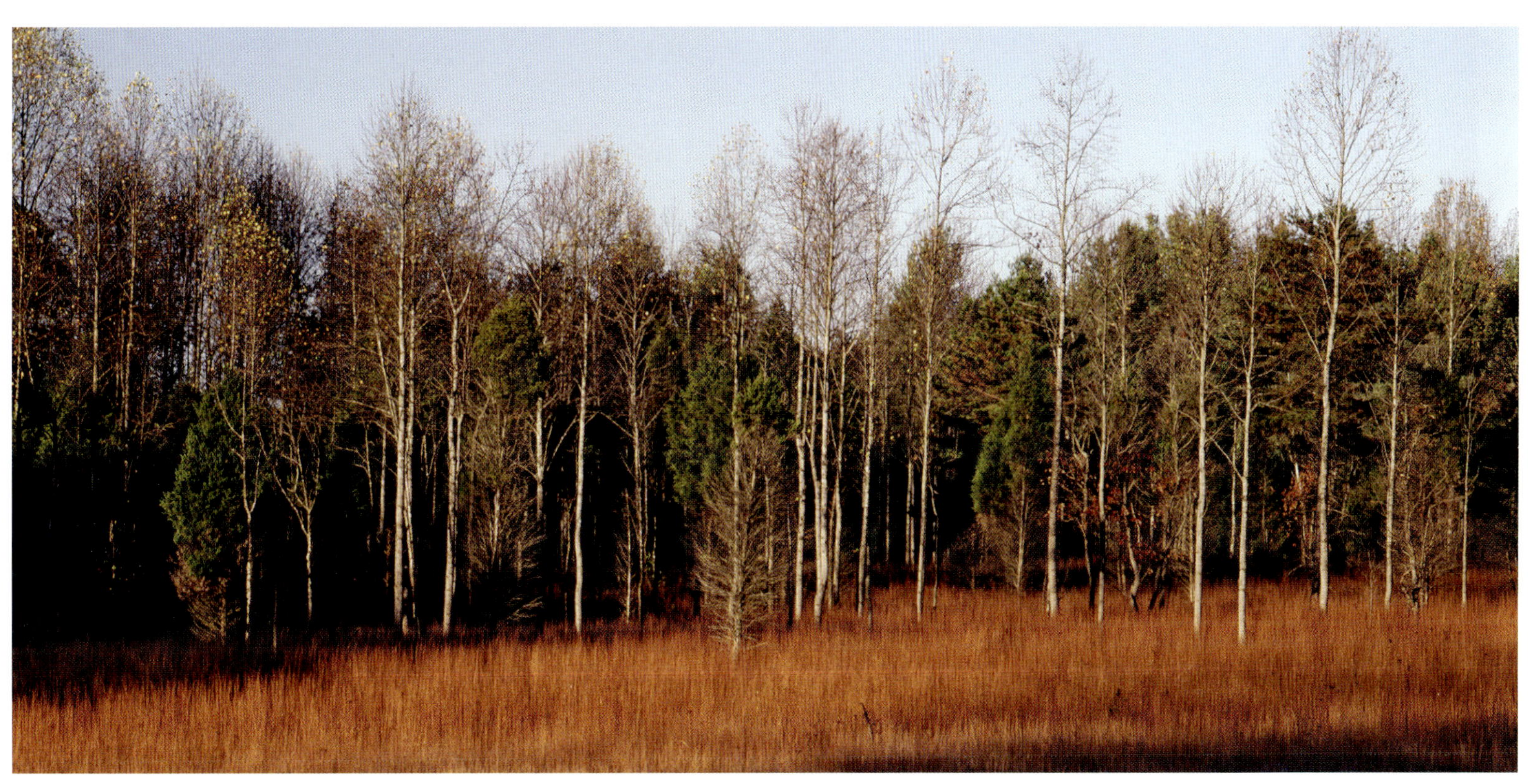

Yellowwood State Forest. *Summer.*

Hoosier National Forest. *October.*

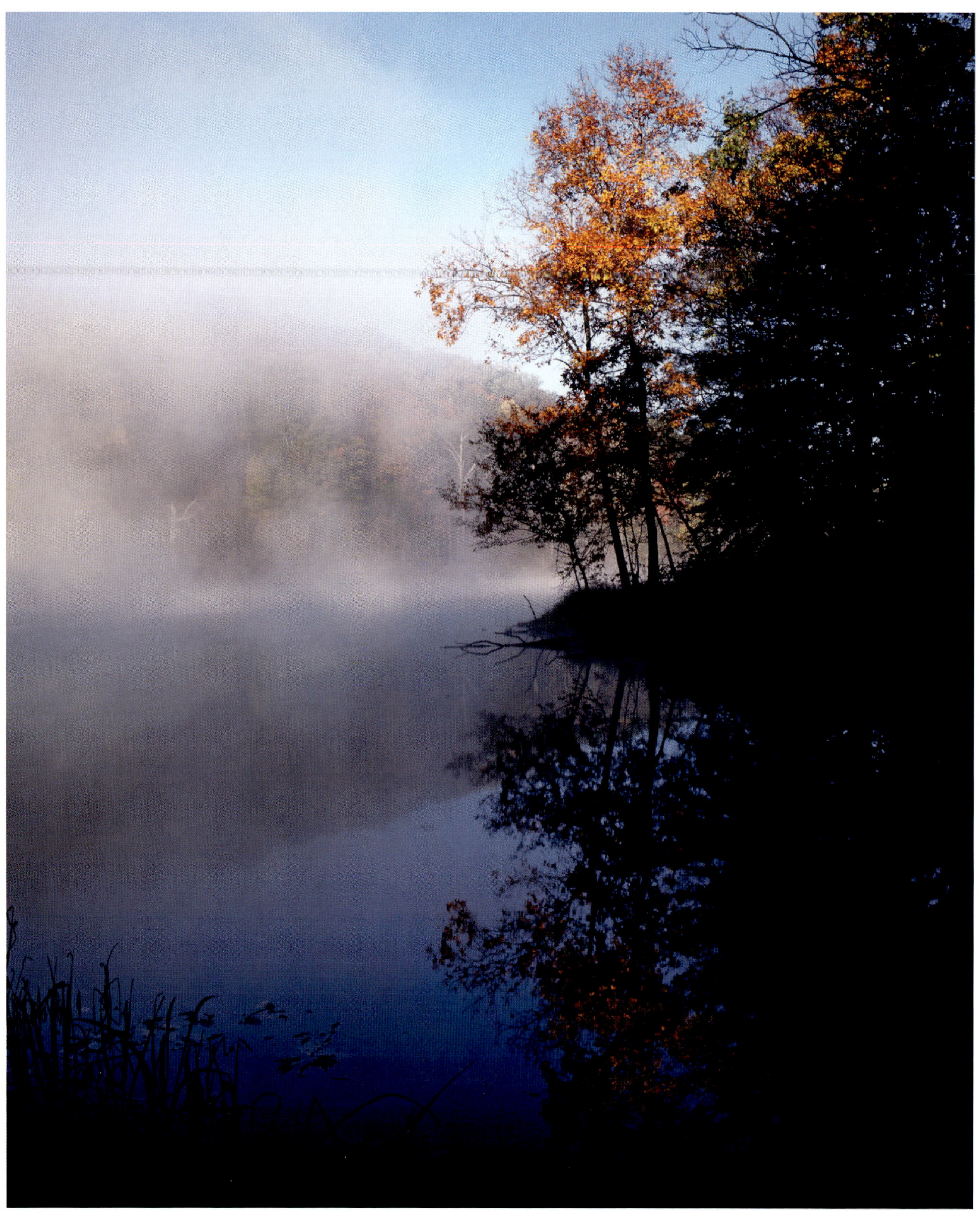

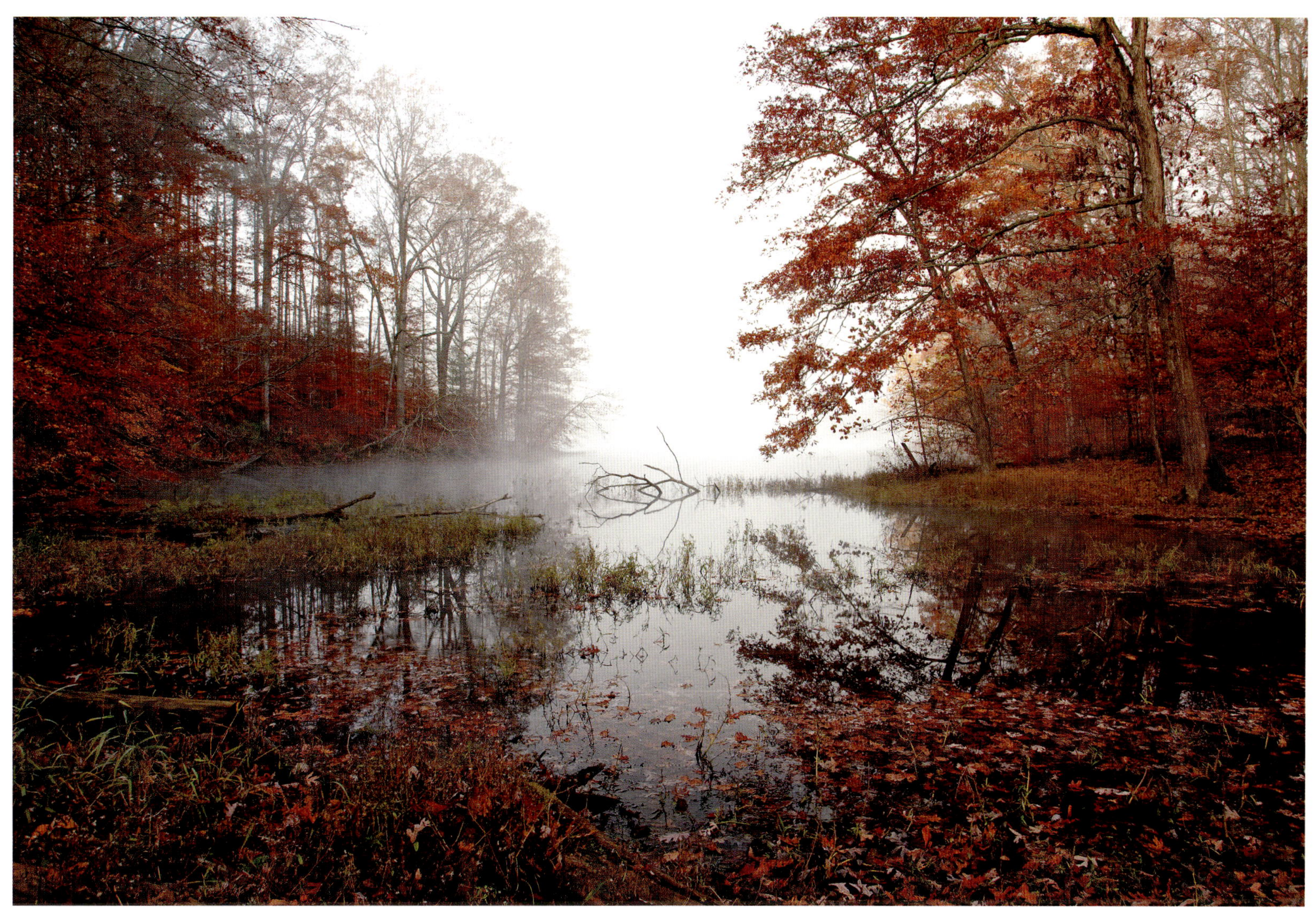

Bear Lake in Yellowwood State Park. *October.*

Yellowwood Lake in Yellowwood State Forest. *October.*

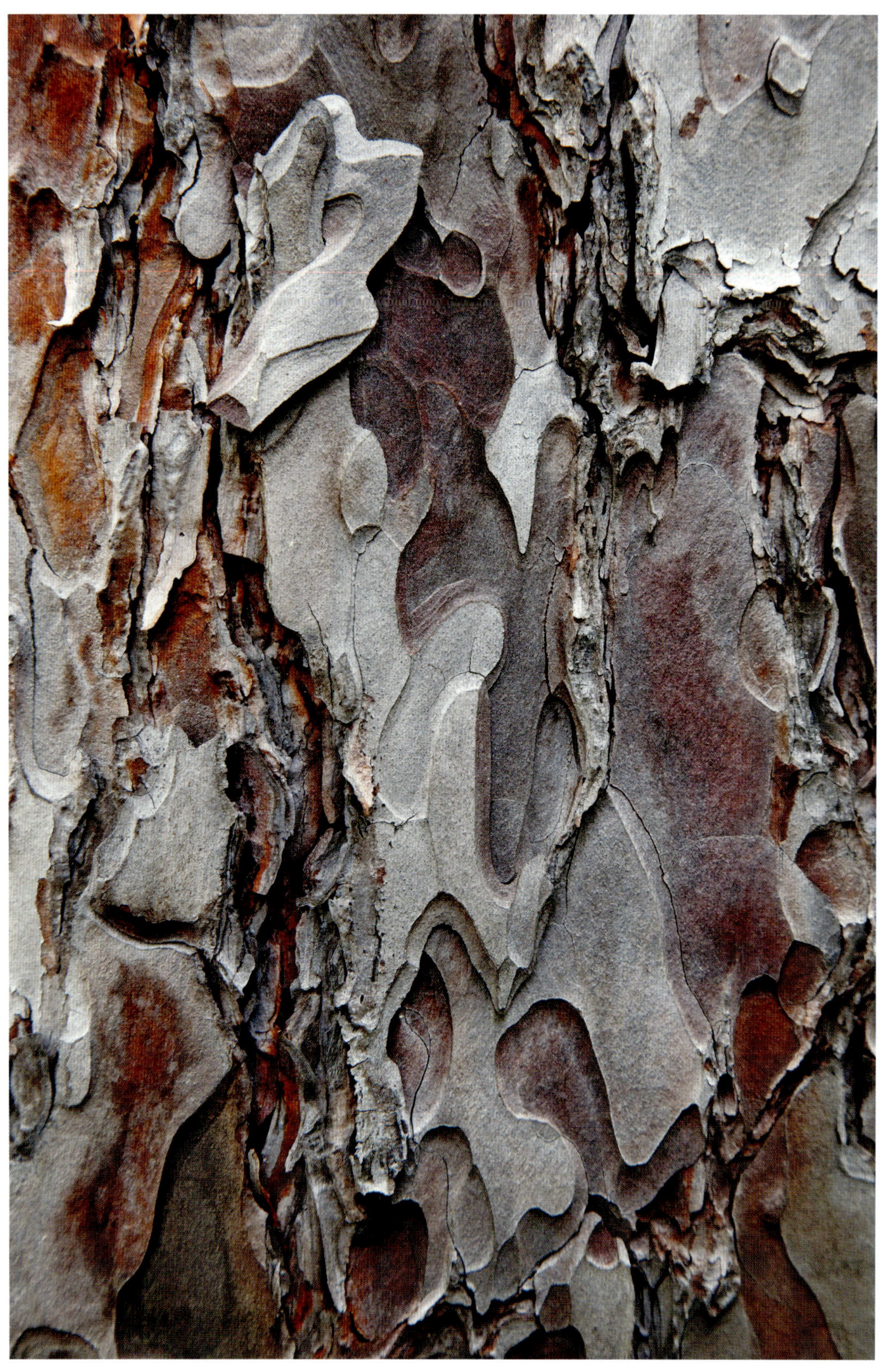

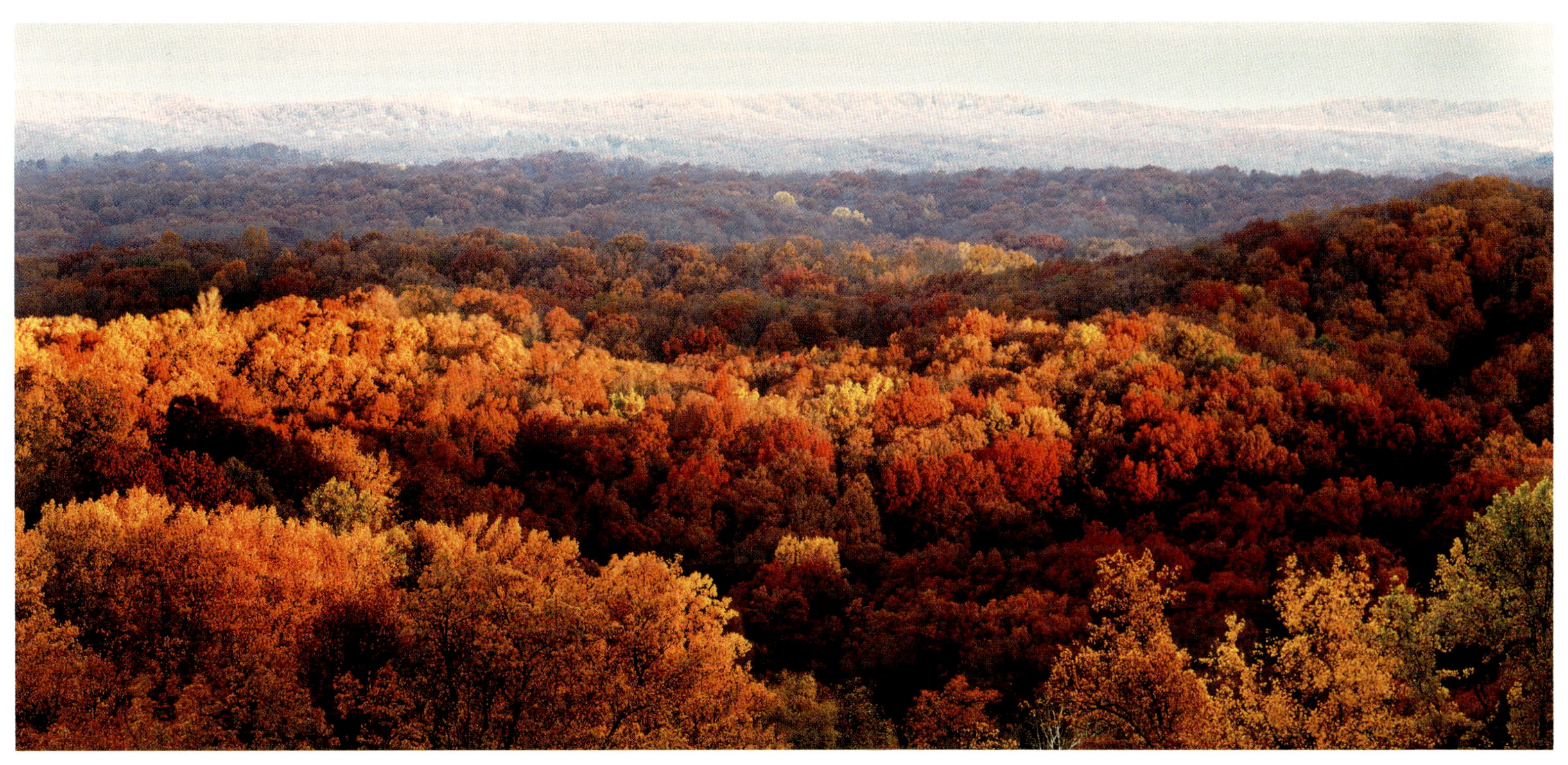

Brown County State Park. *April.*

Brown County State Park. *October.*

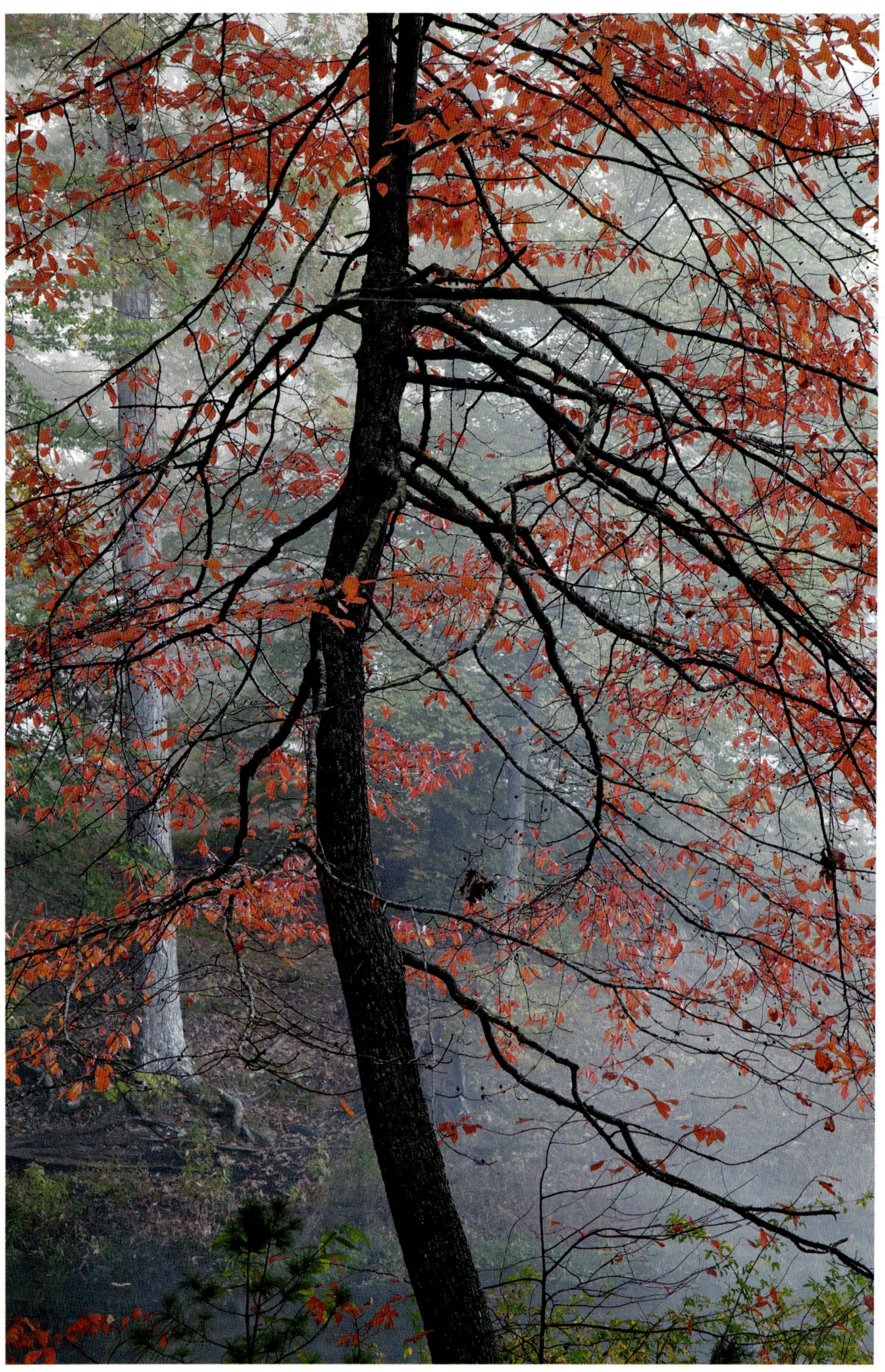

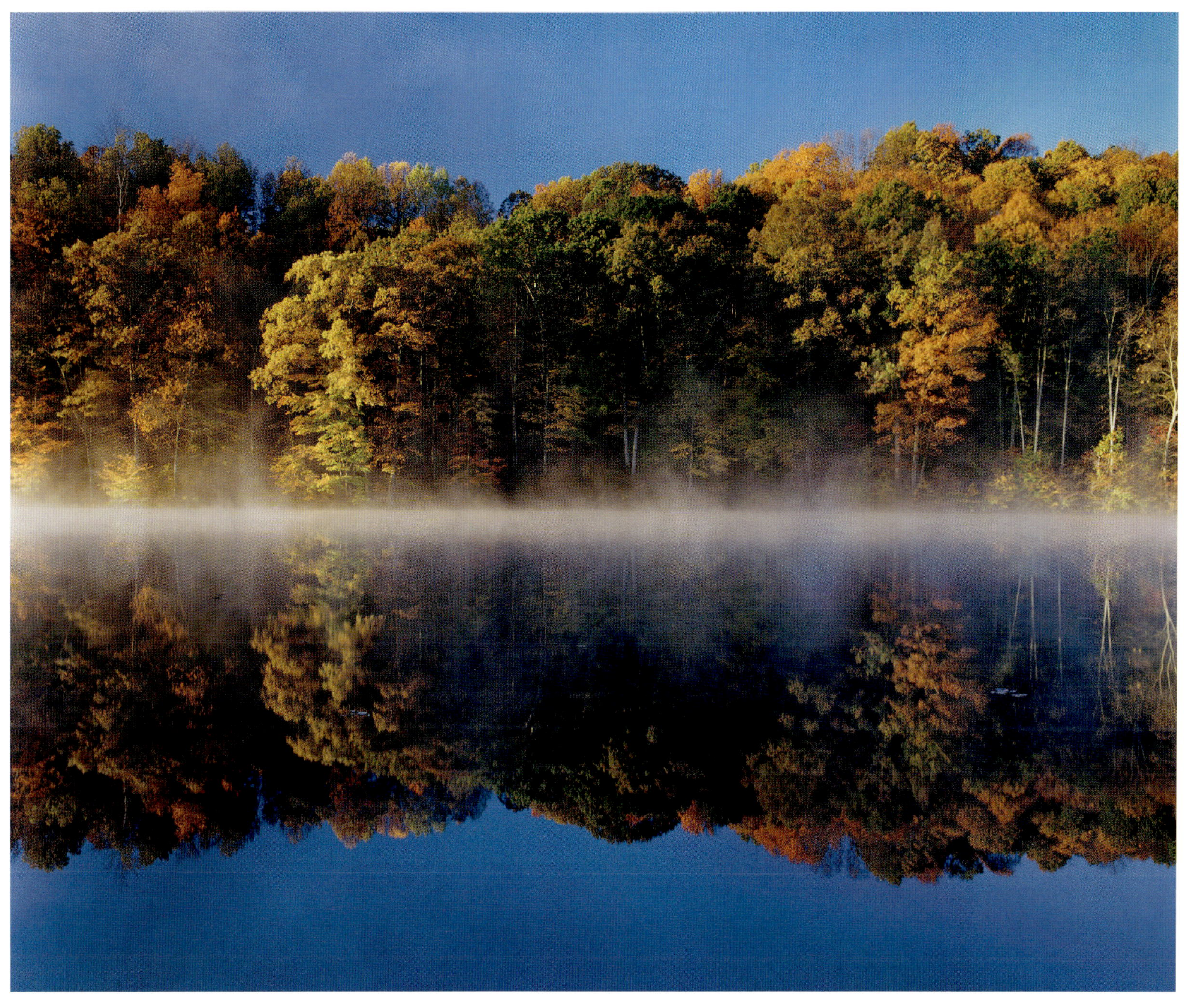

Yellowwood State Forest. *October.* Private Property.

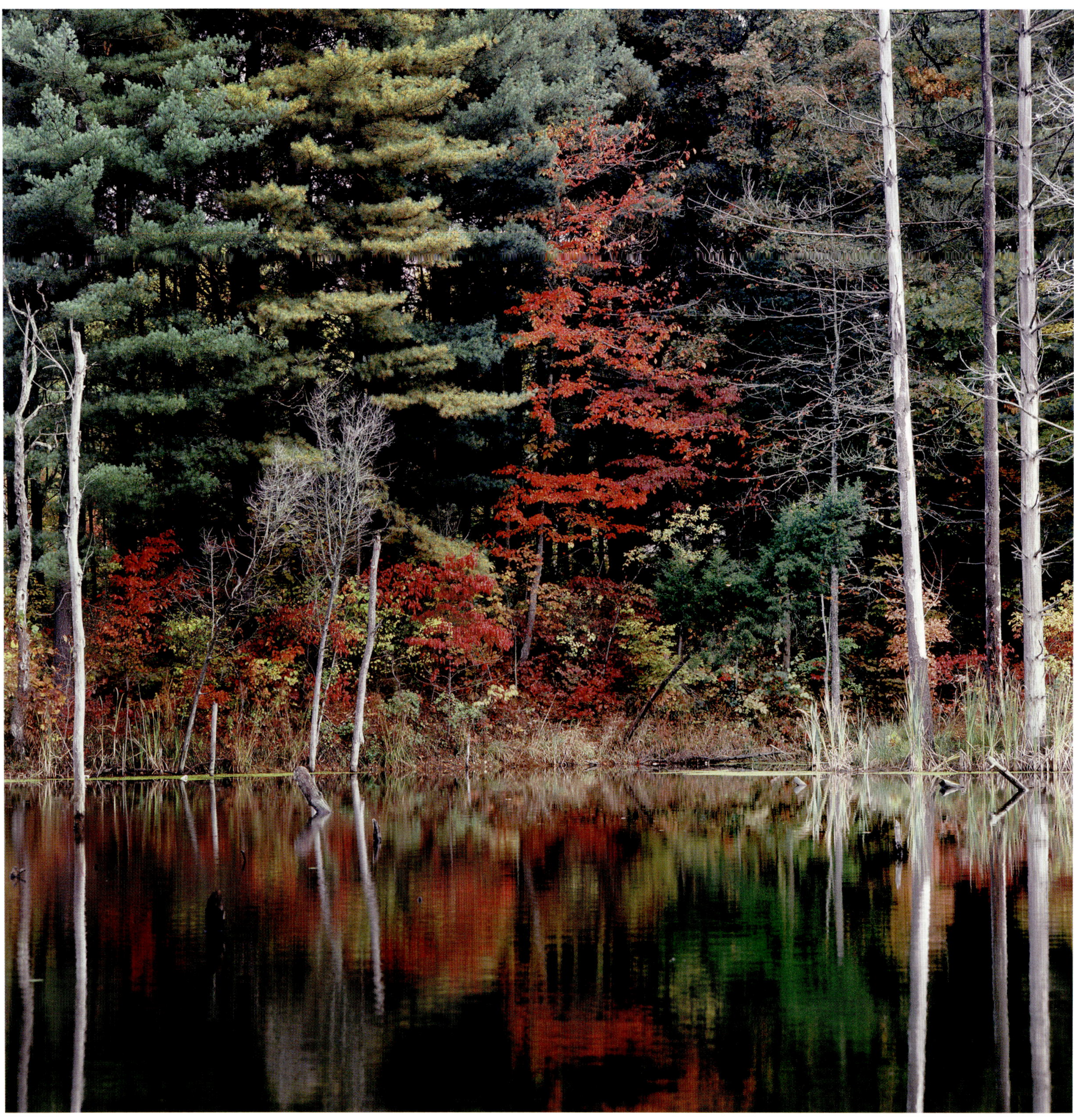

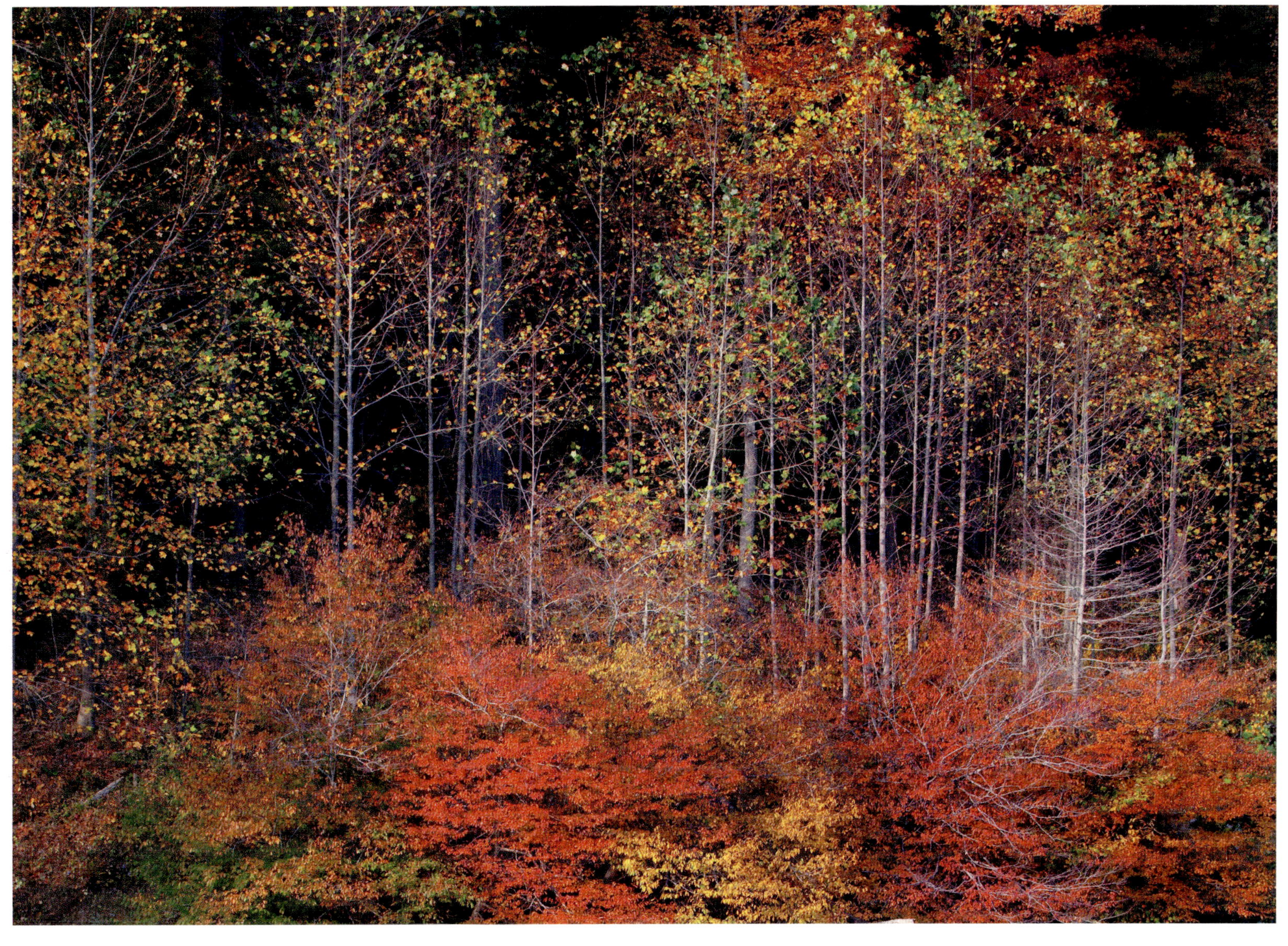

Sundance Lake.

Bear Lake in Yellowwood State Forest. *October.*

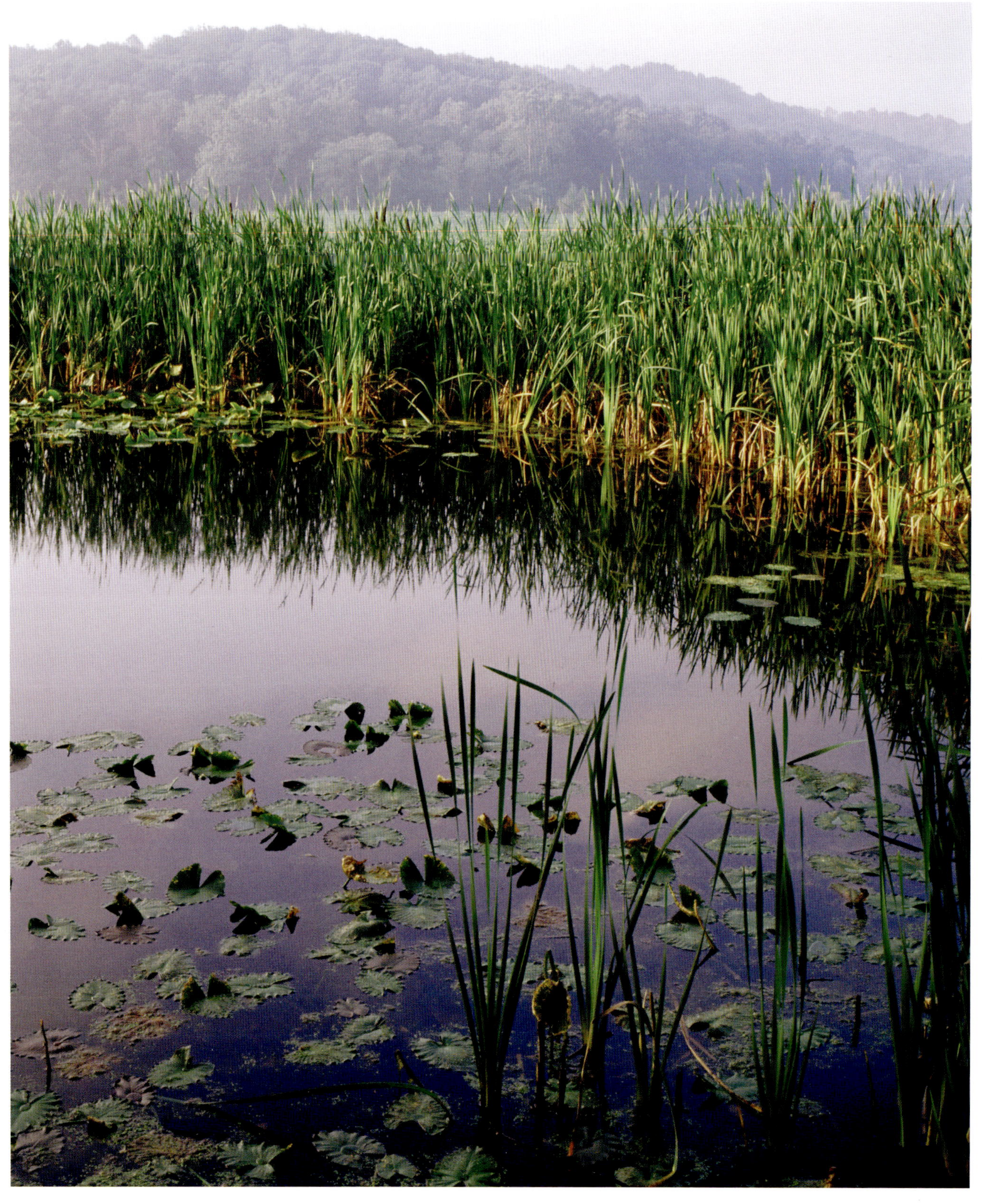

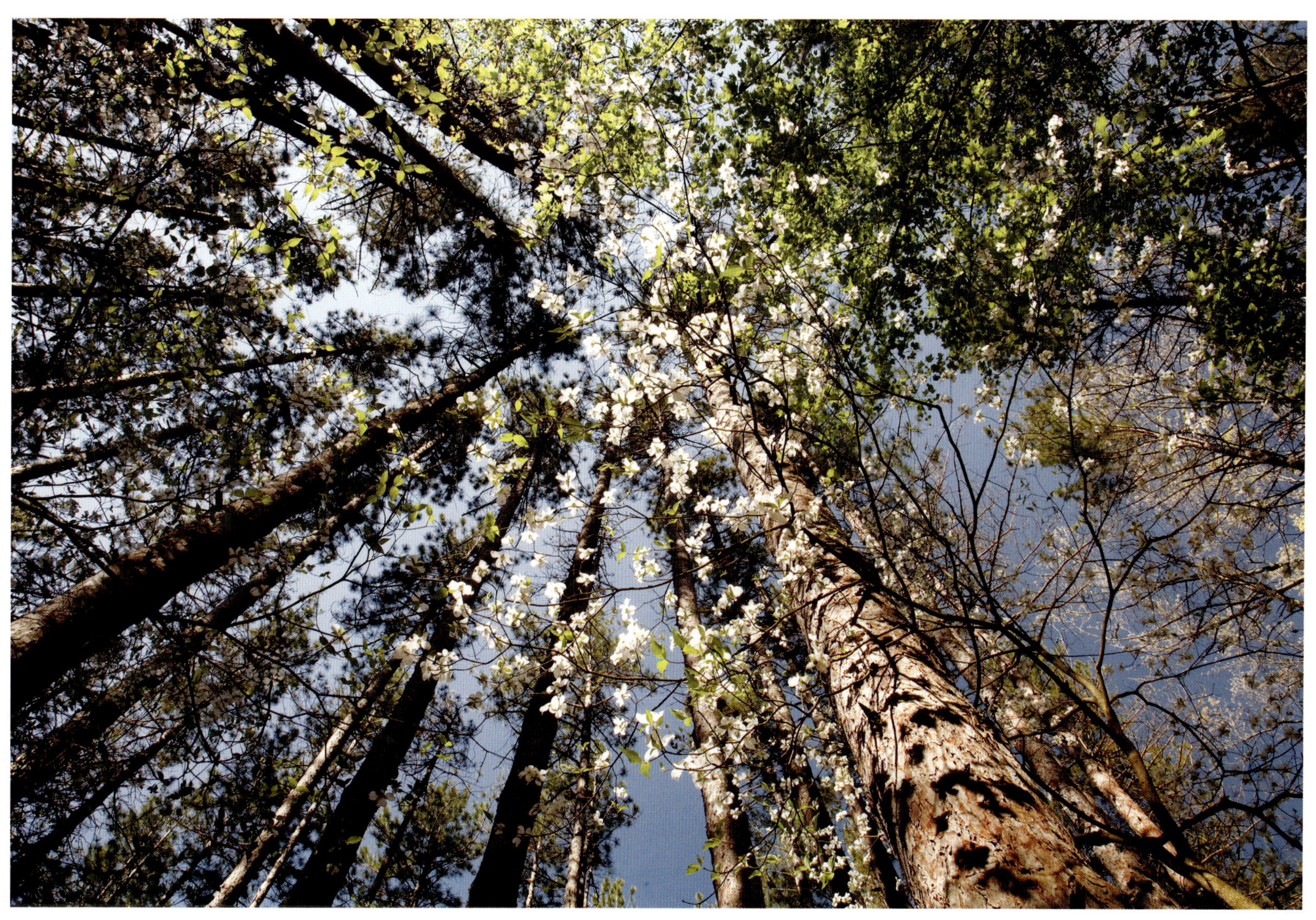

Private Property. *Summer.*

Brown County State Park. *April.*

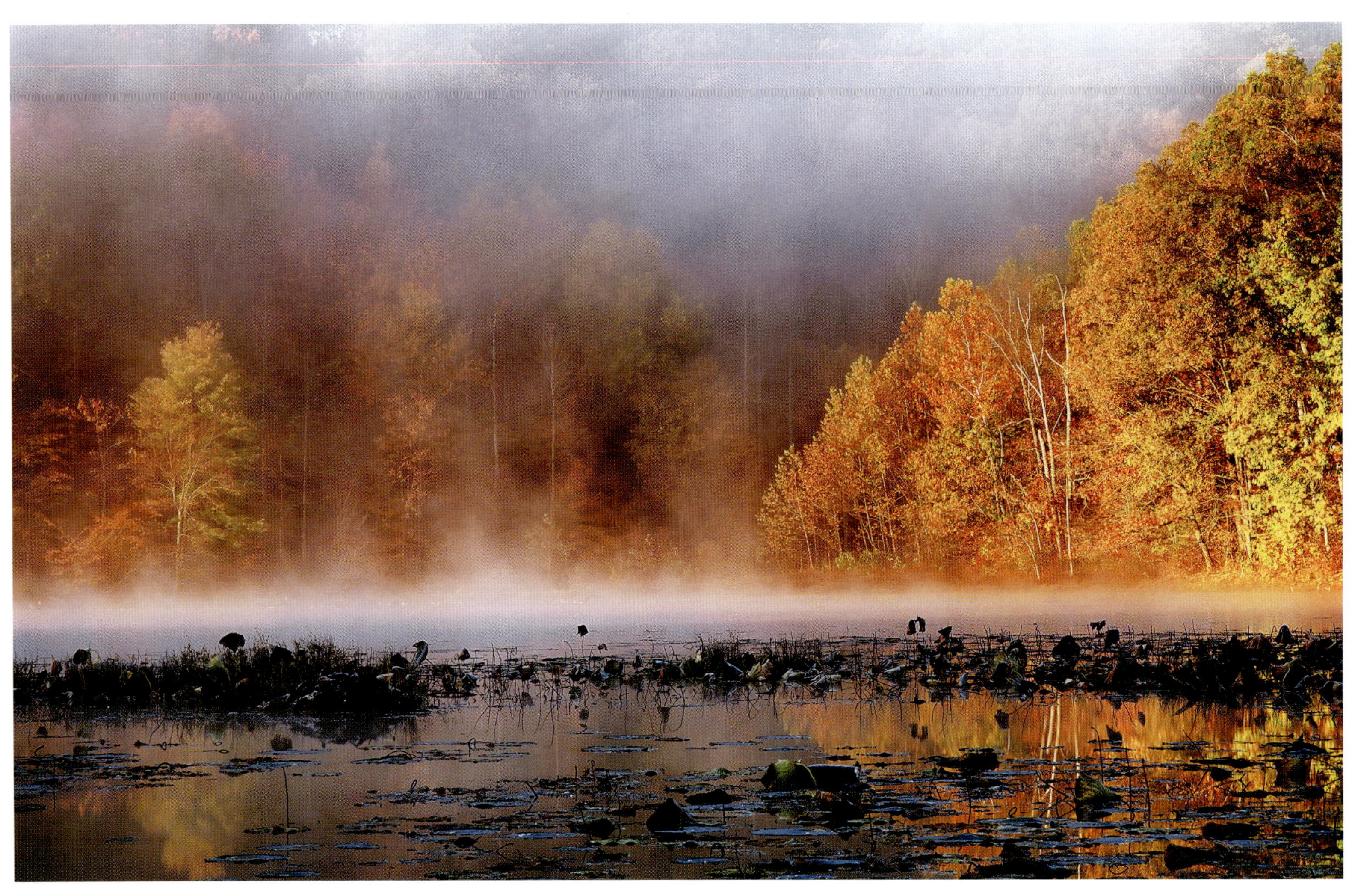

Yellowwood Lake in Yellowwood State Forest. *October.*

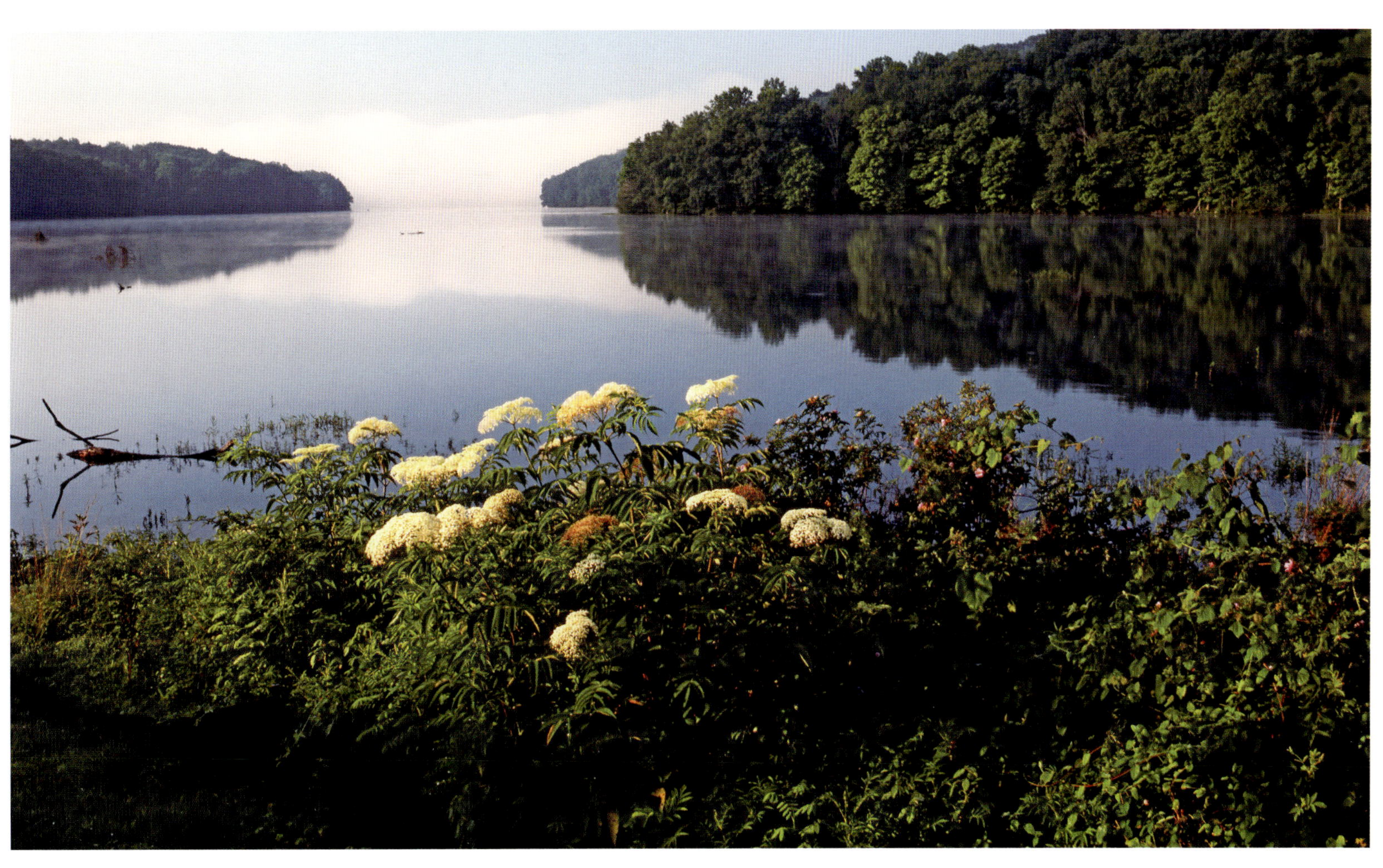

Yellowwood Lake in Yellowwood State Forest. *Summer.*

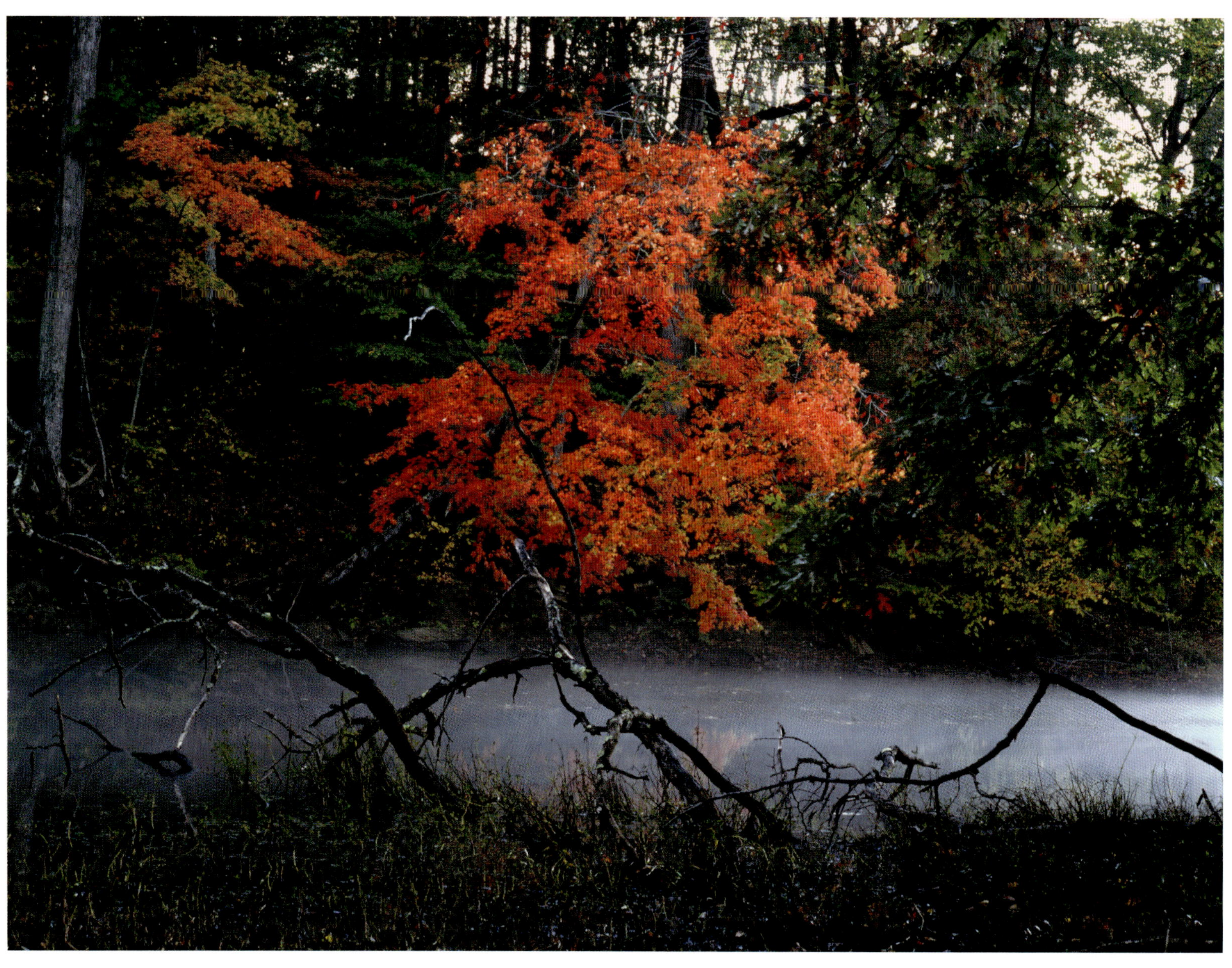

Yellowwood Lake in Yellowwood State Forest. *October.*

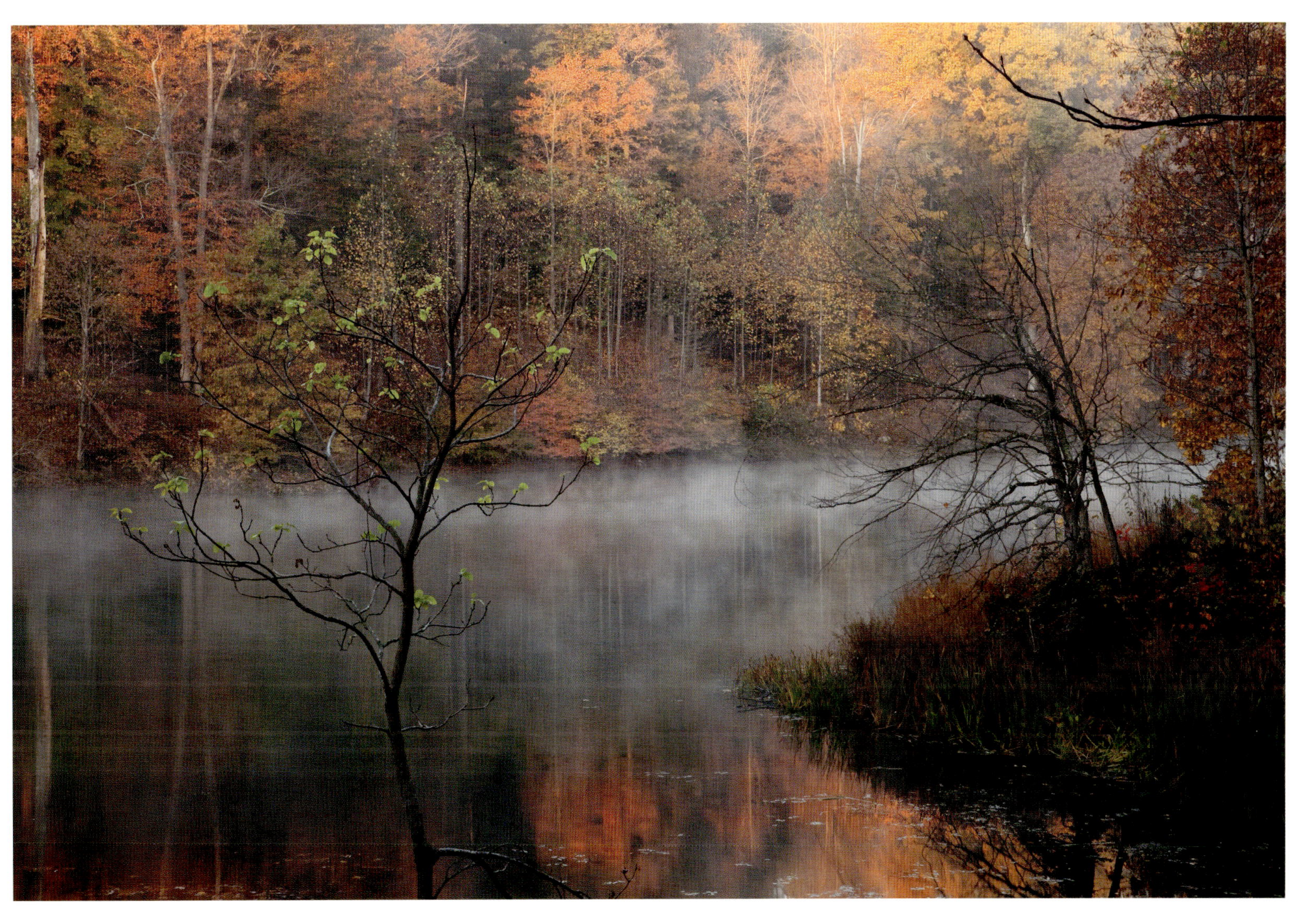

Bear Lake in Yellowwood State Forest. *October.*

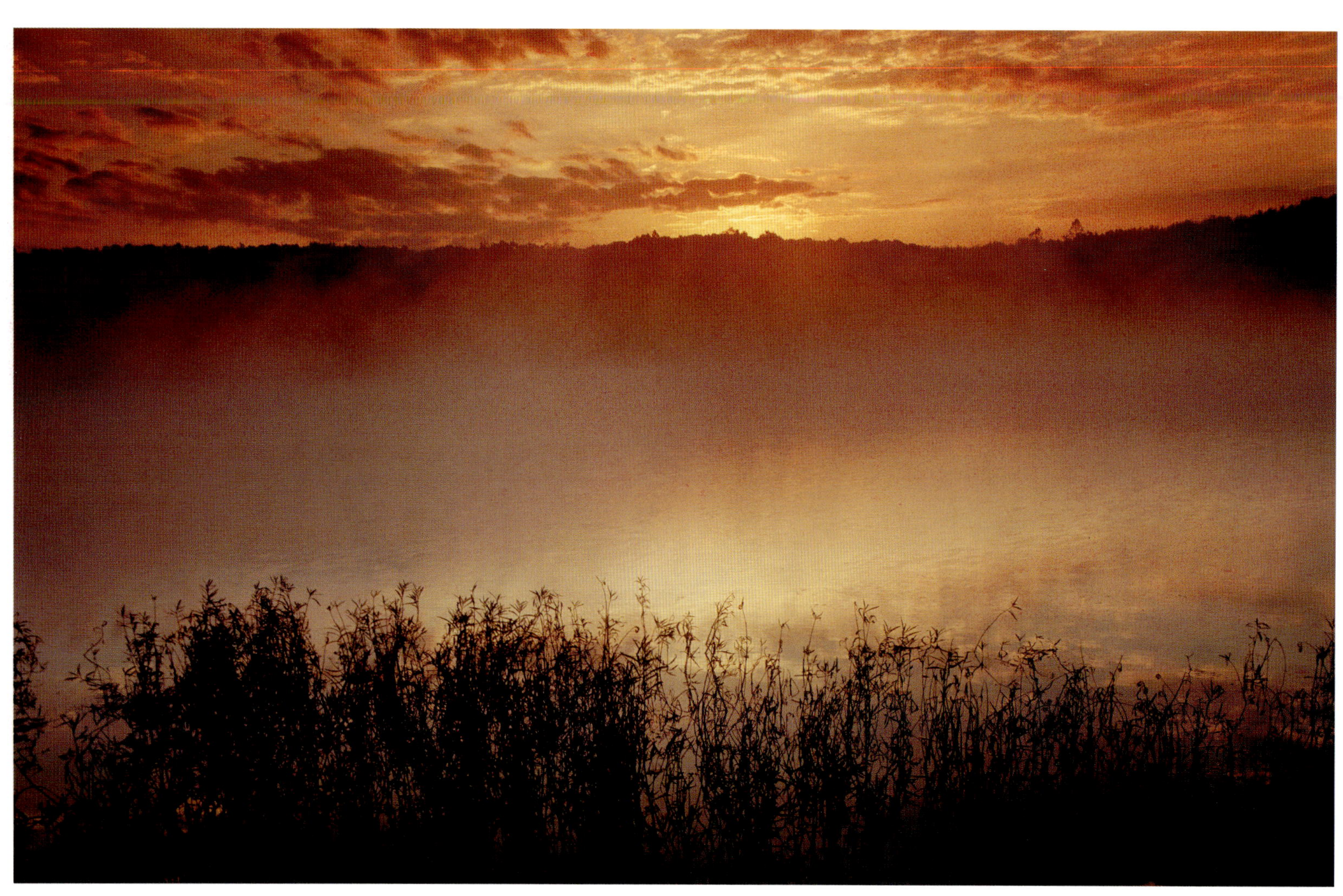

Yellowwood Lake in Yellowwood State Forest. *October.*

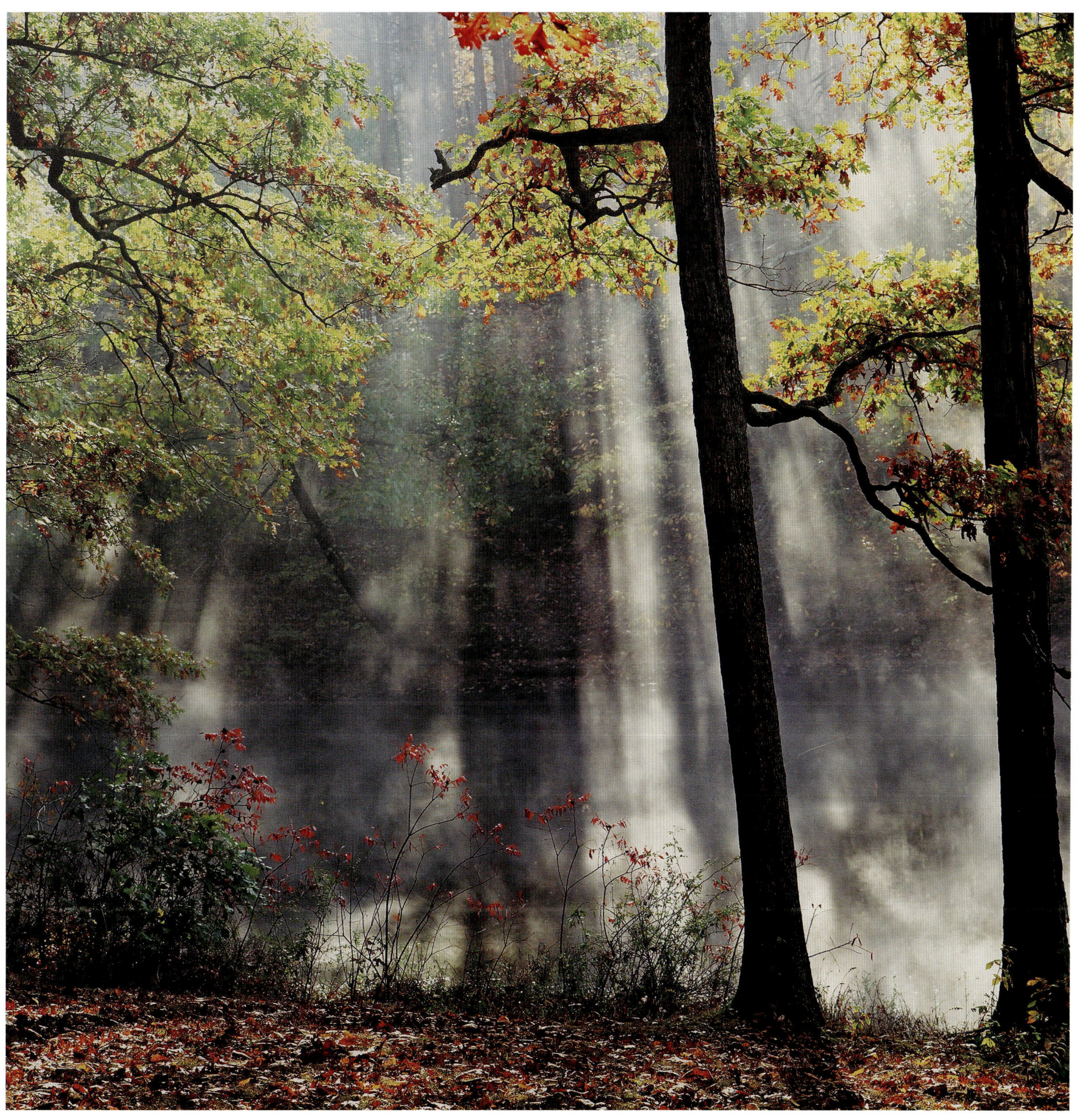

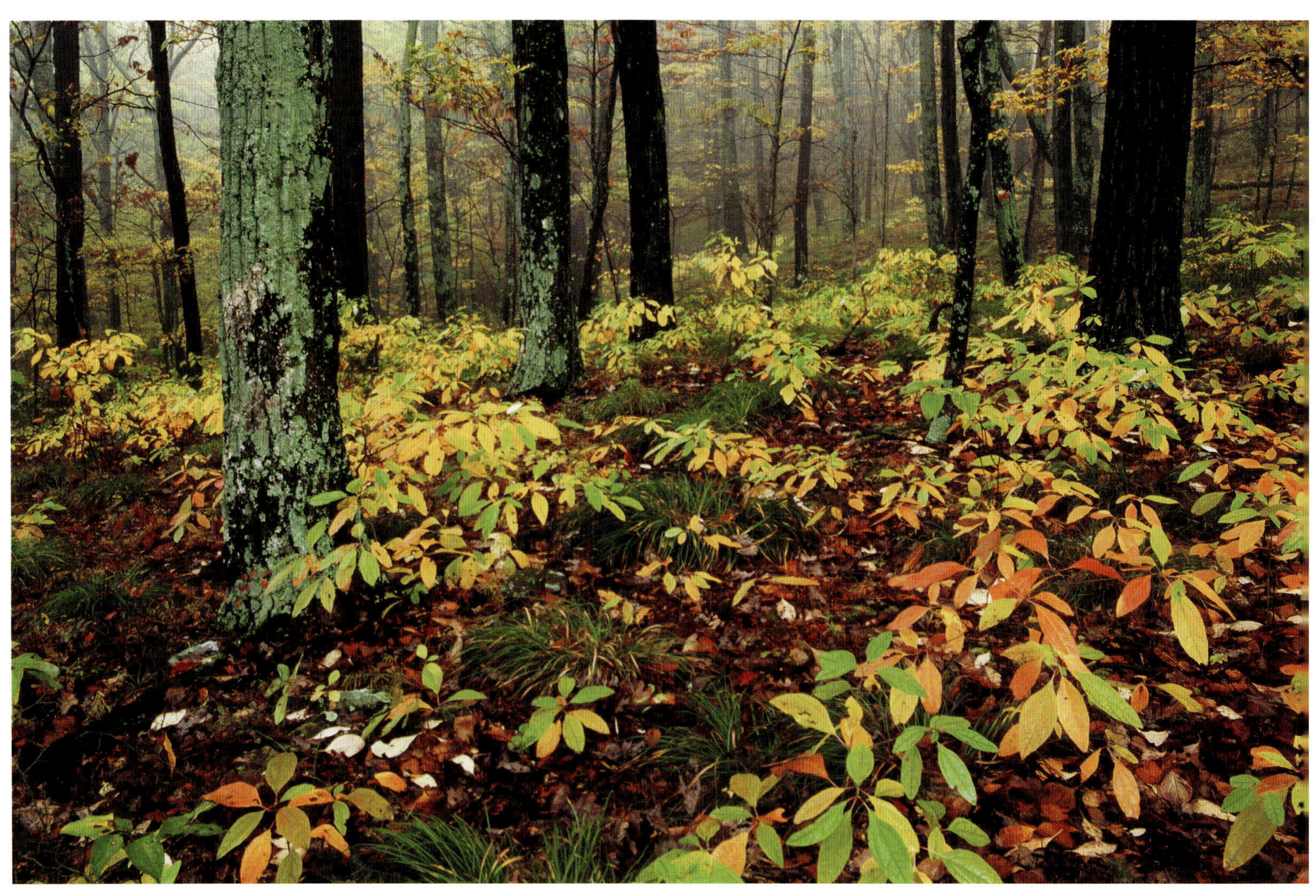

Hoosier National Forest. *October.*

Private Property. *October.*

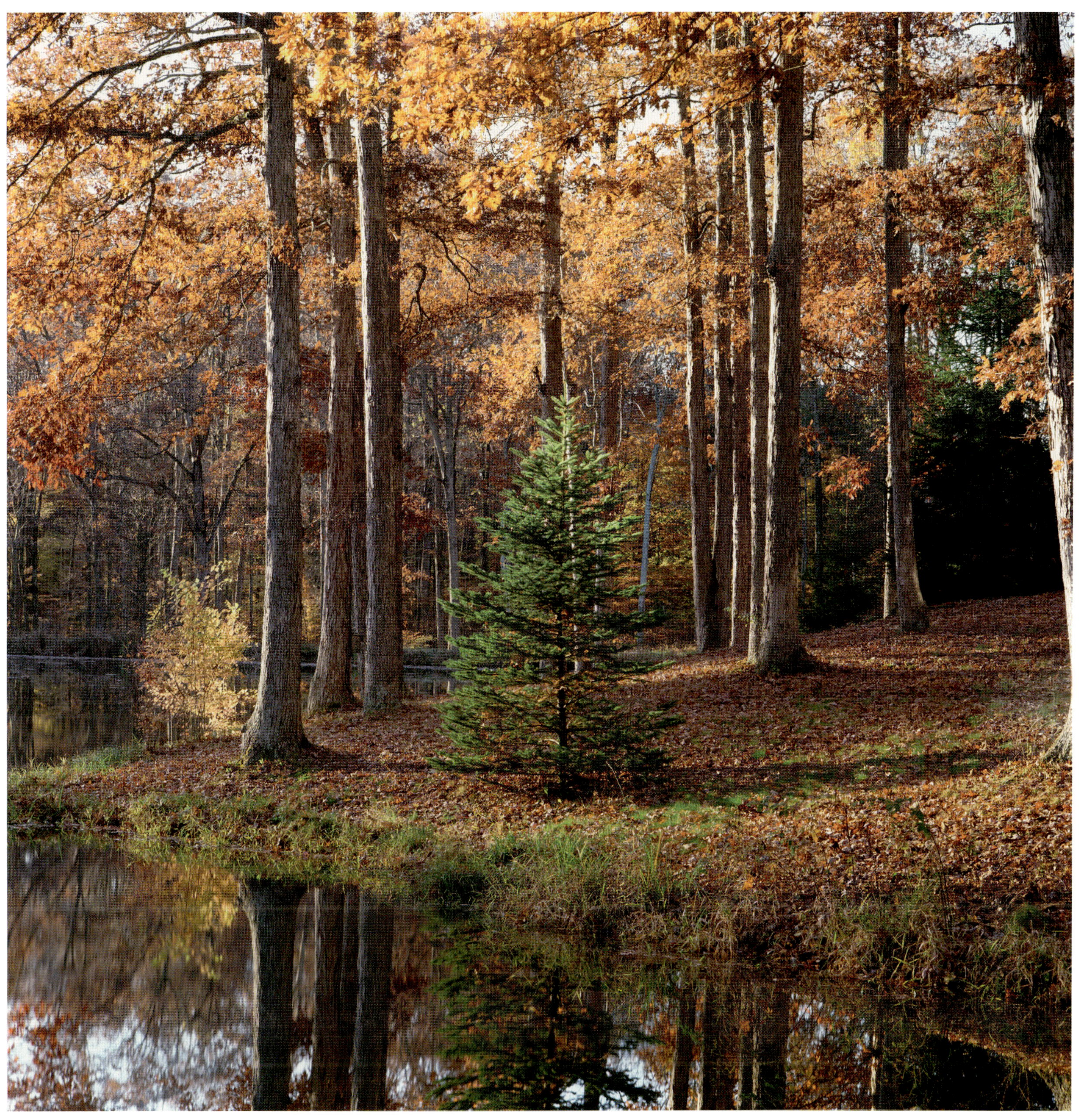

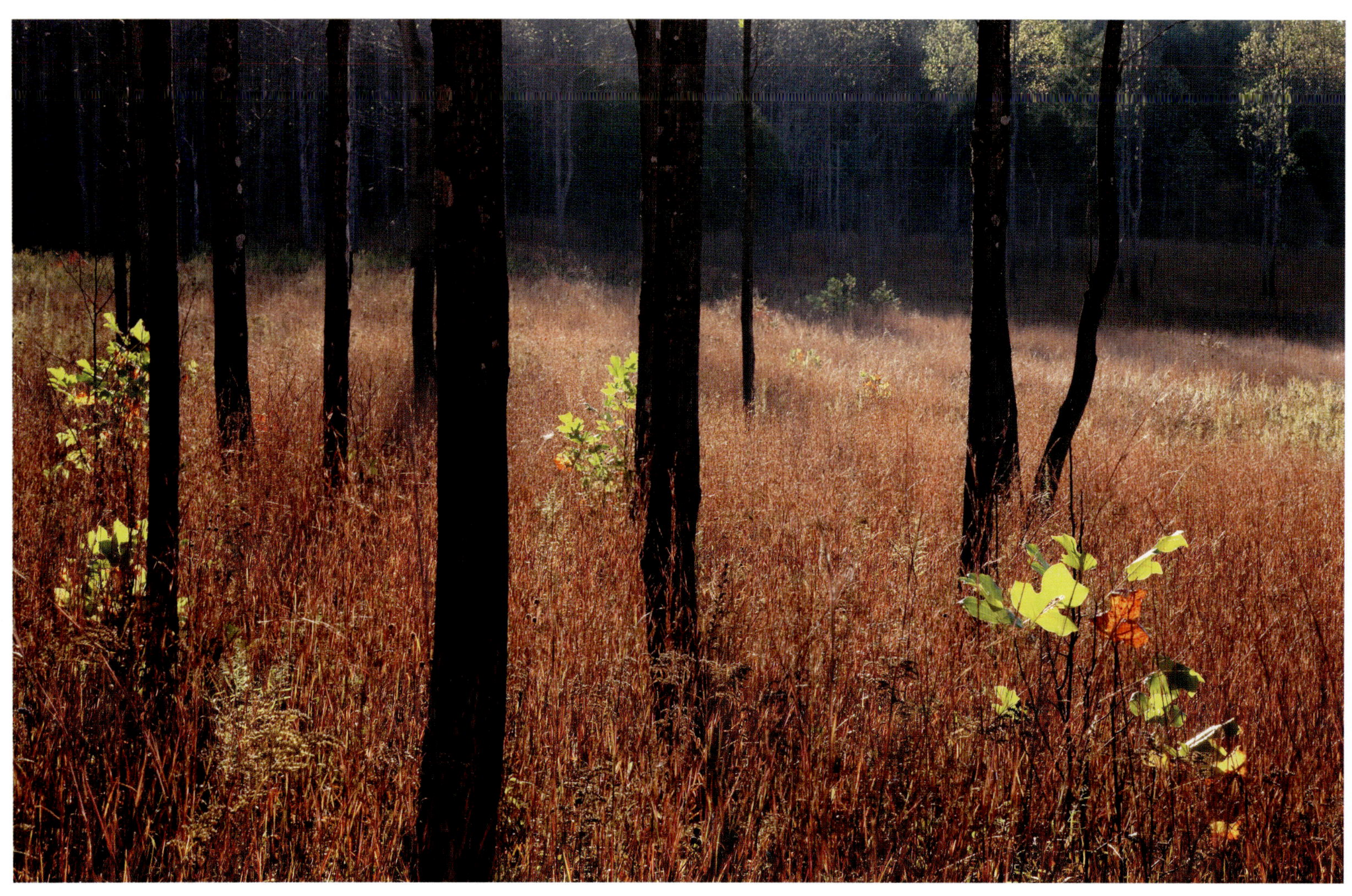

Hoosier National Forest. *October.*

Yellowwood State Forest. *October.*

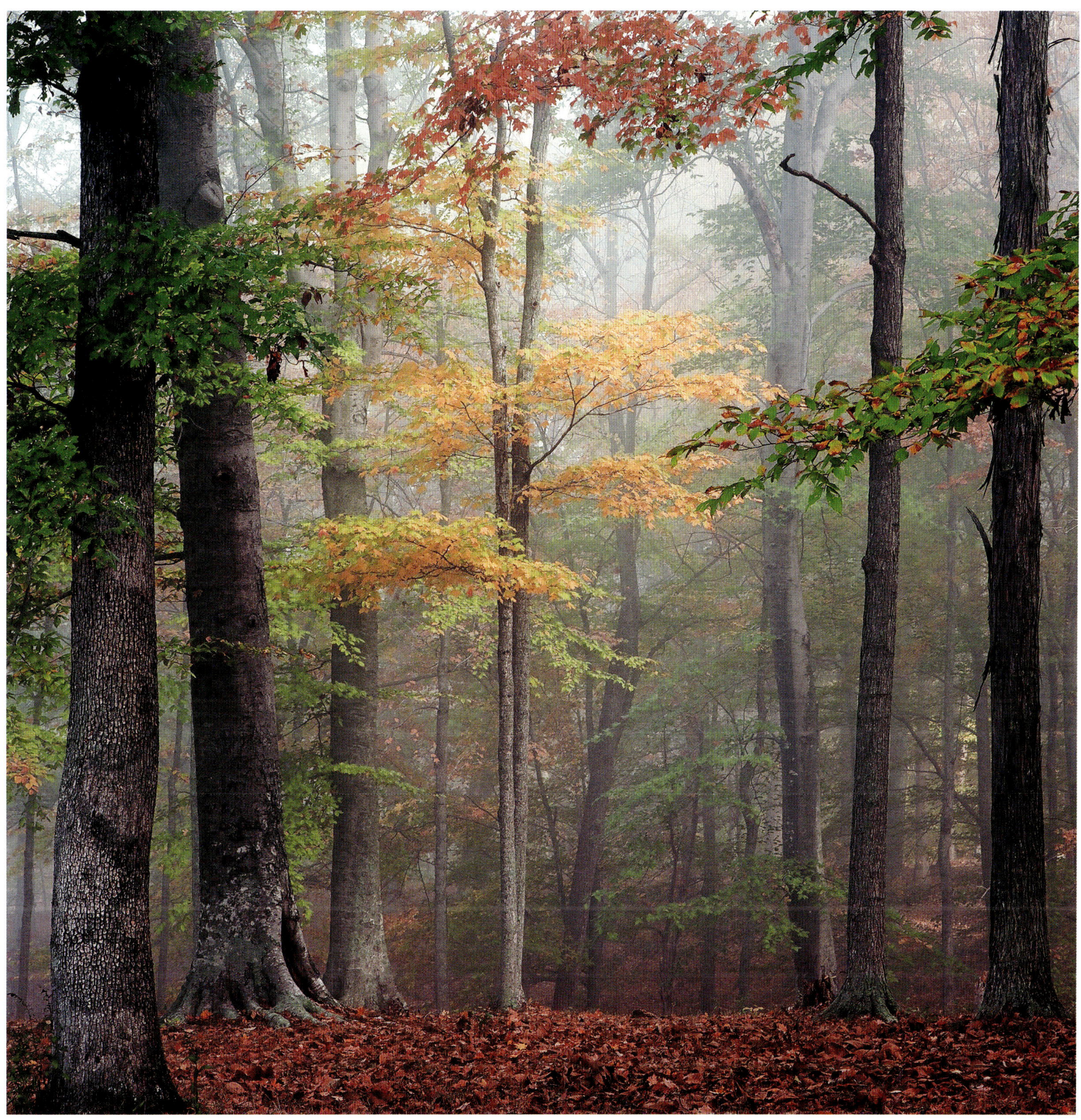

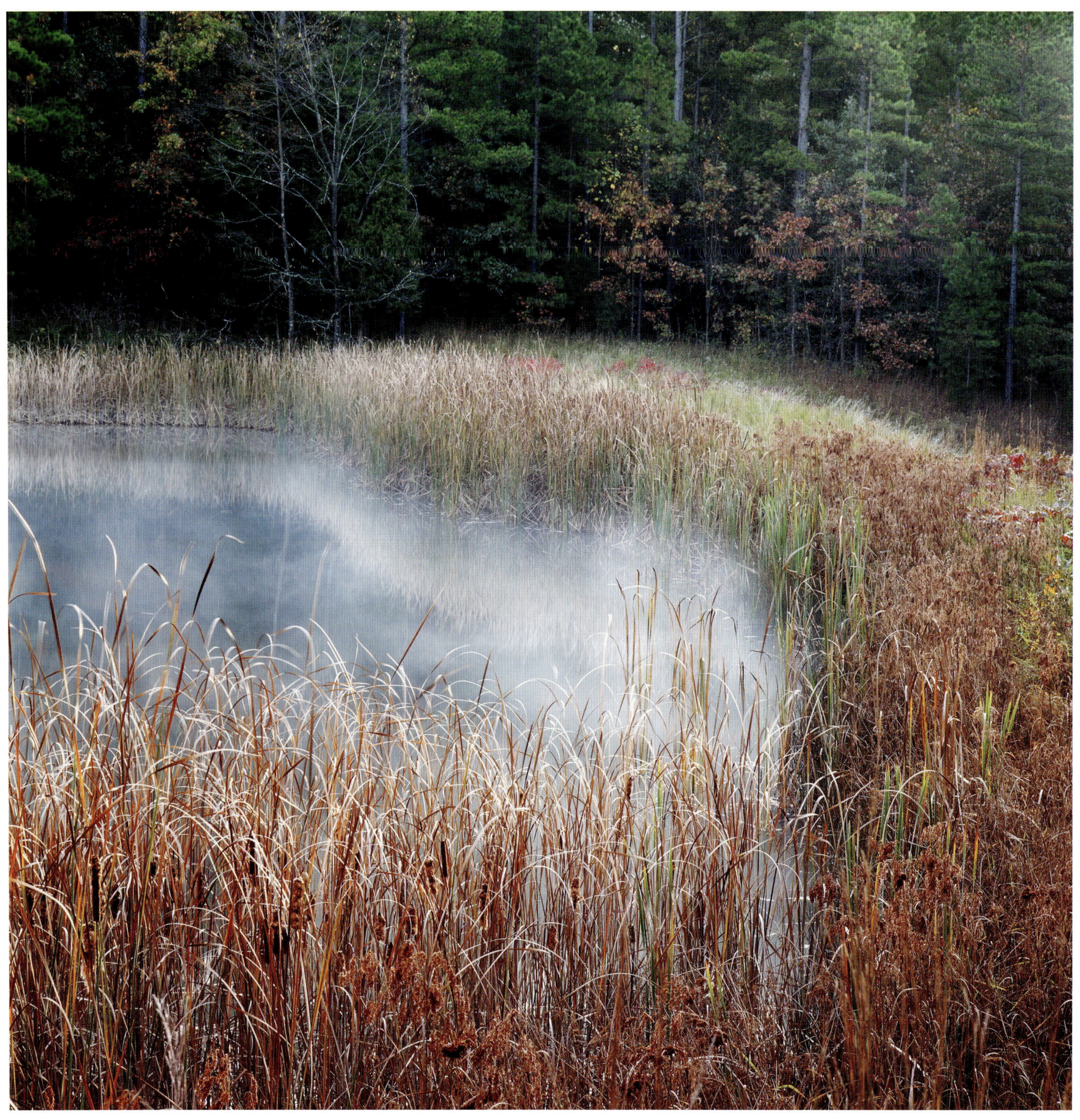

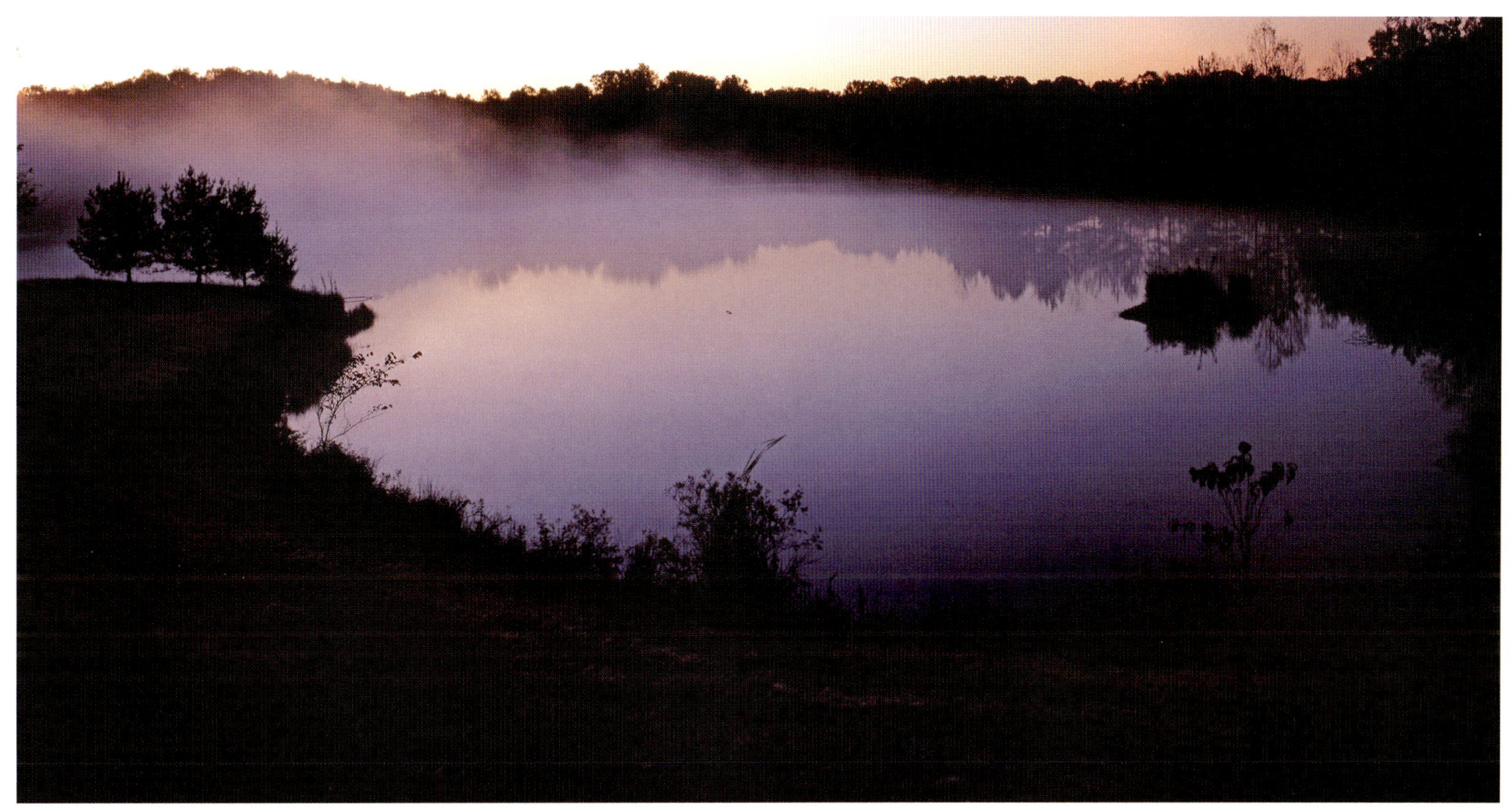

Hoosier National Forest. *October.*

Private Property.

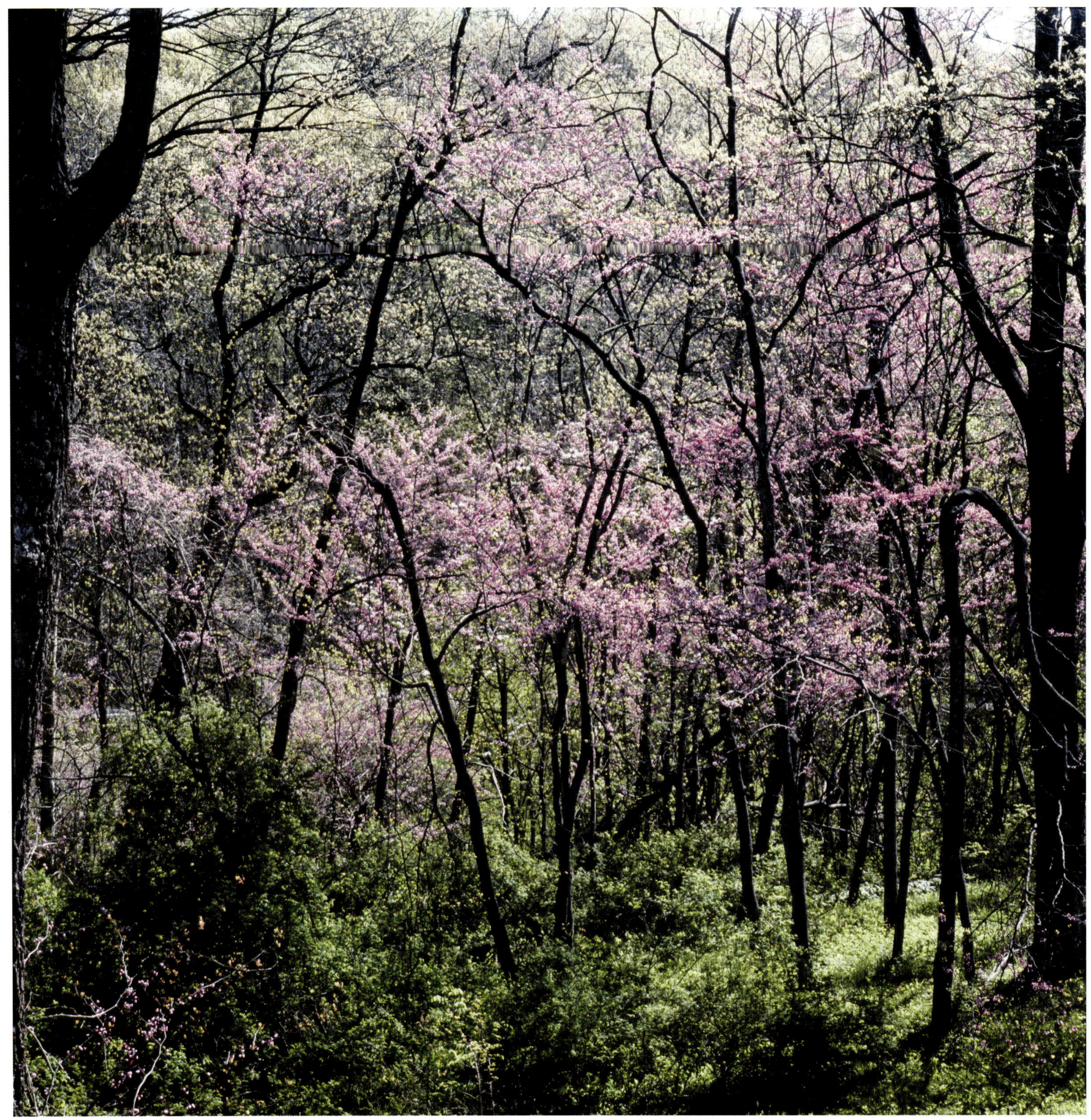

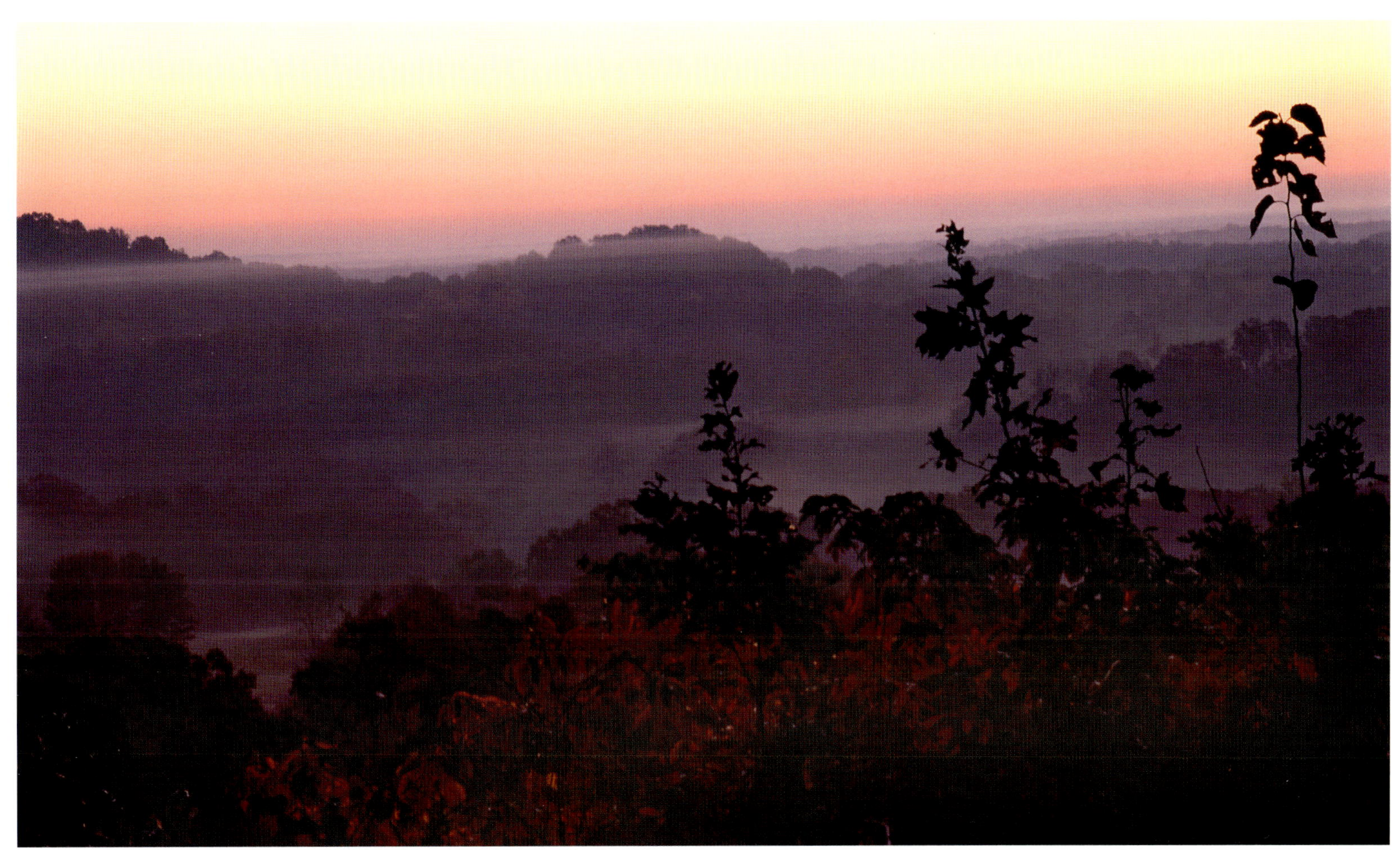

Private Property. *April.*

Private Property. *October.*

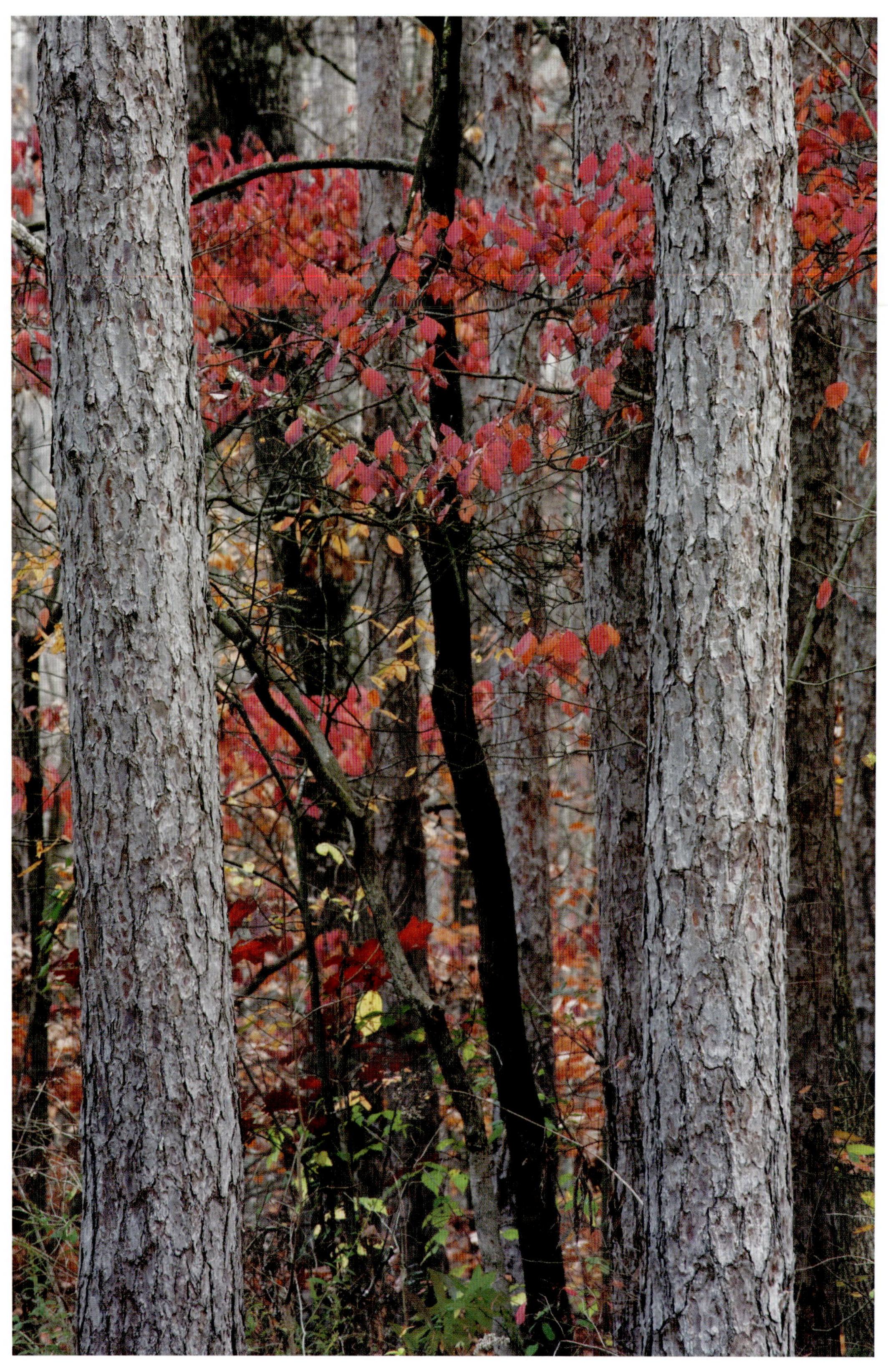

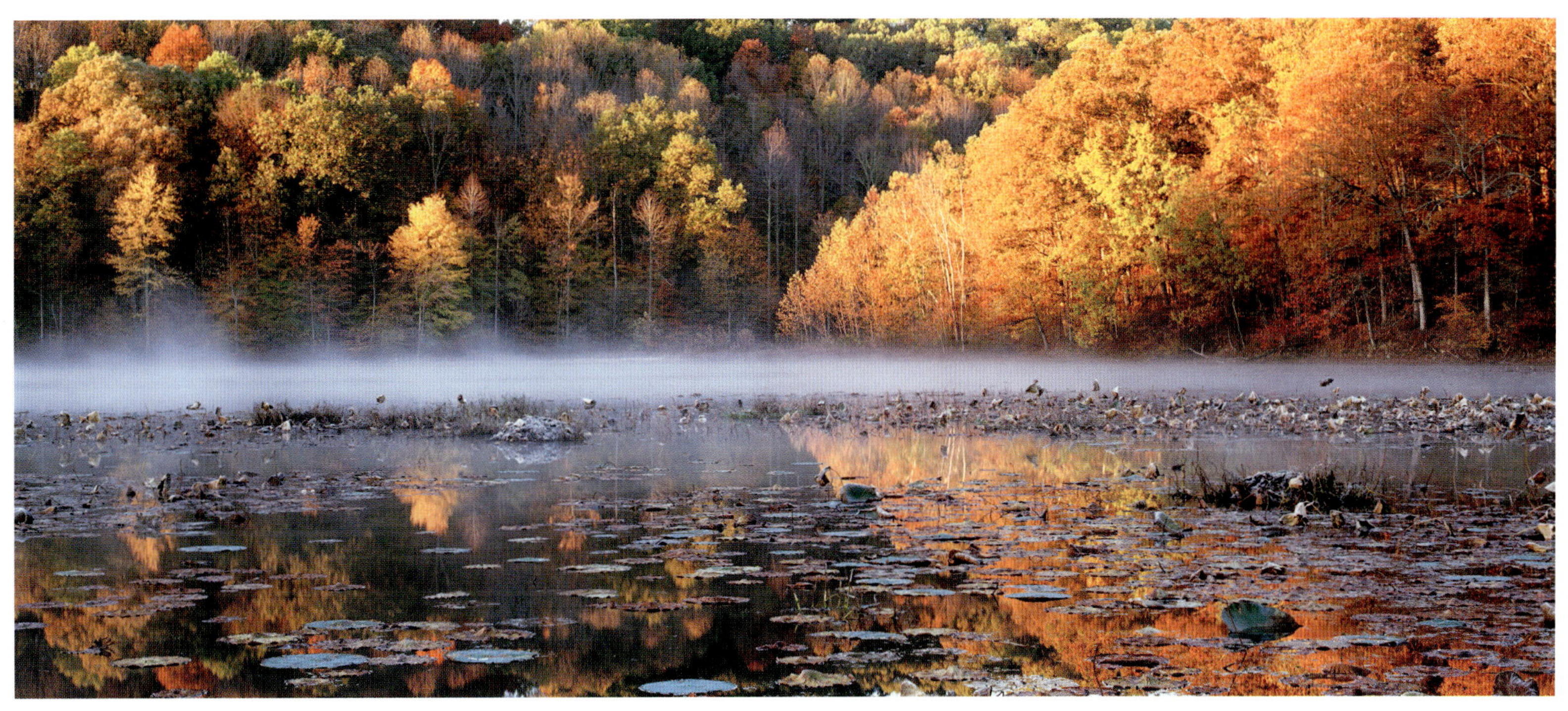

Yellowwood State Forest. *October.*

Yellowwood Lake in Yellowwood State Forest. *October.*

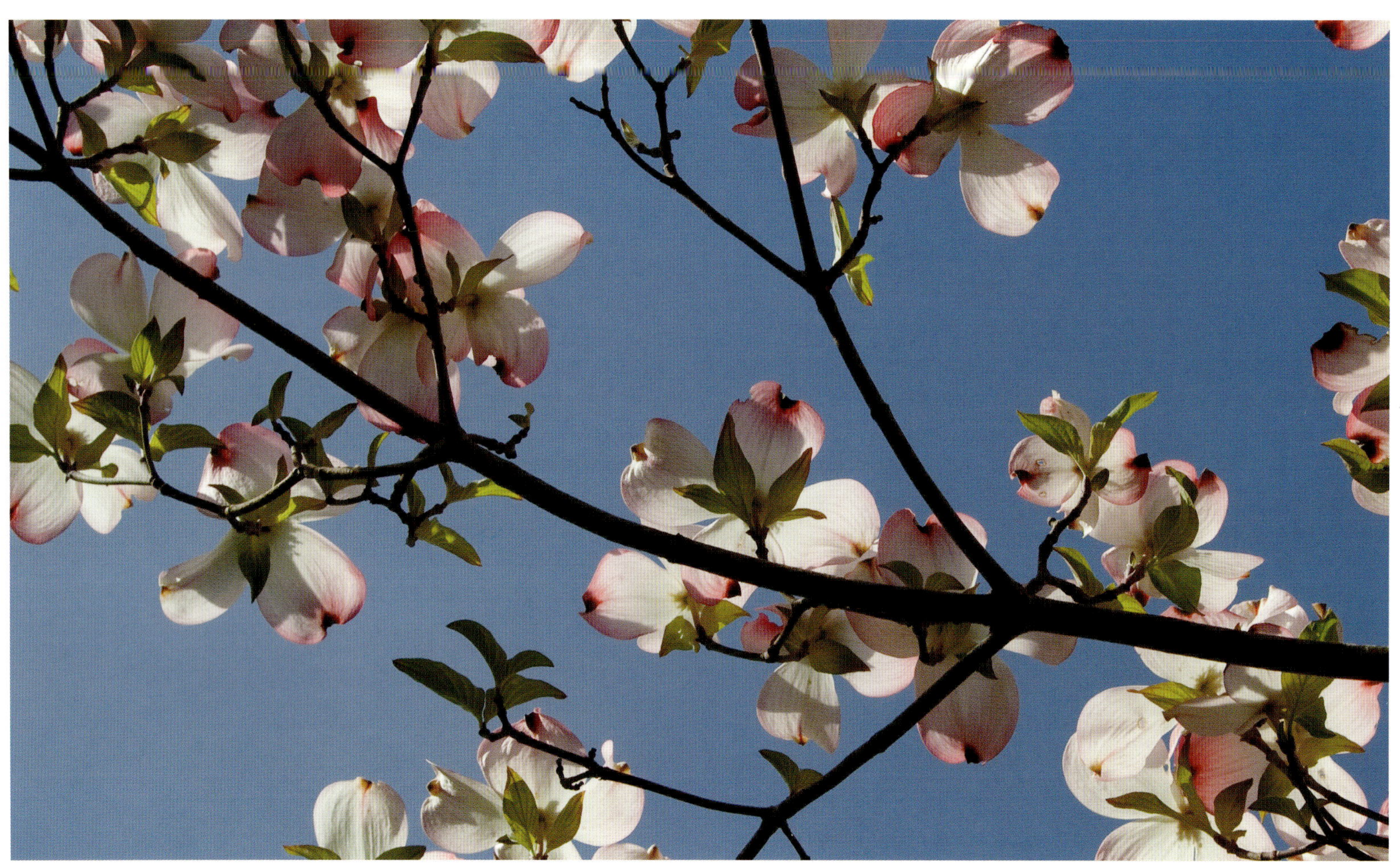

Yellowwood State Forest. *April.*

Hoosier National Forest. *October.*

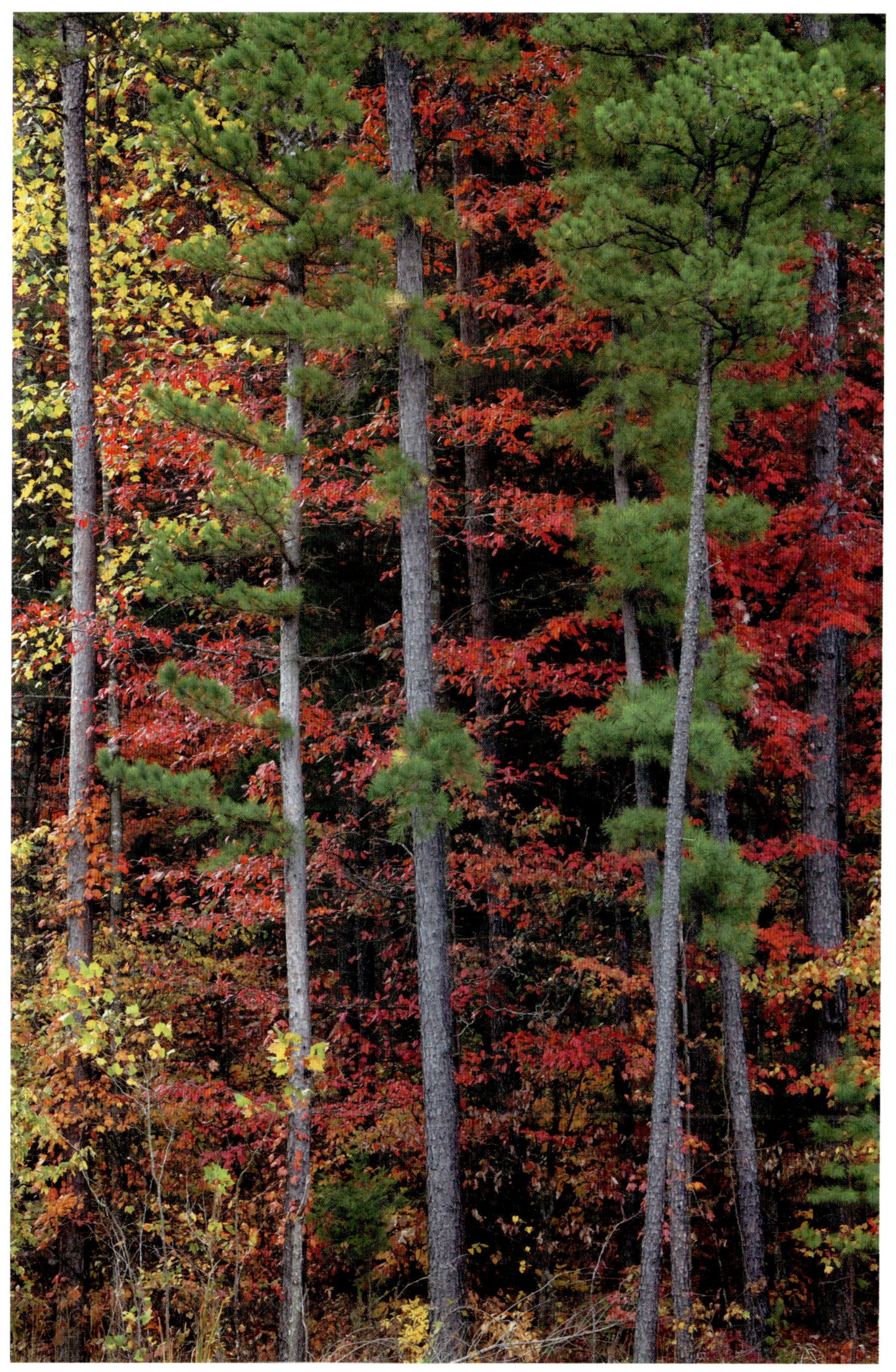

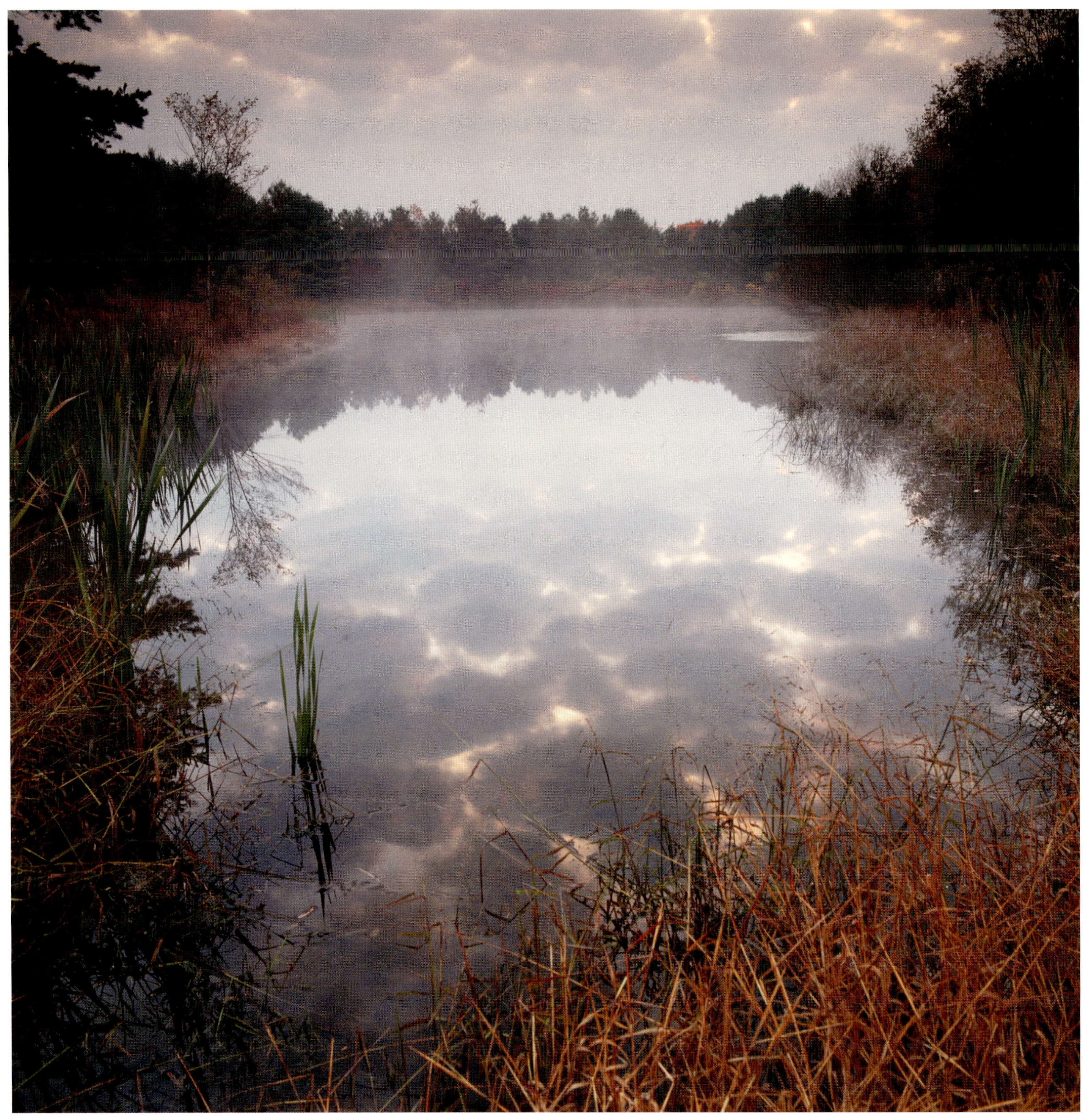

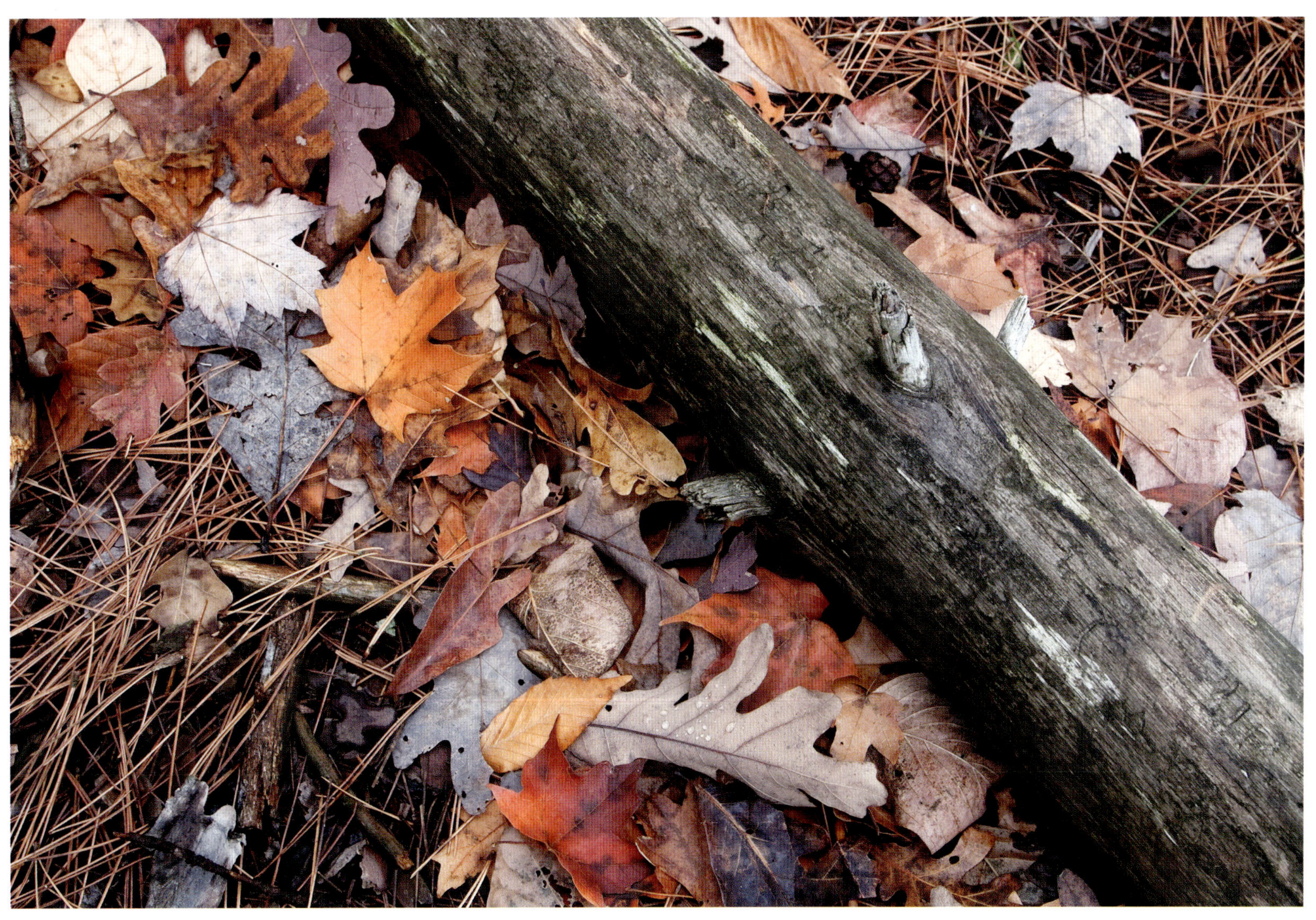

Scott Pond in Hoosier National Forest. *October.*

Brown County State Park. *October.*

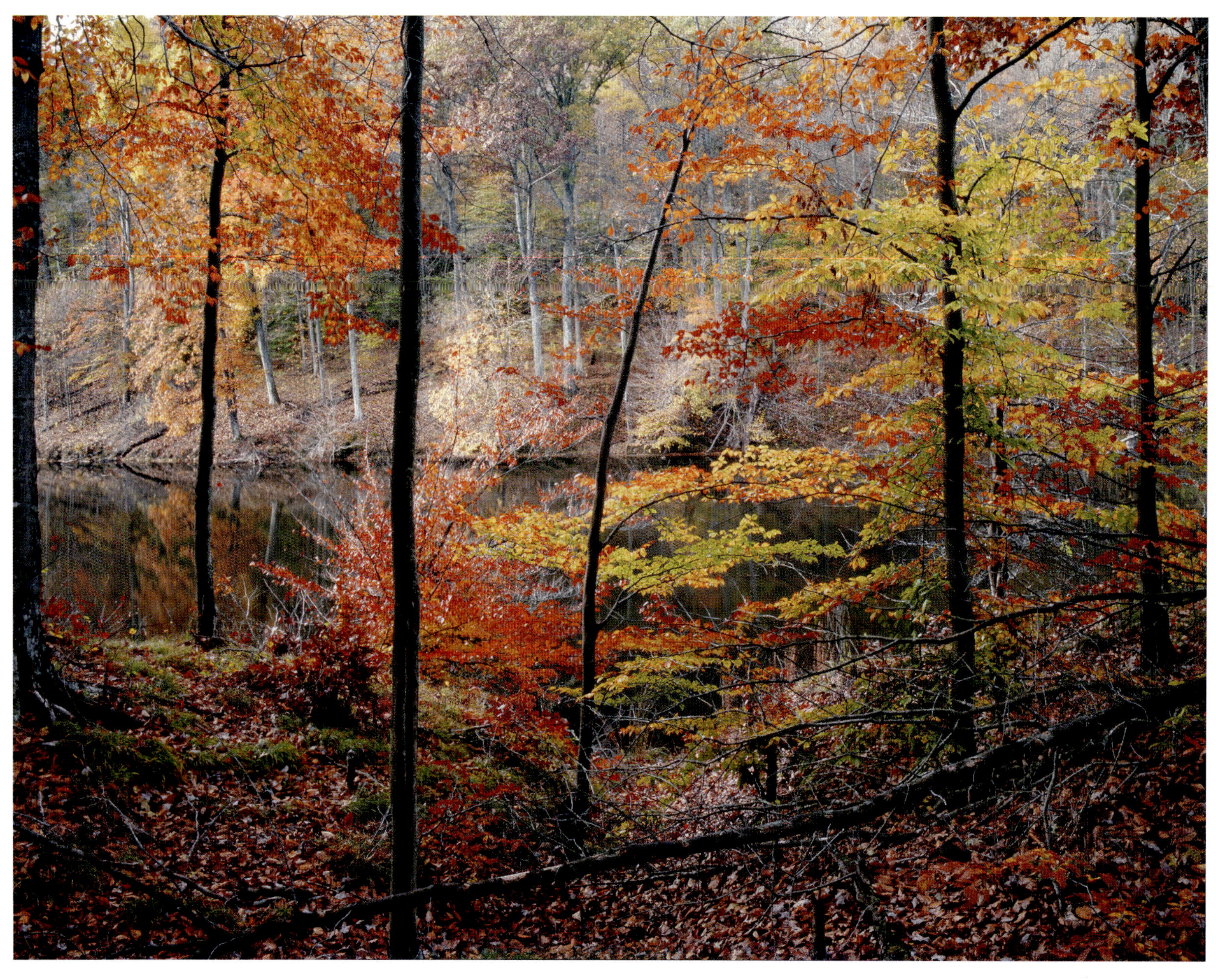

Bear Lake in Yellowwood State Forest. *October.* Private Property.

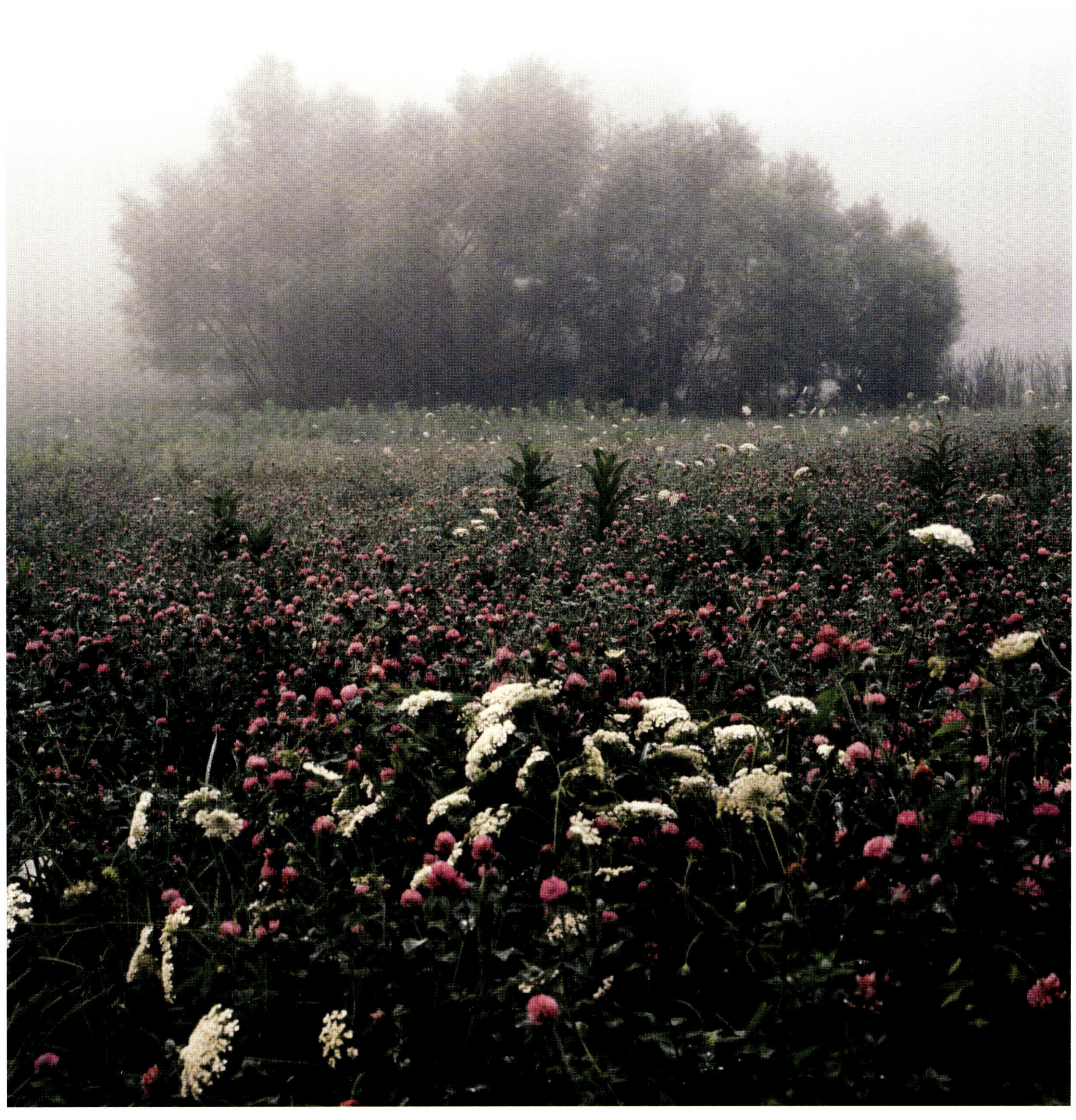

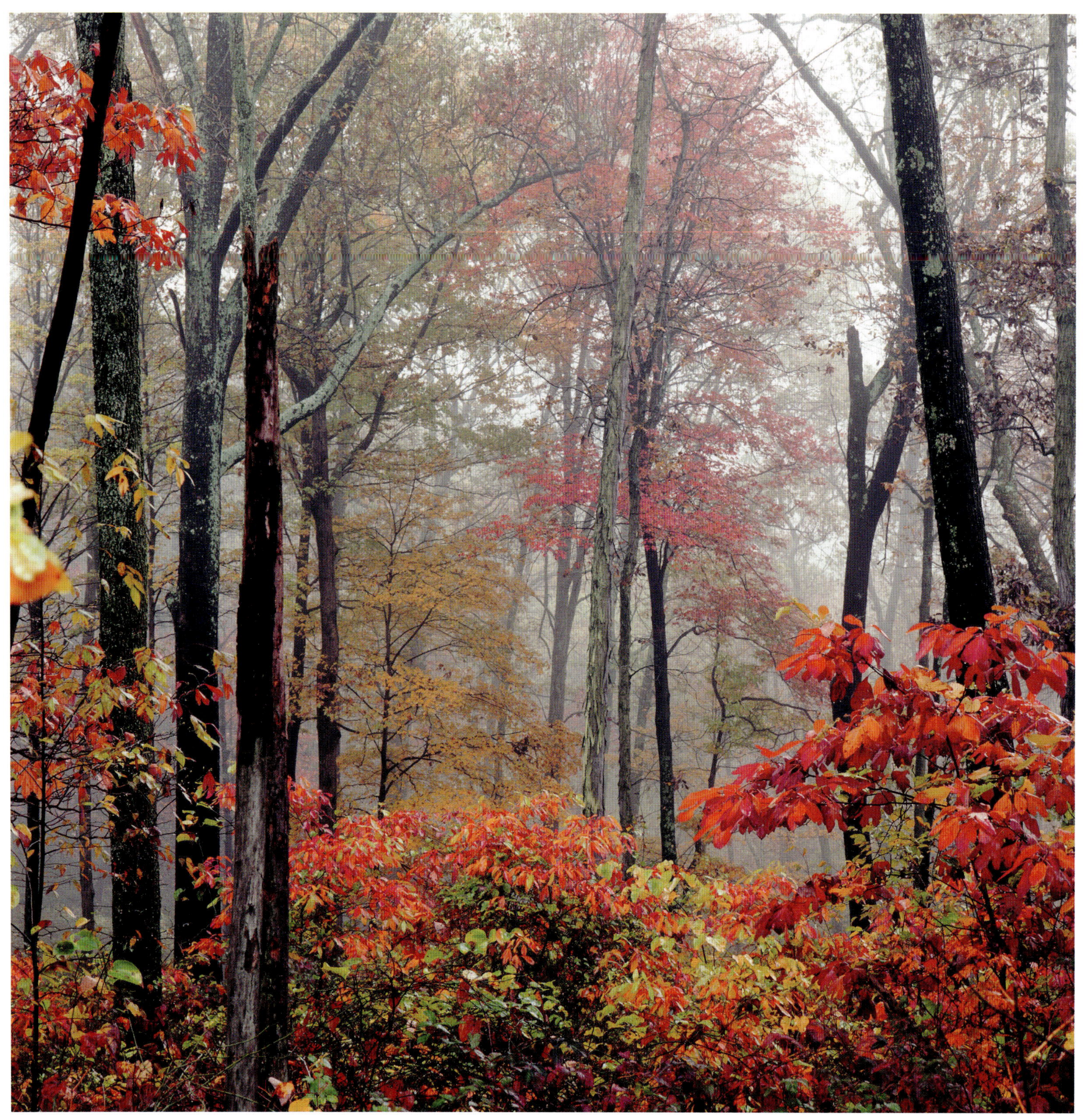

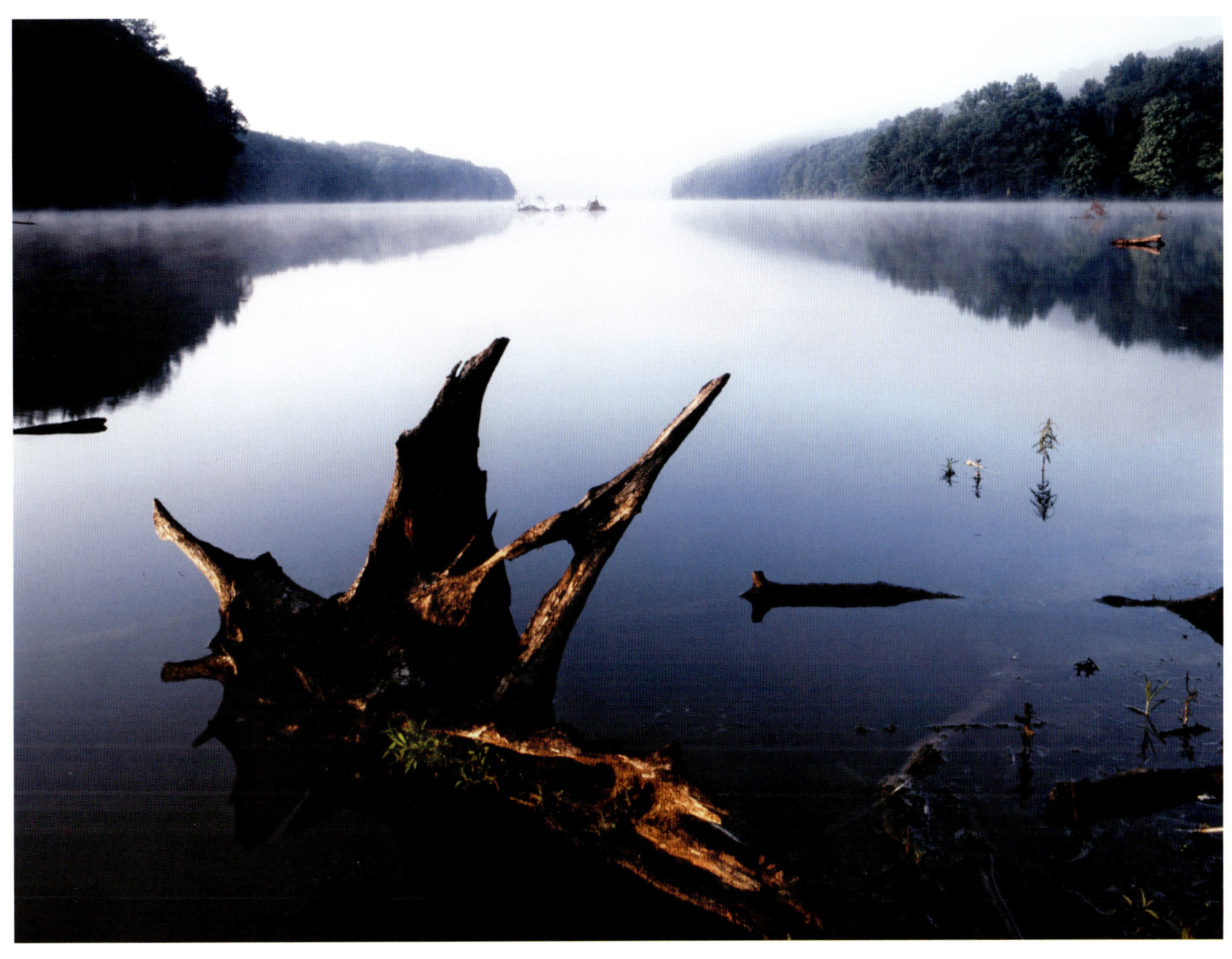

Brown County State Park. *October.*

Yellowwood Lake in Yellowwood State Forest. *Summer.*

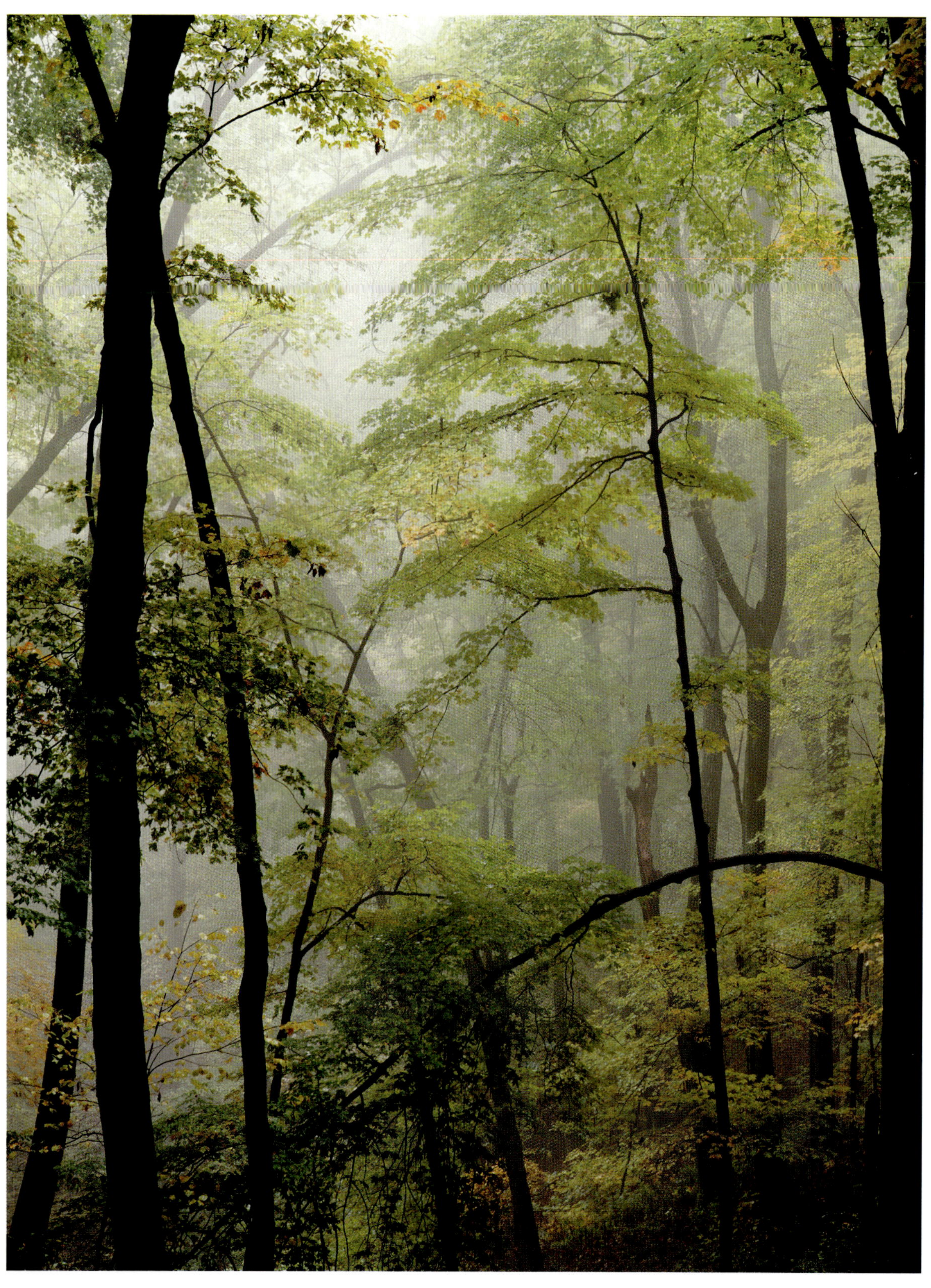

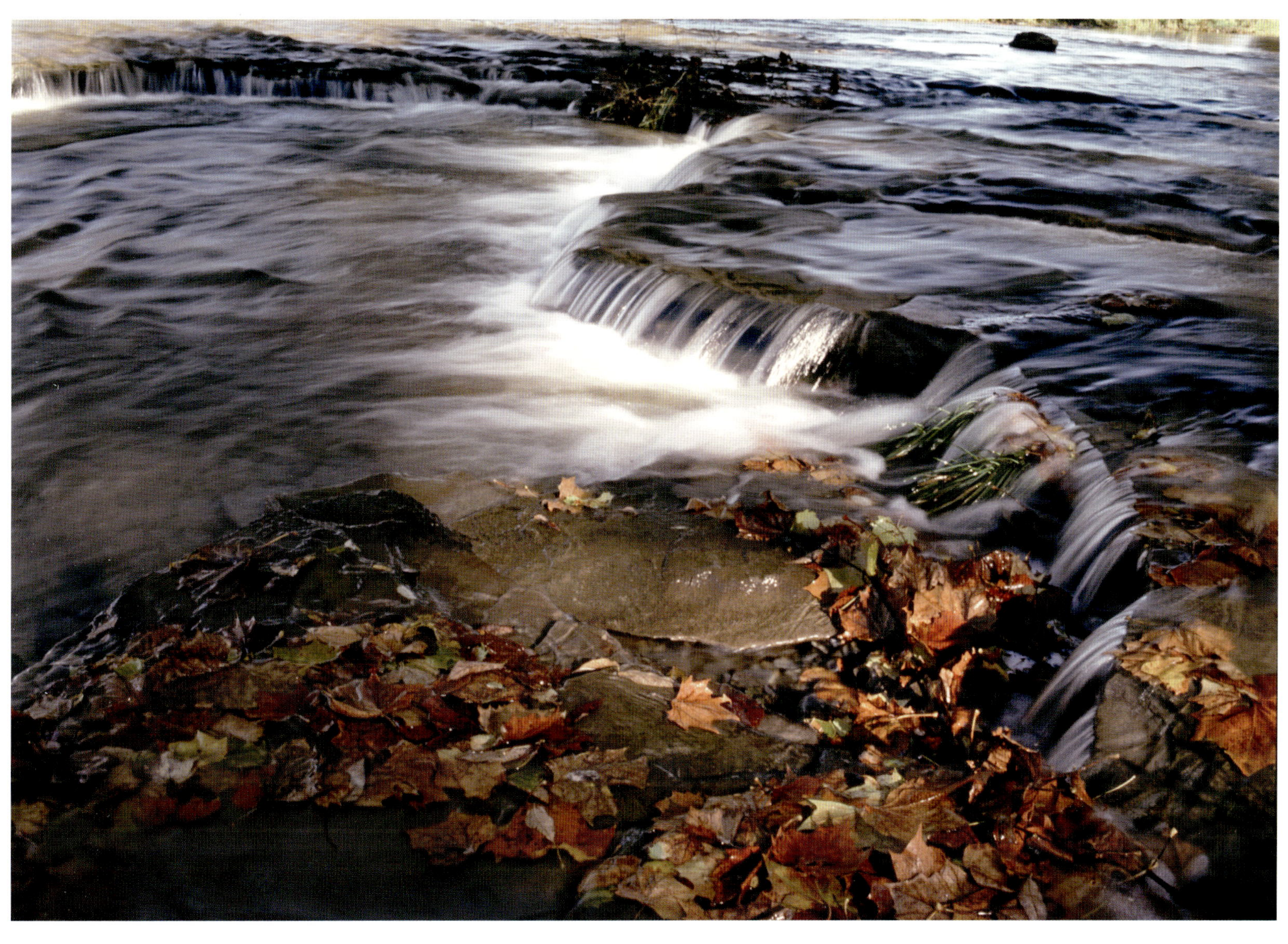

Brown County State Park. *October.*

Private Property. *October.*

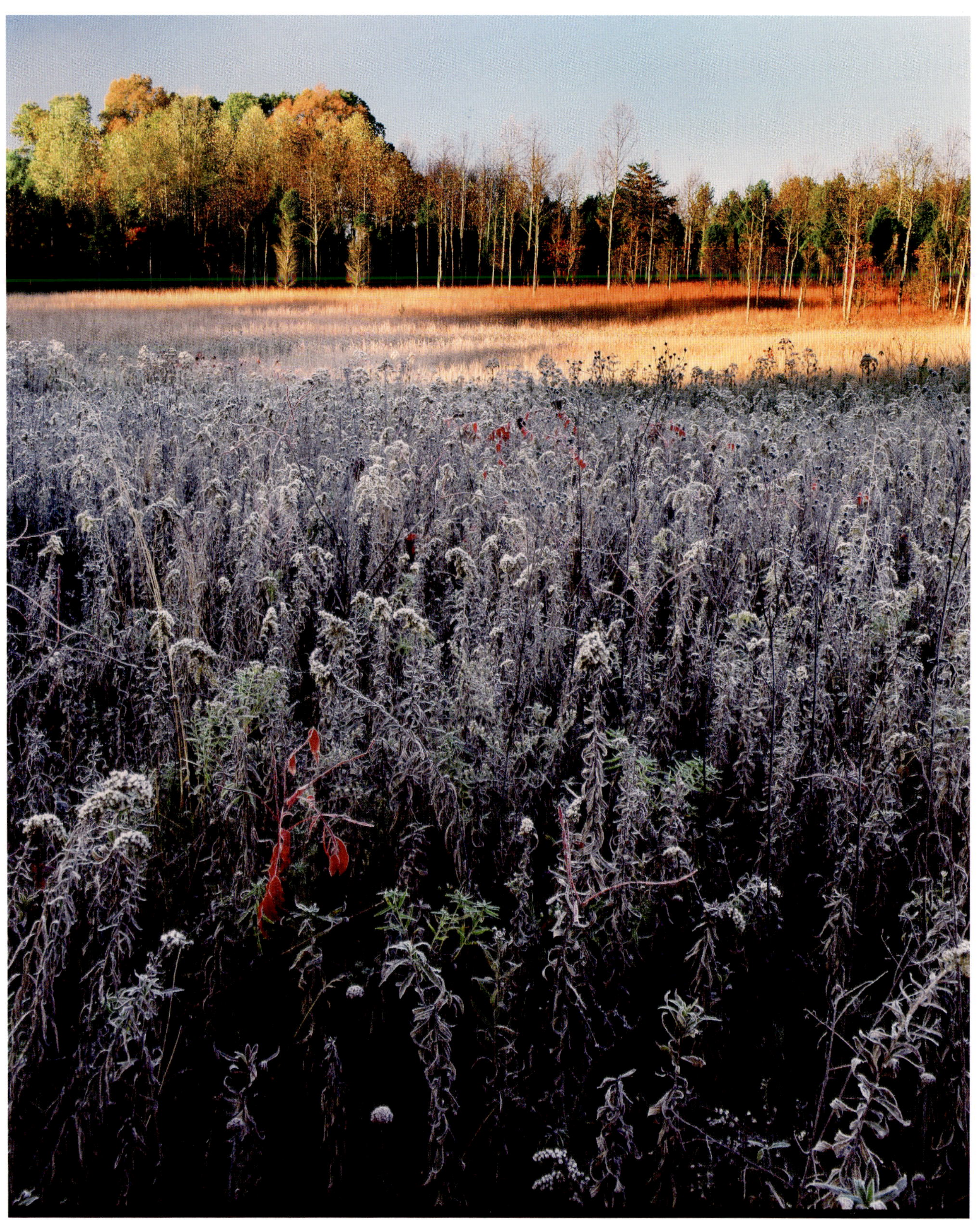

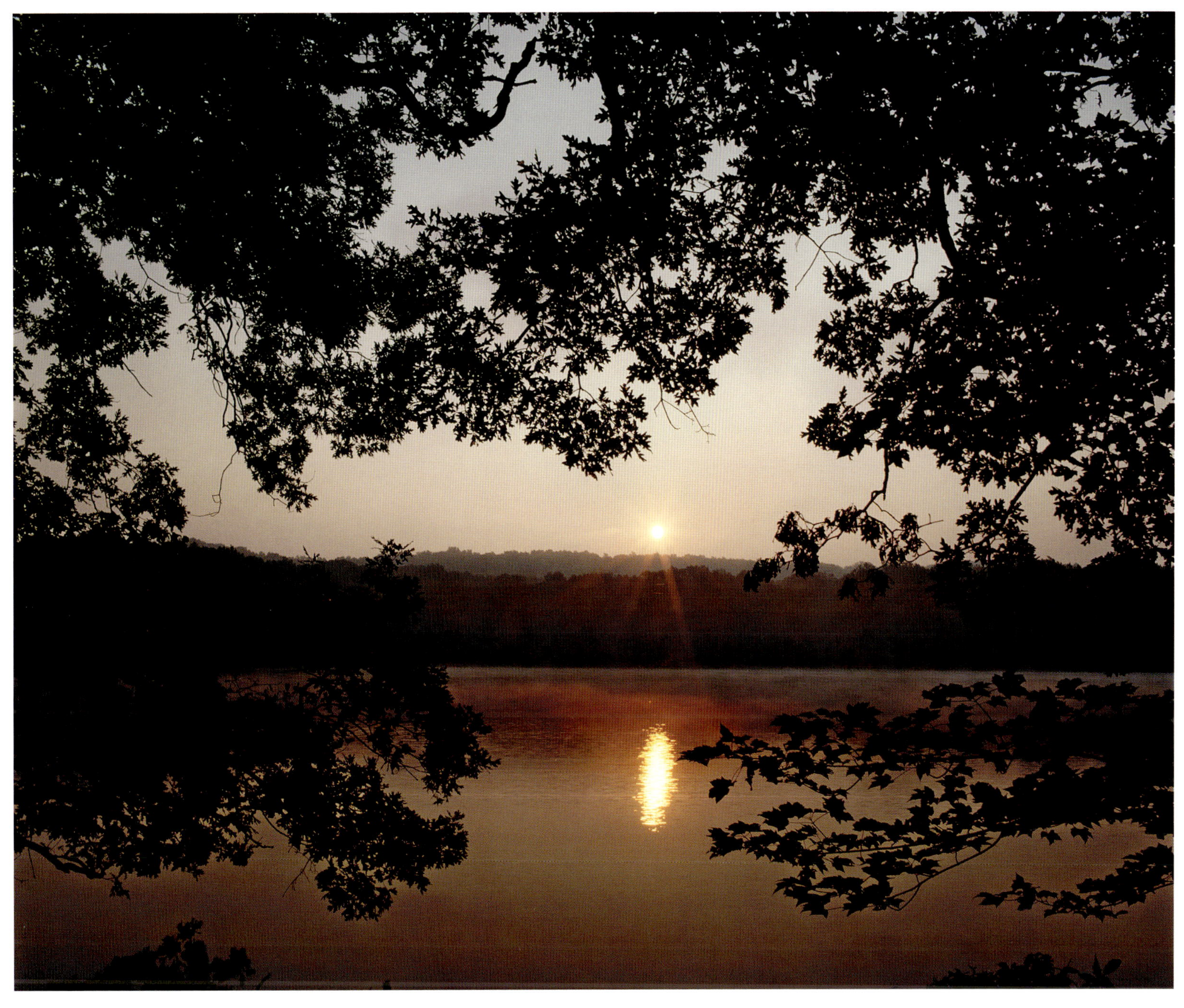

Hoosier National Forest. *October.*

Yellowwood State Forest.

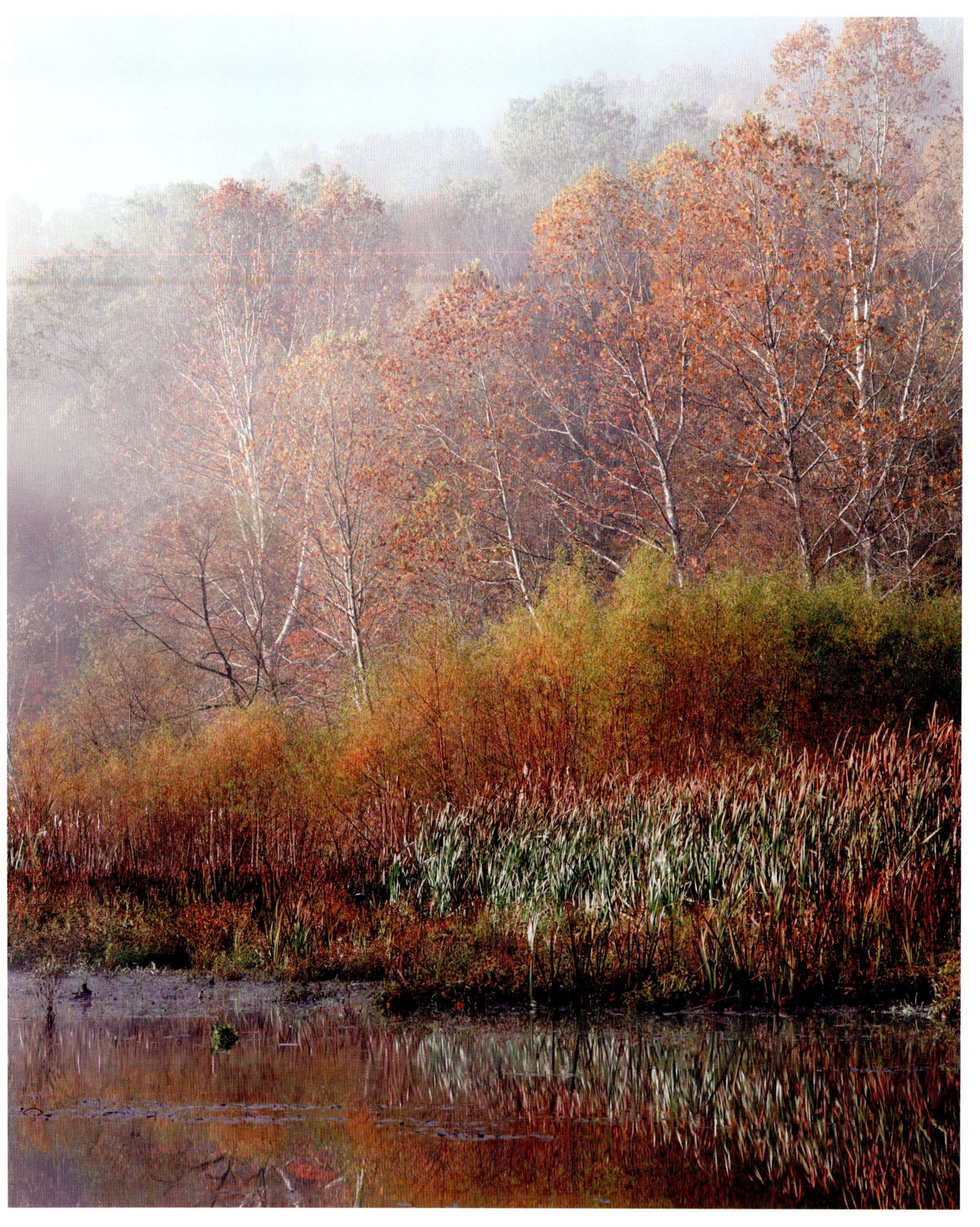

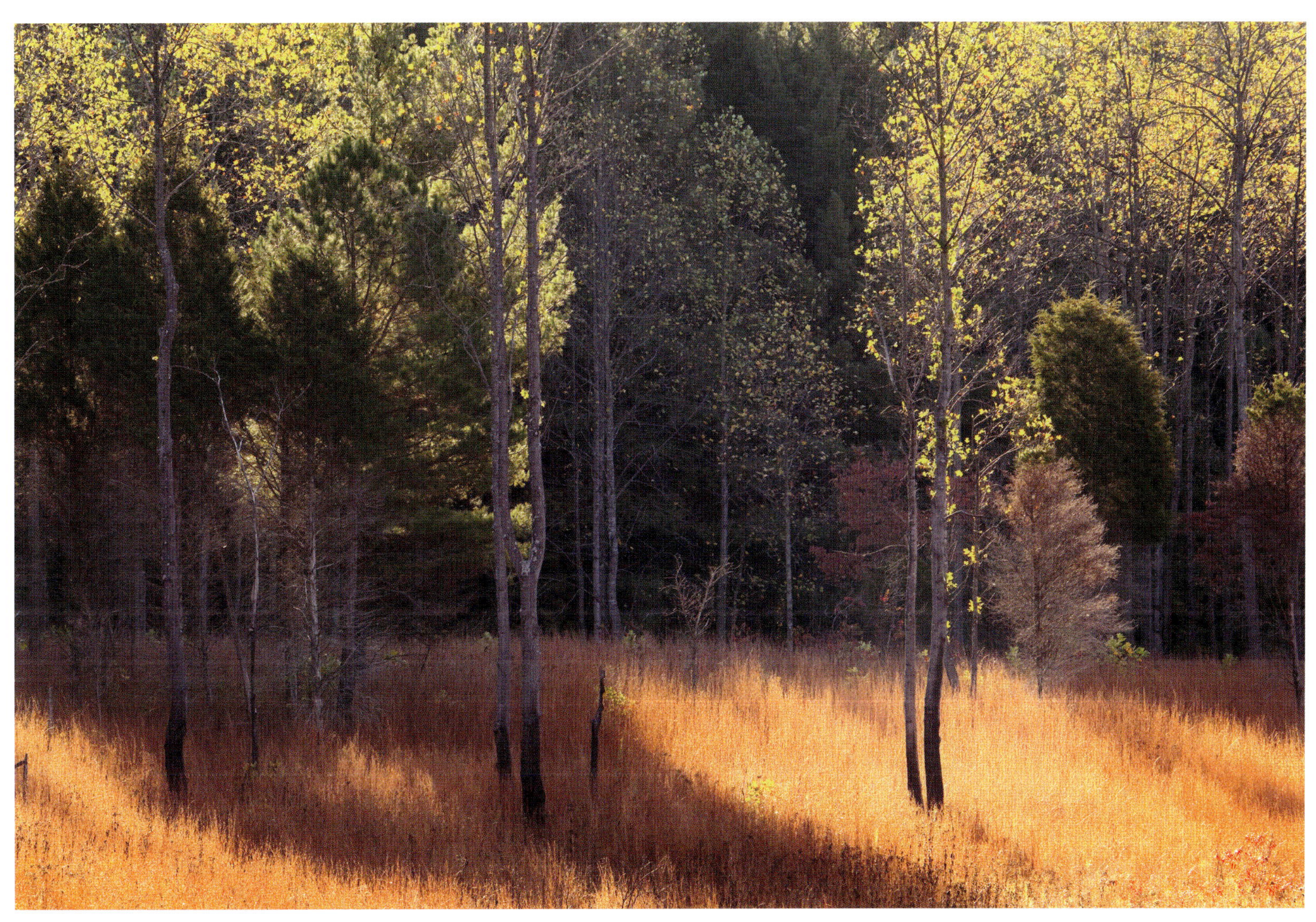

Yellowwood Lake in Yellowwood State Forest. *October.*

Hoosier National Forest. *October.*

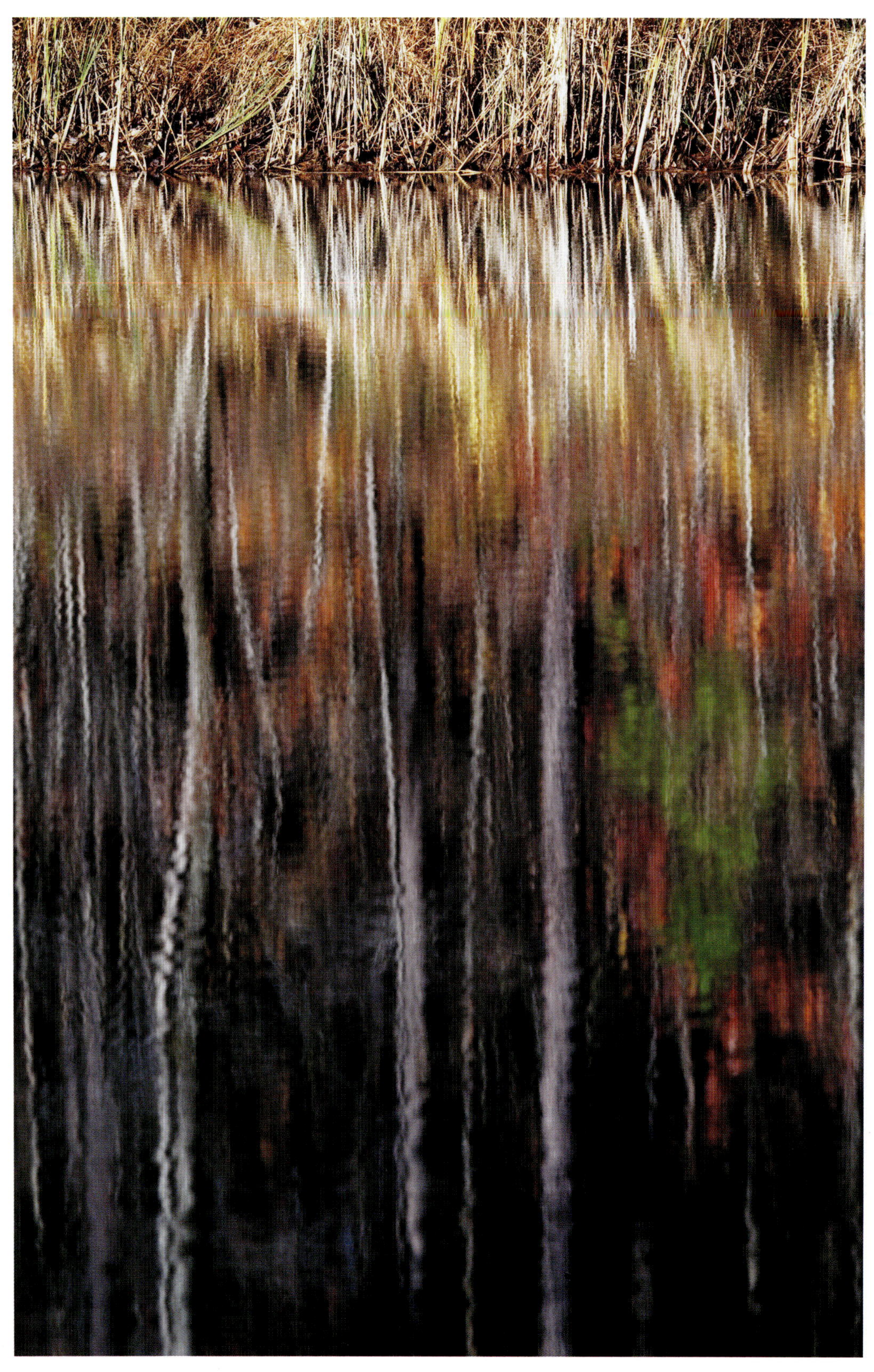

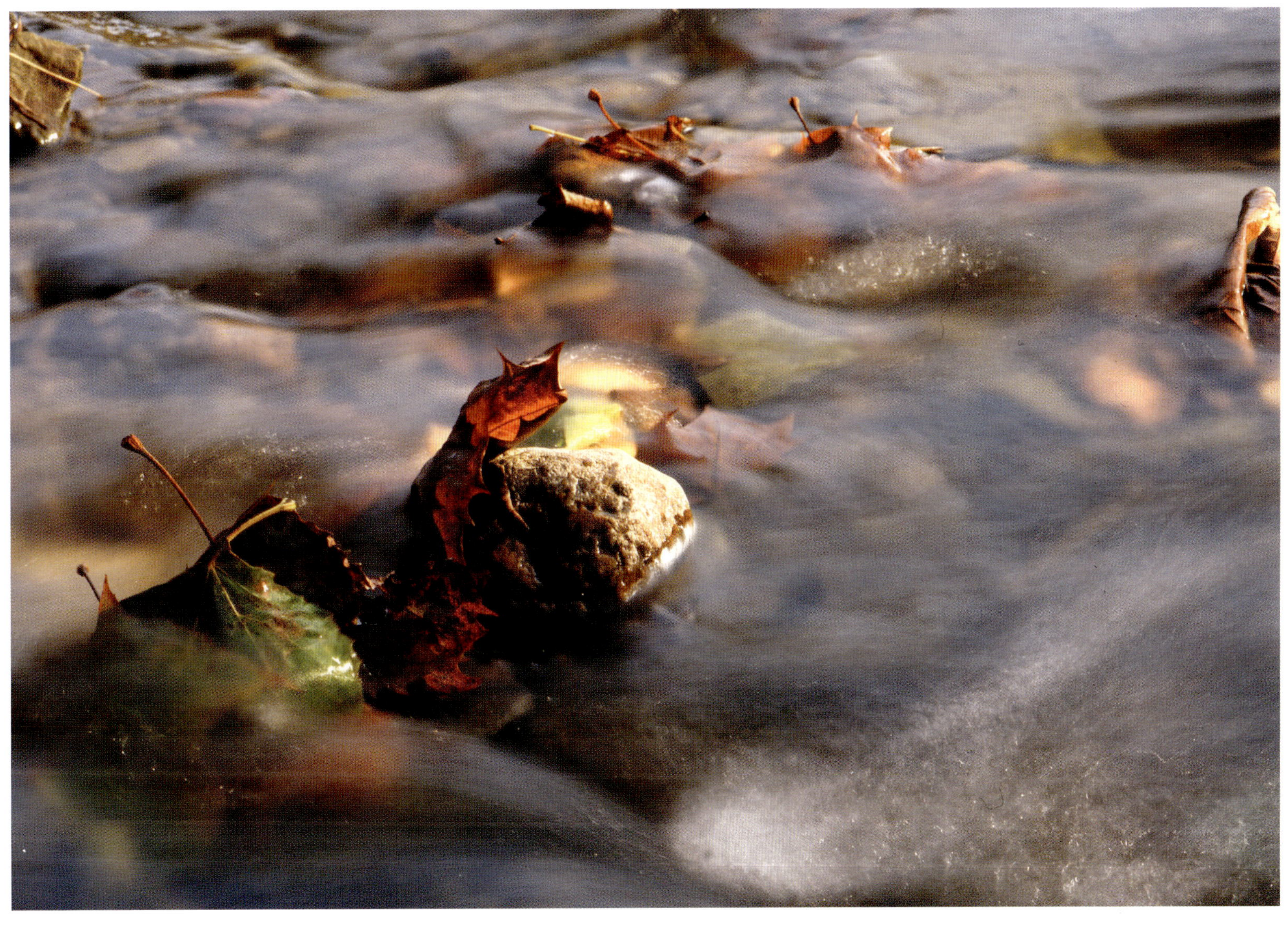

Hoosier National Forest. *October.*

Private Property. *October.*

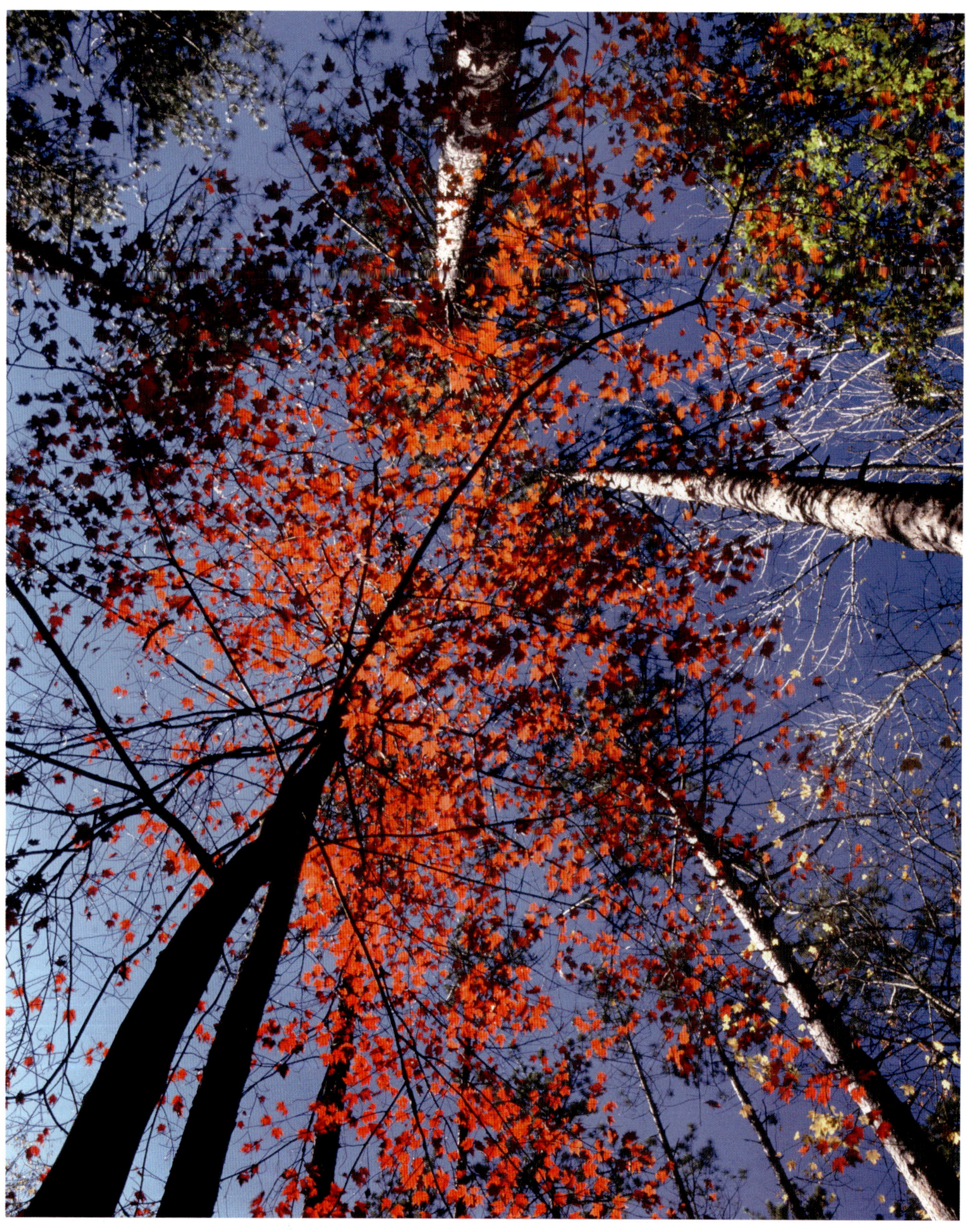

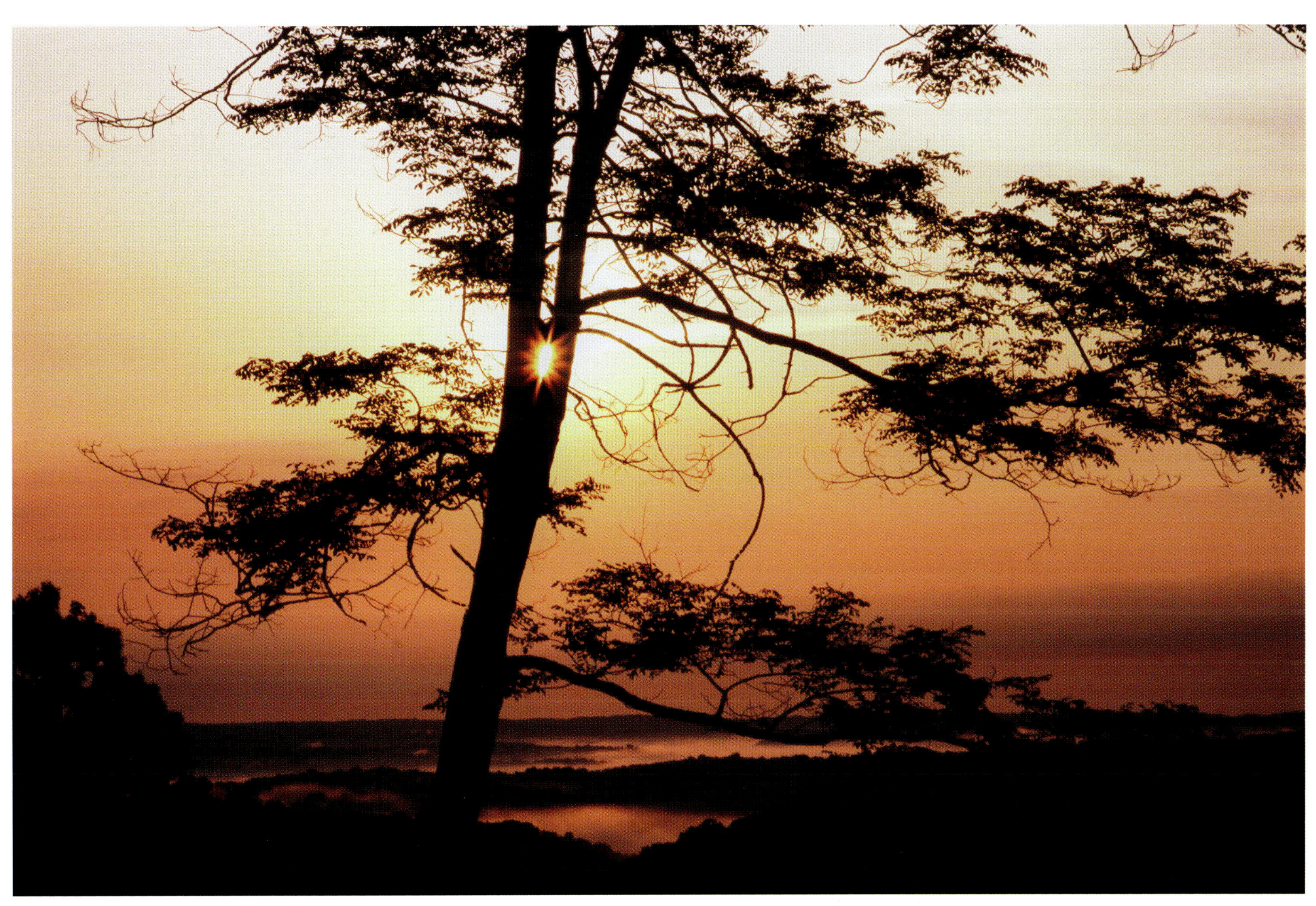

Yellowwood State Forest. *October.*

Brown County State Park. *October.*

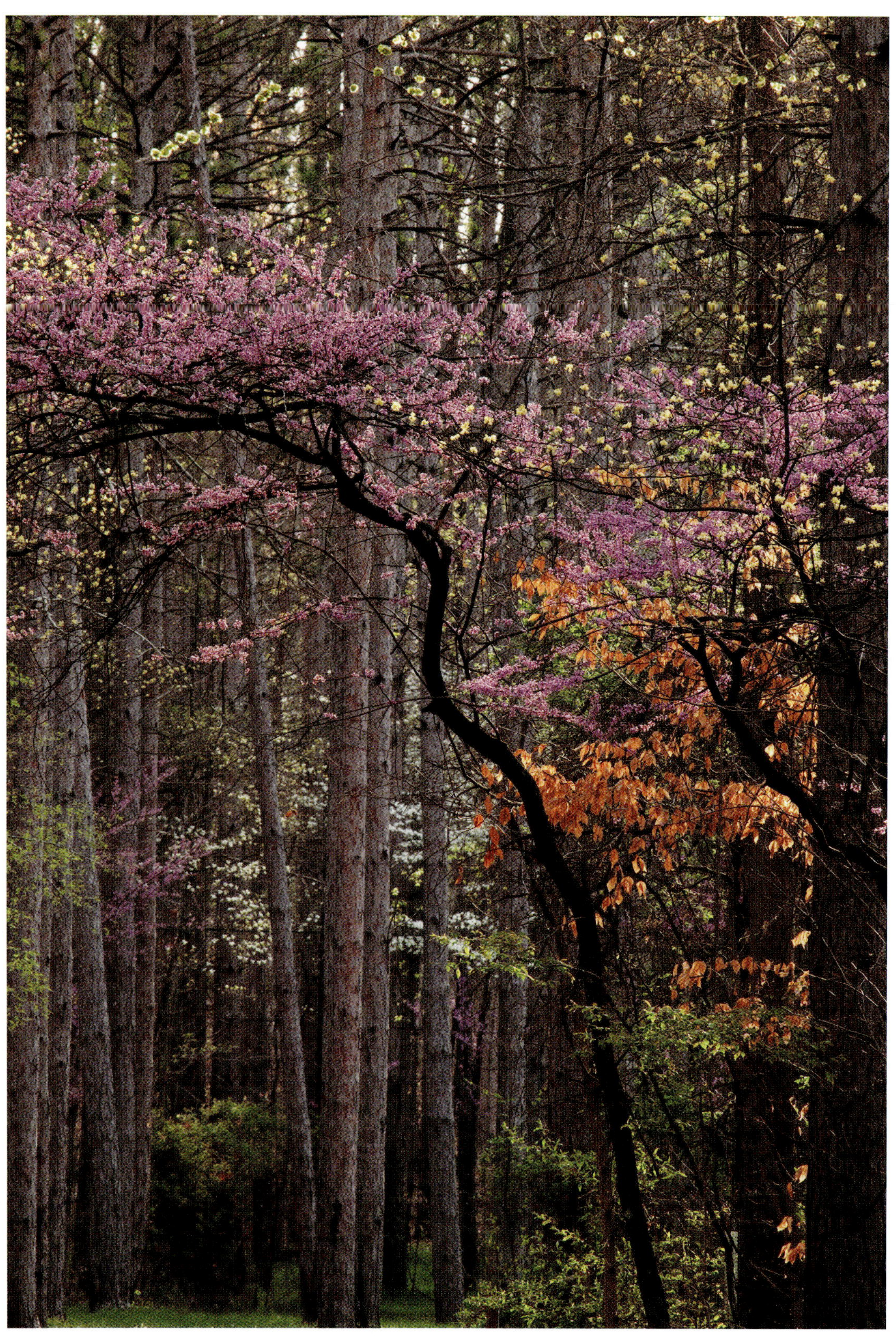

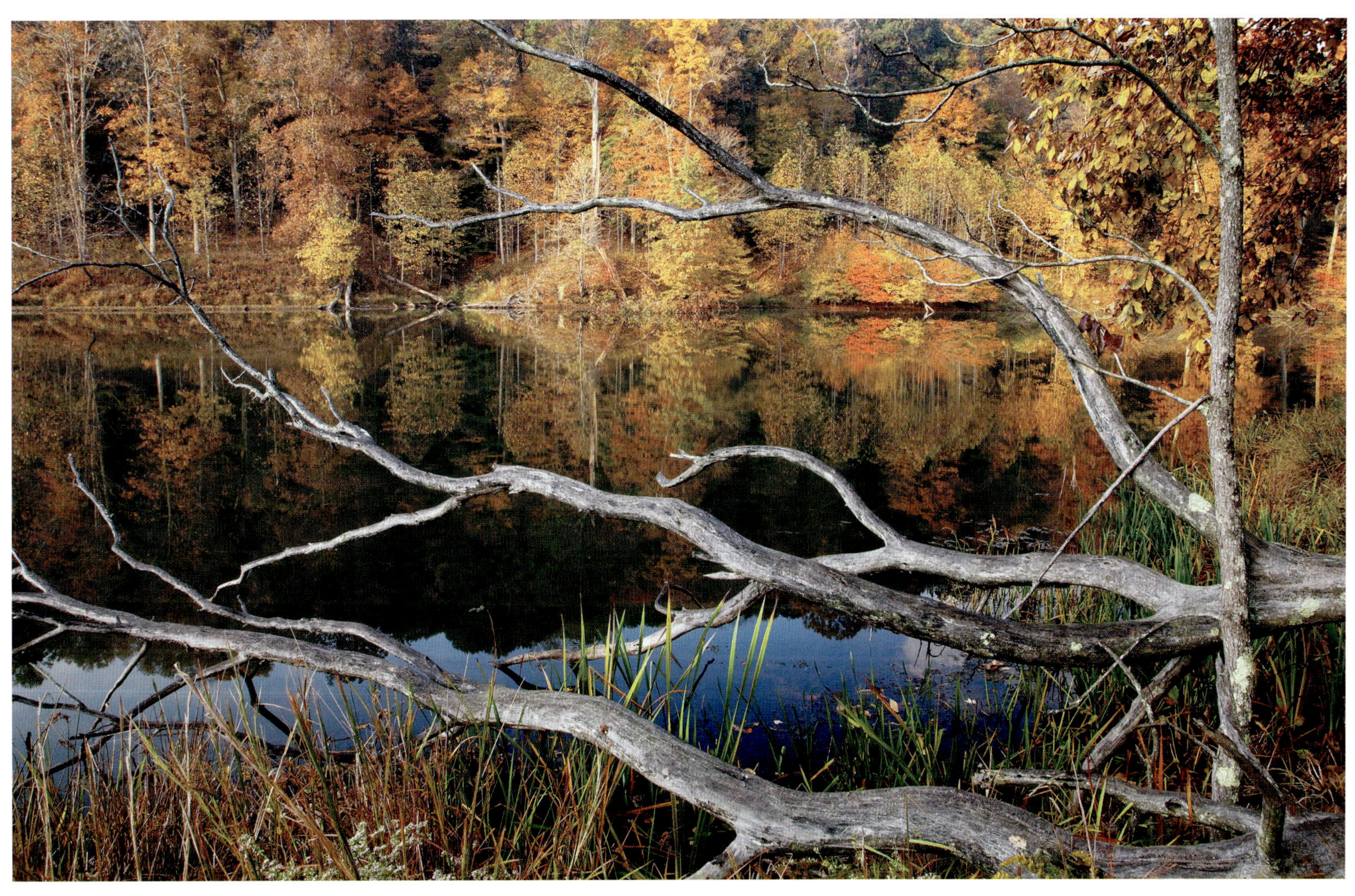

Yellowwood State Forest. *October.*

Bear Lake in Yellowwood State Forest. *October.*

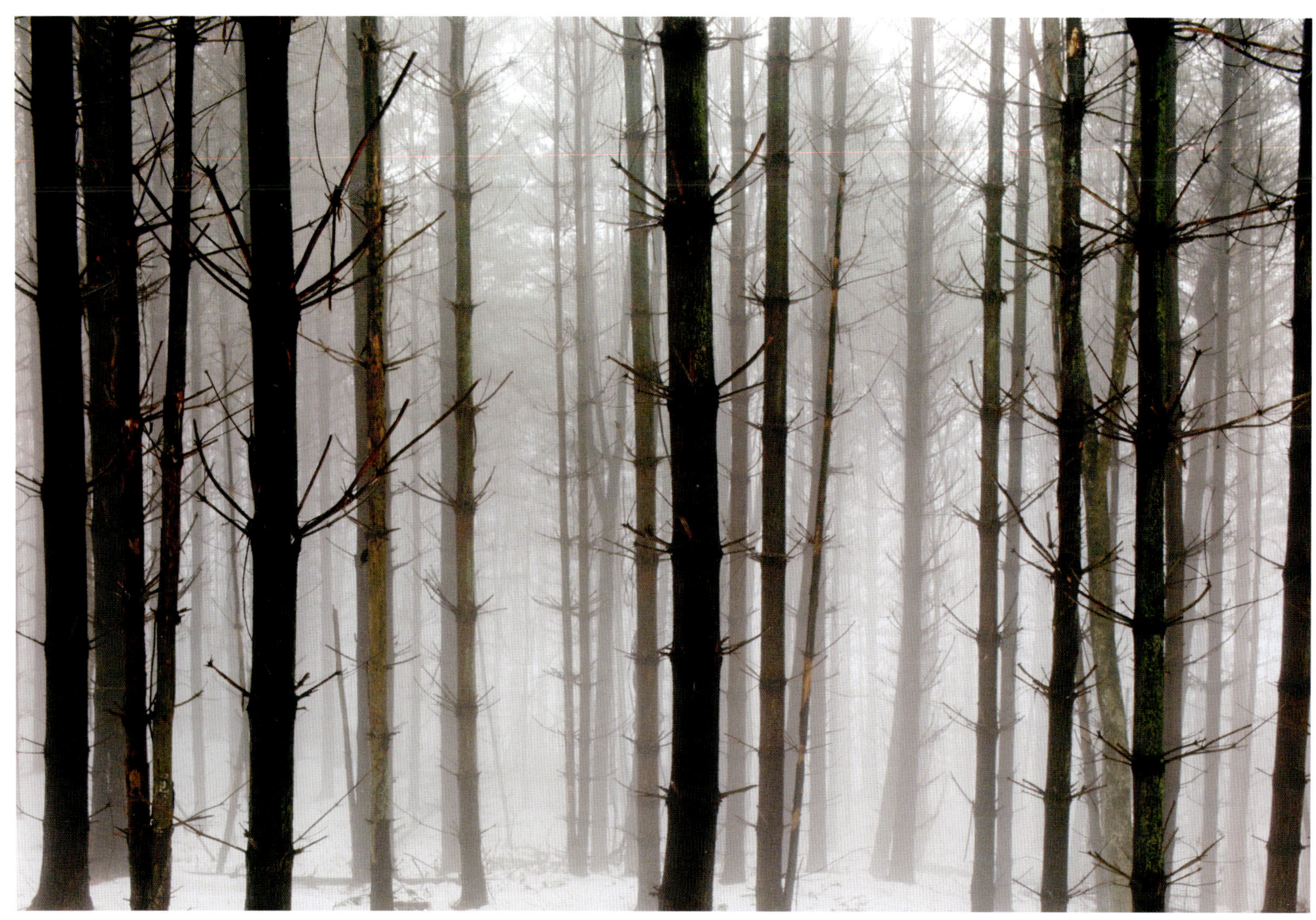

Private Property. *Winter.*

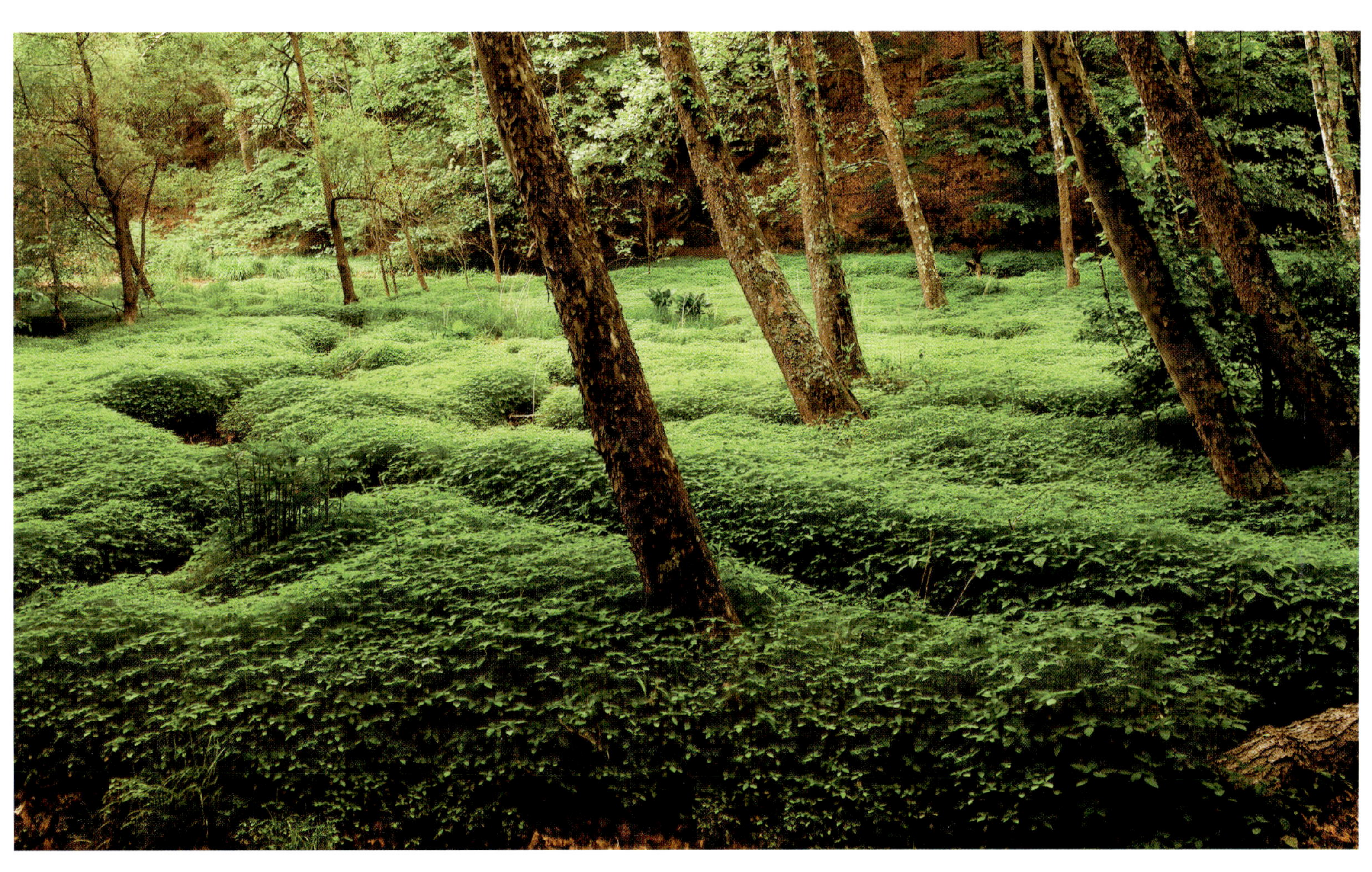

Brown County State Park. *Spring.*

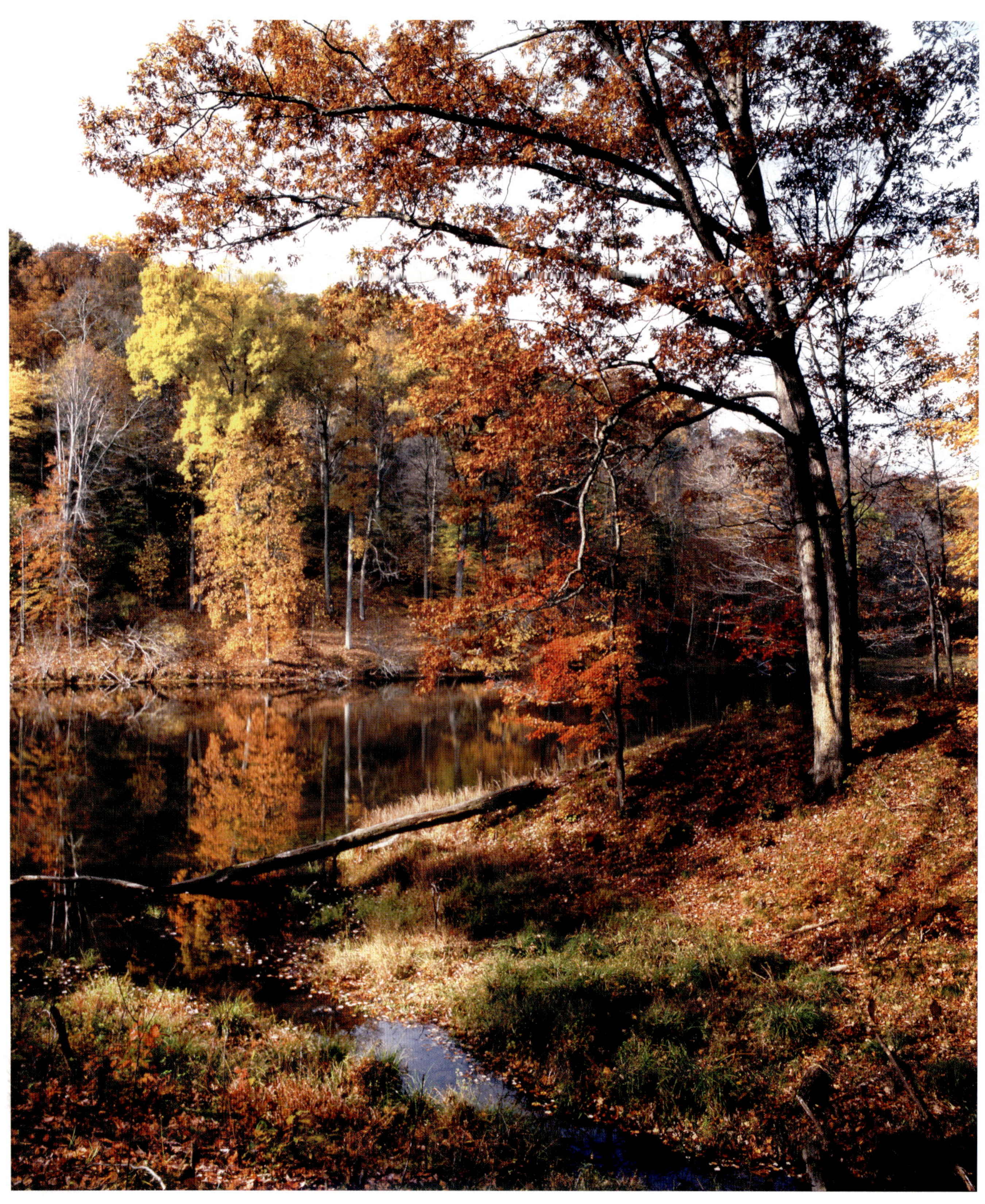

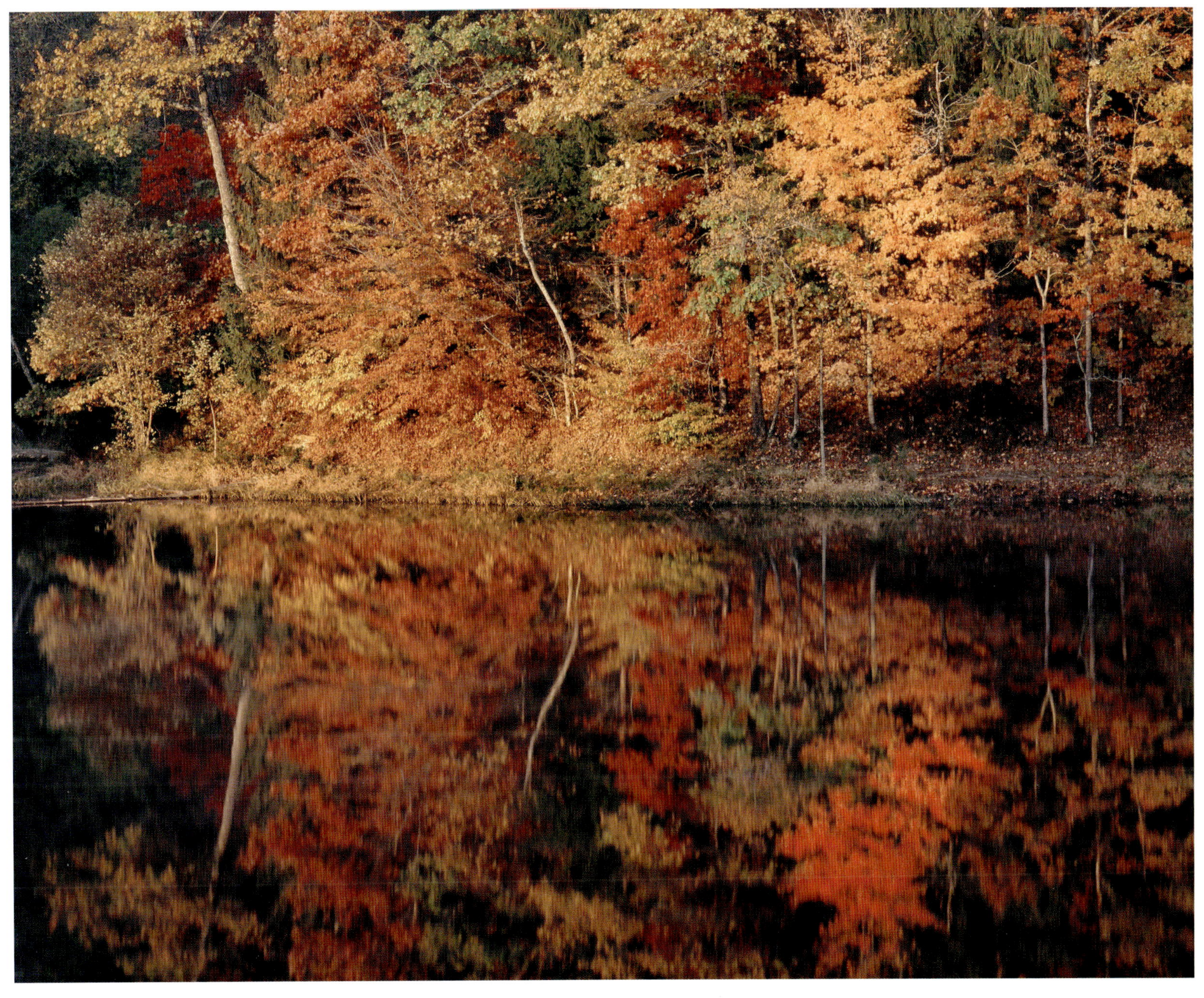

Bear Lake in Yellowwood State Forest. *October.*

Strahl Lake in Brown County State Park. *October.*

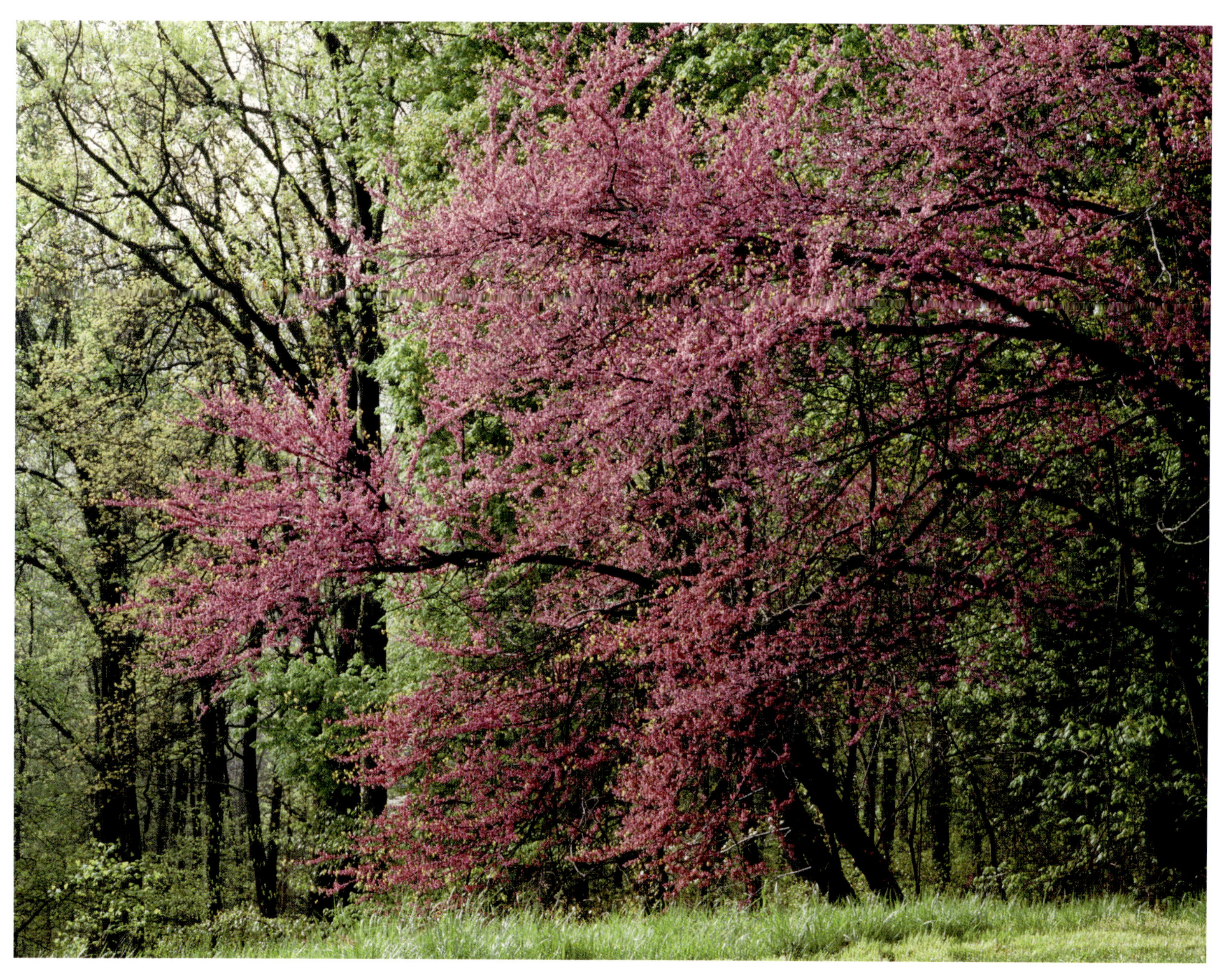

Brown County State Park. *April.*

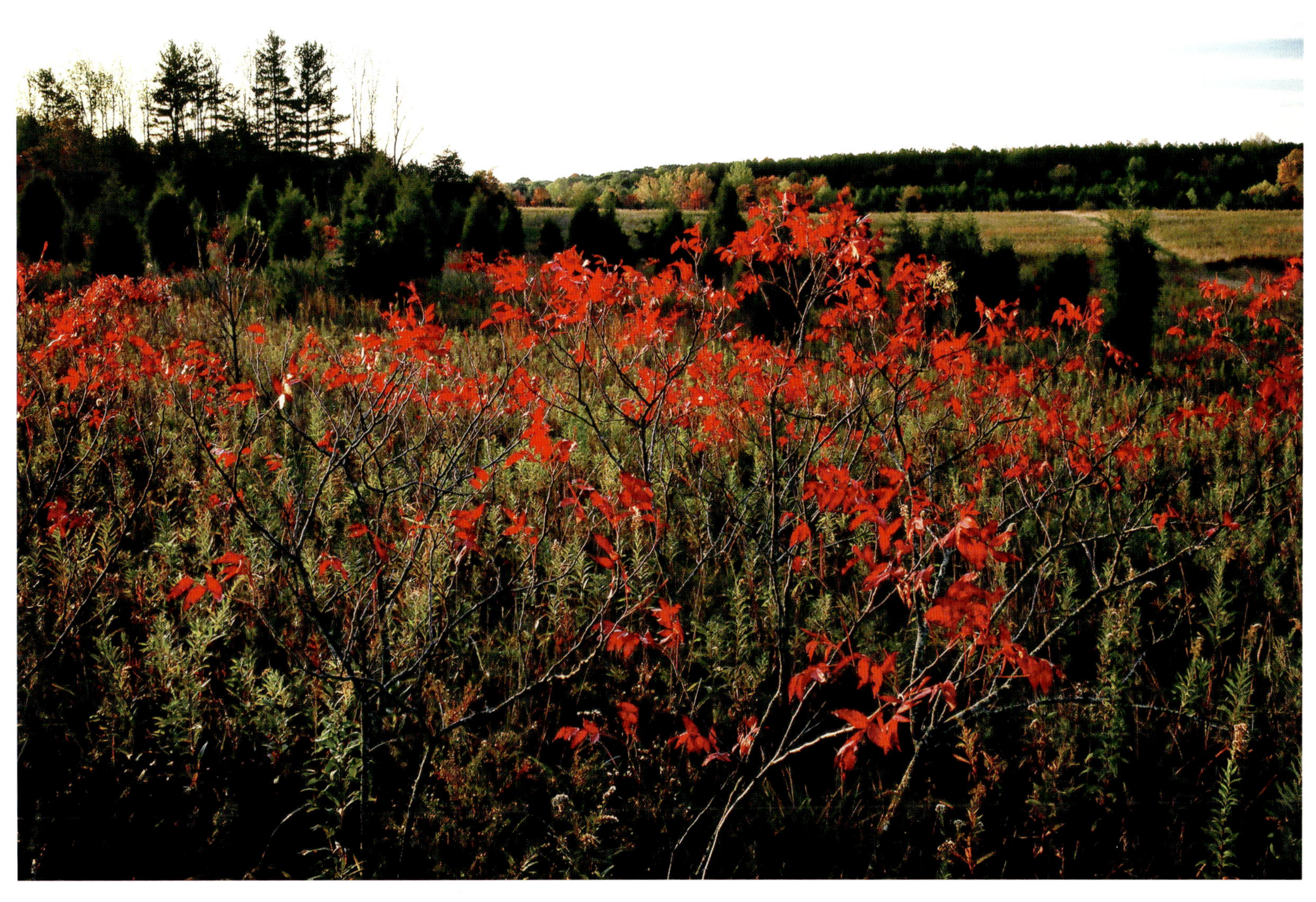

Hoosier National Forest. *October.*

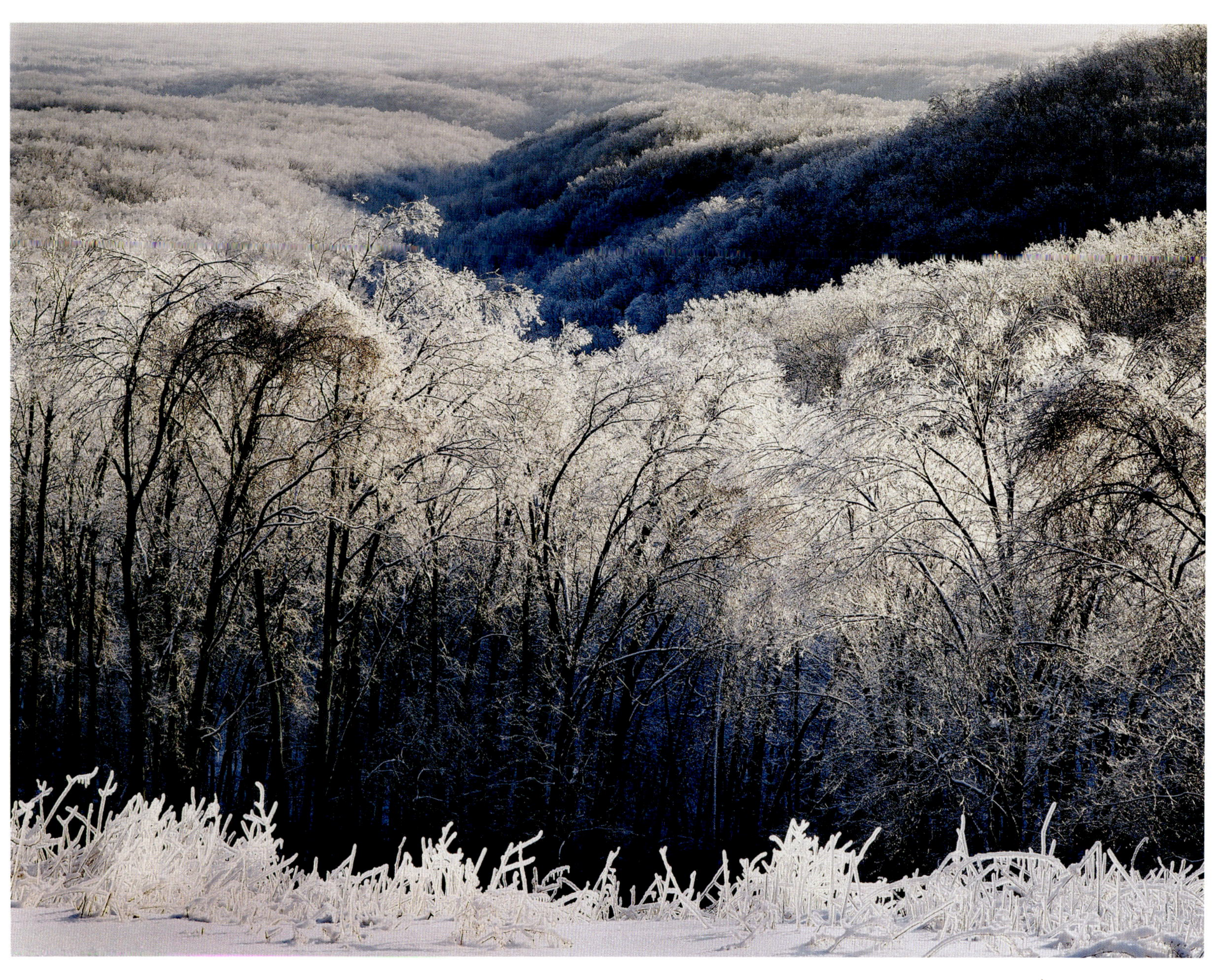

Brown County State Park. *January.*

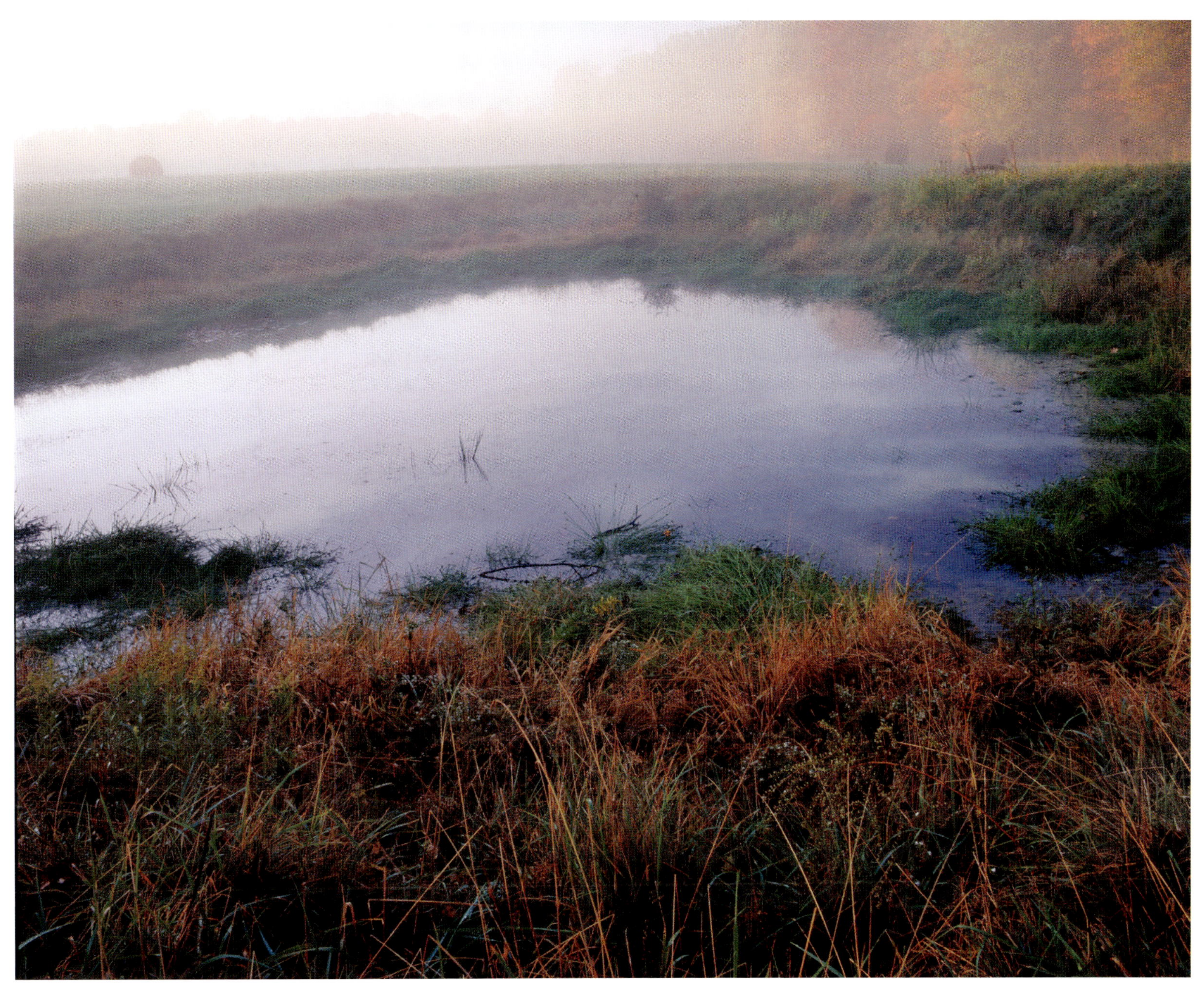

Private Property. *October.*

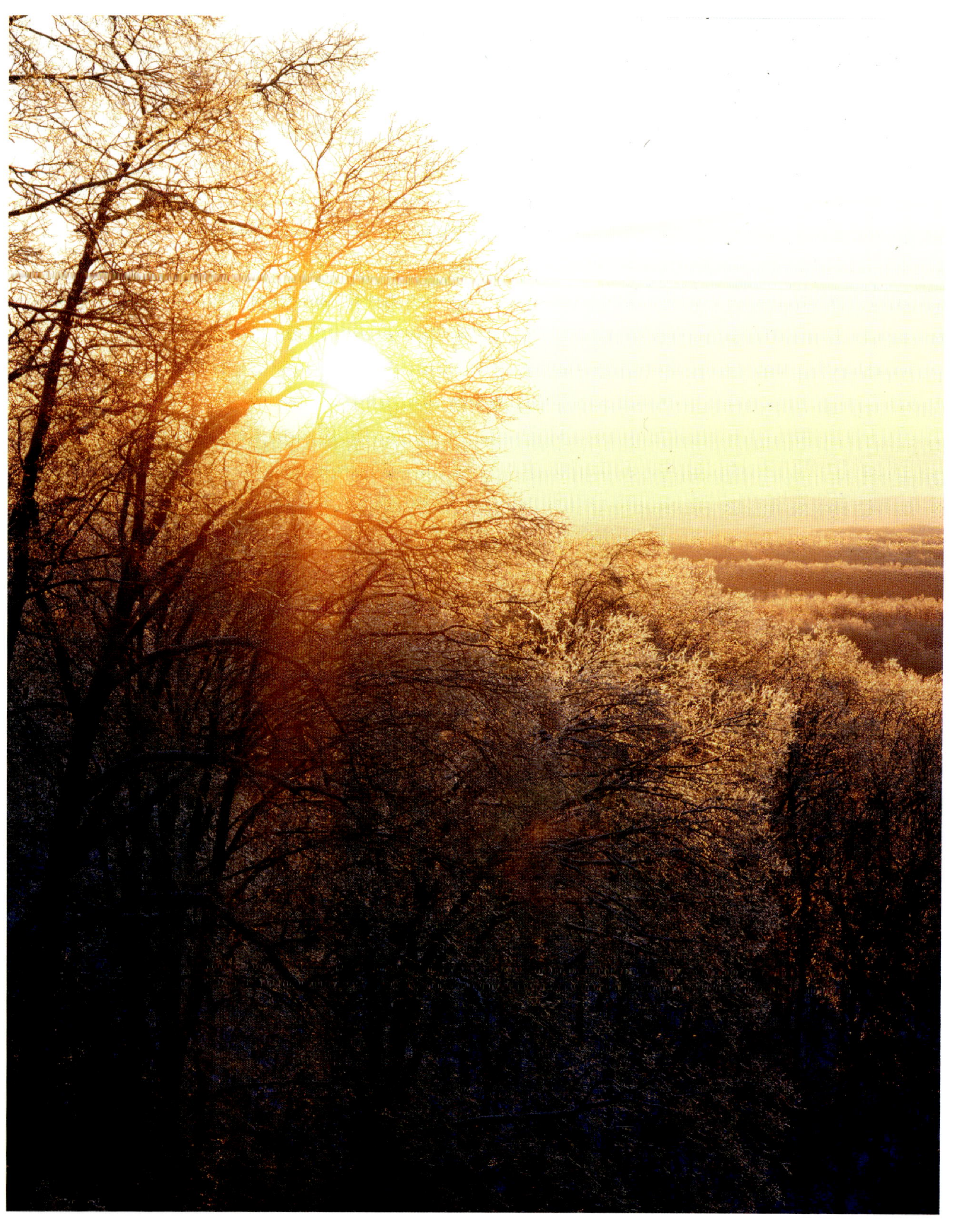

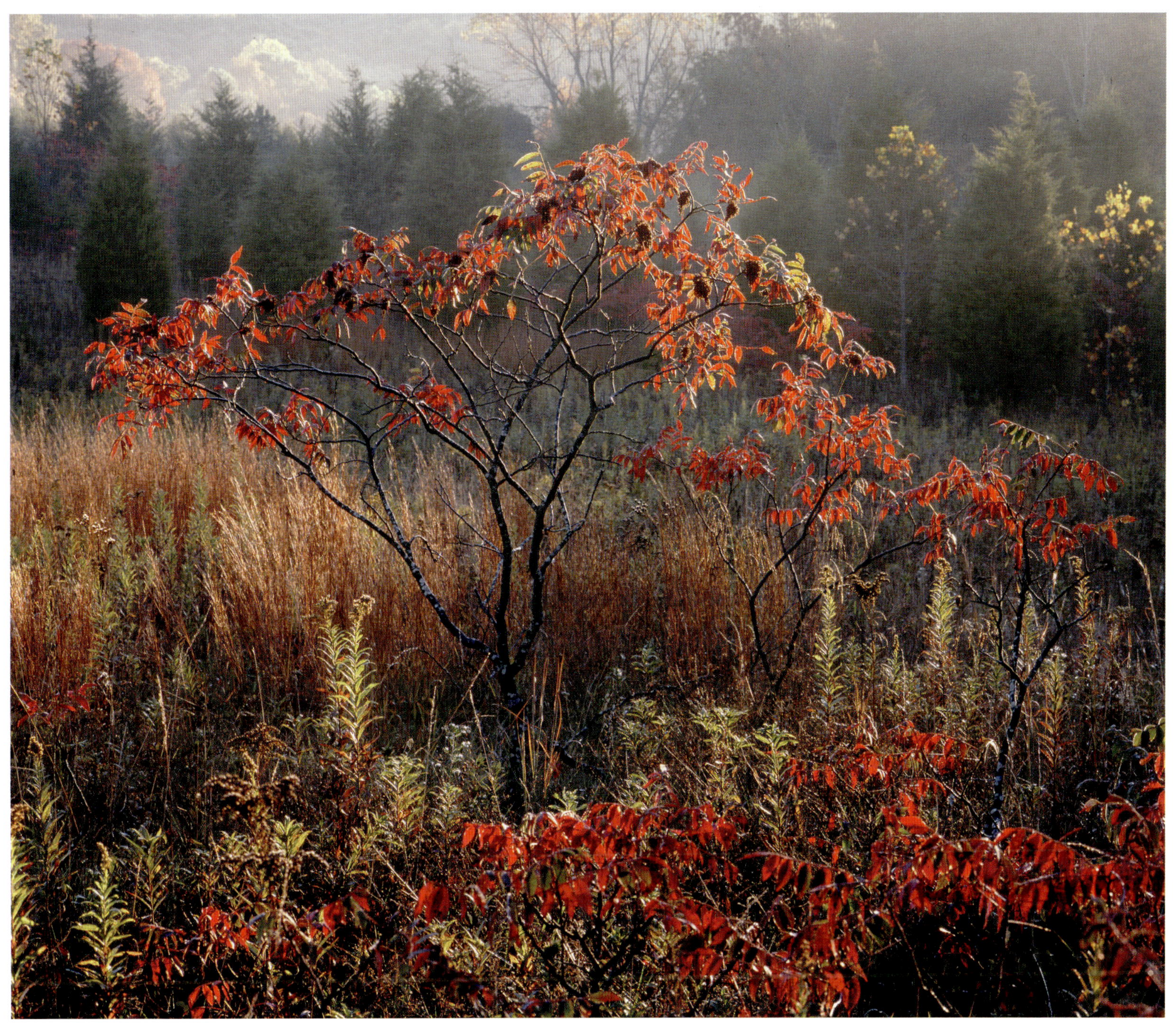

Brown County State Park. *Winter.*

Hoosier National Forest. *October.*

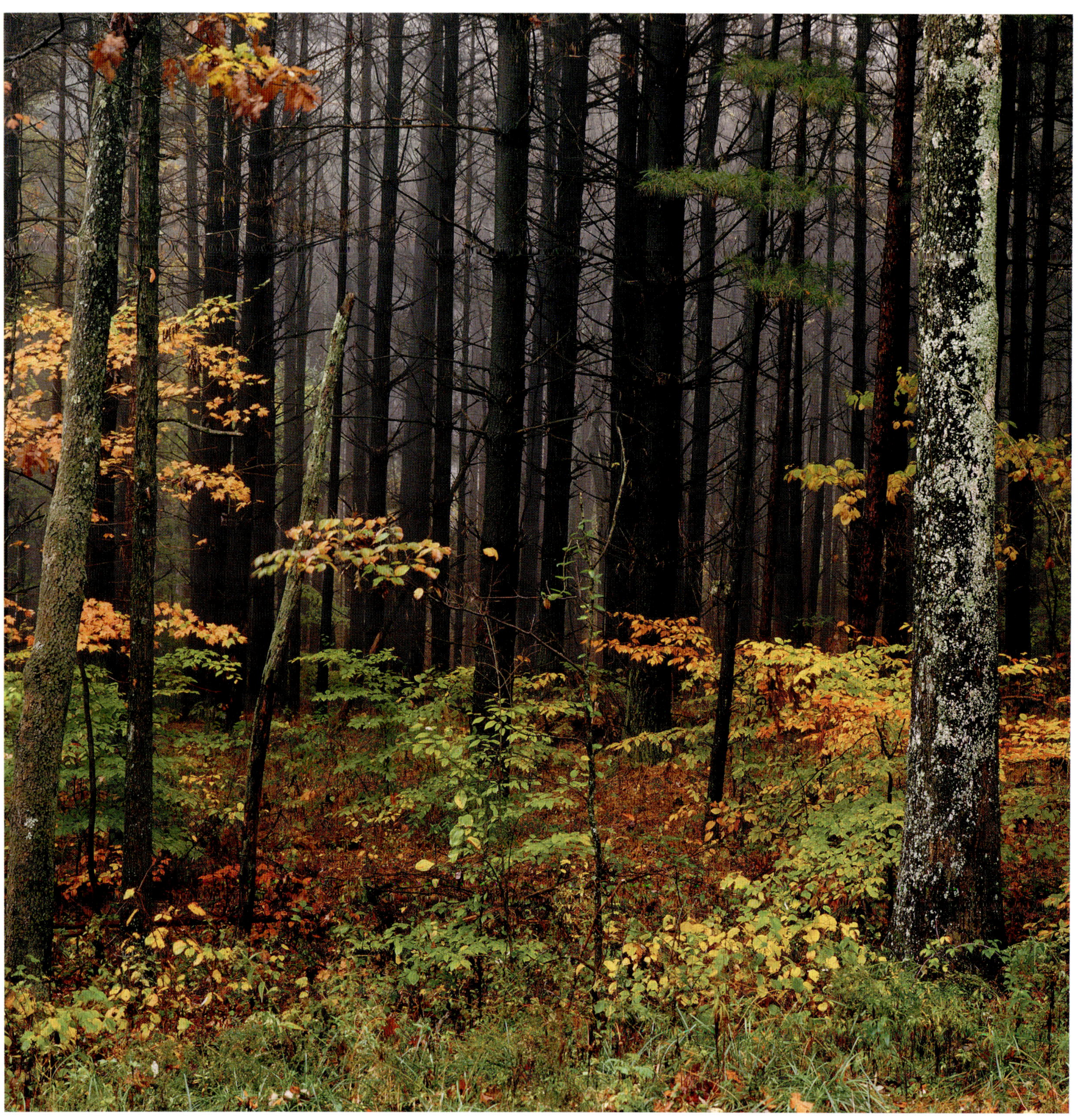

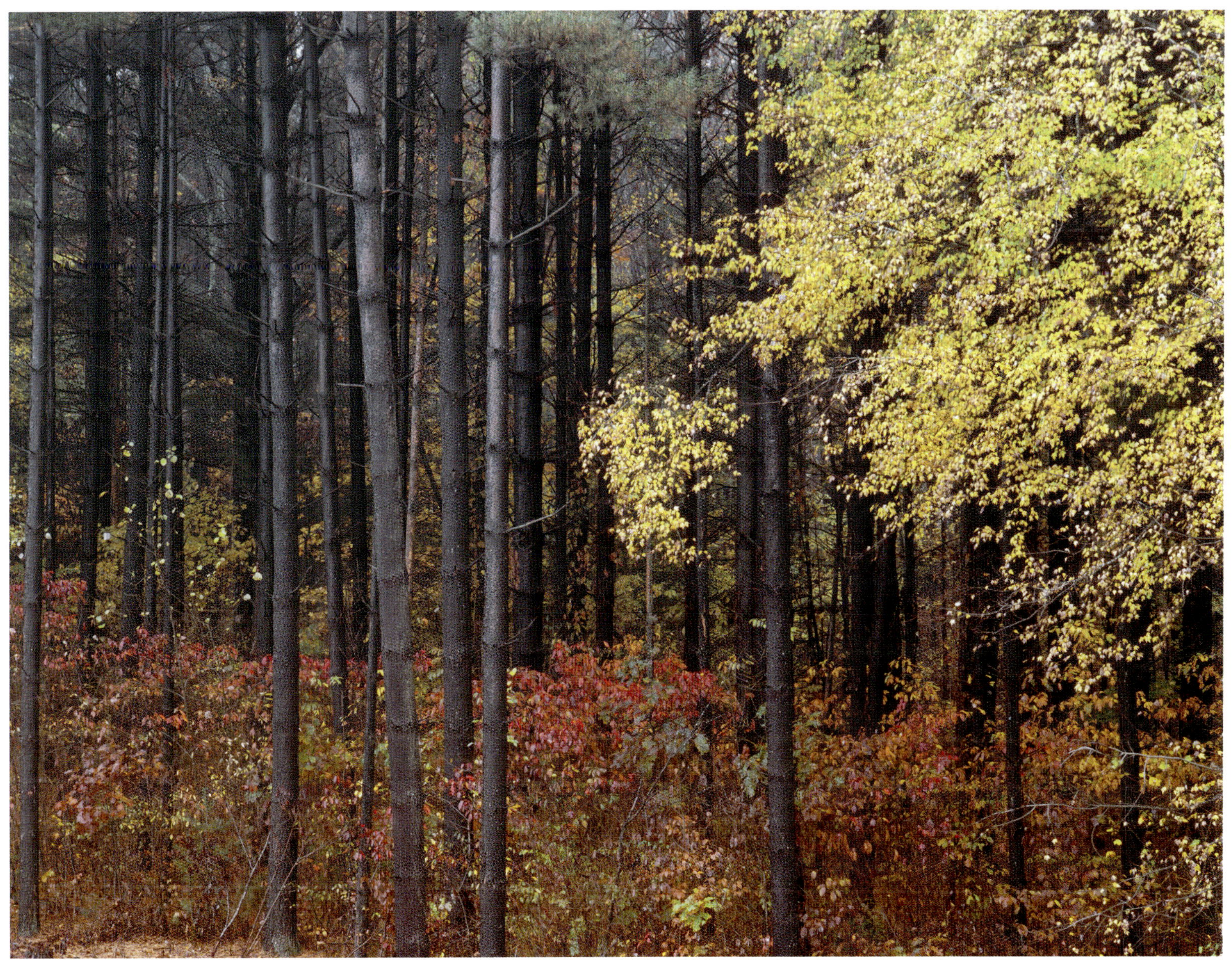

Private Property. *October.*

Hoosier National Forest. *October.*

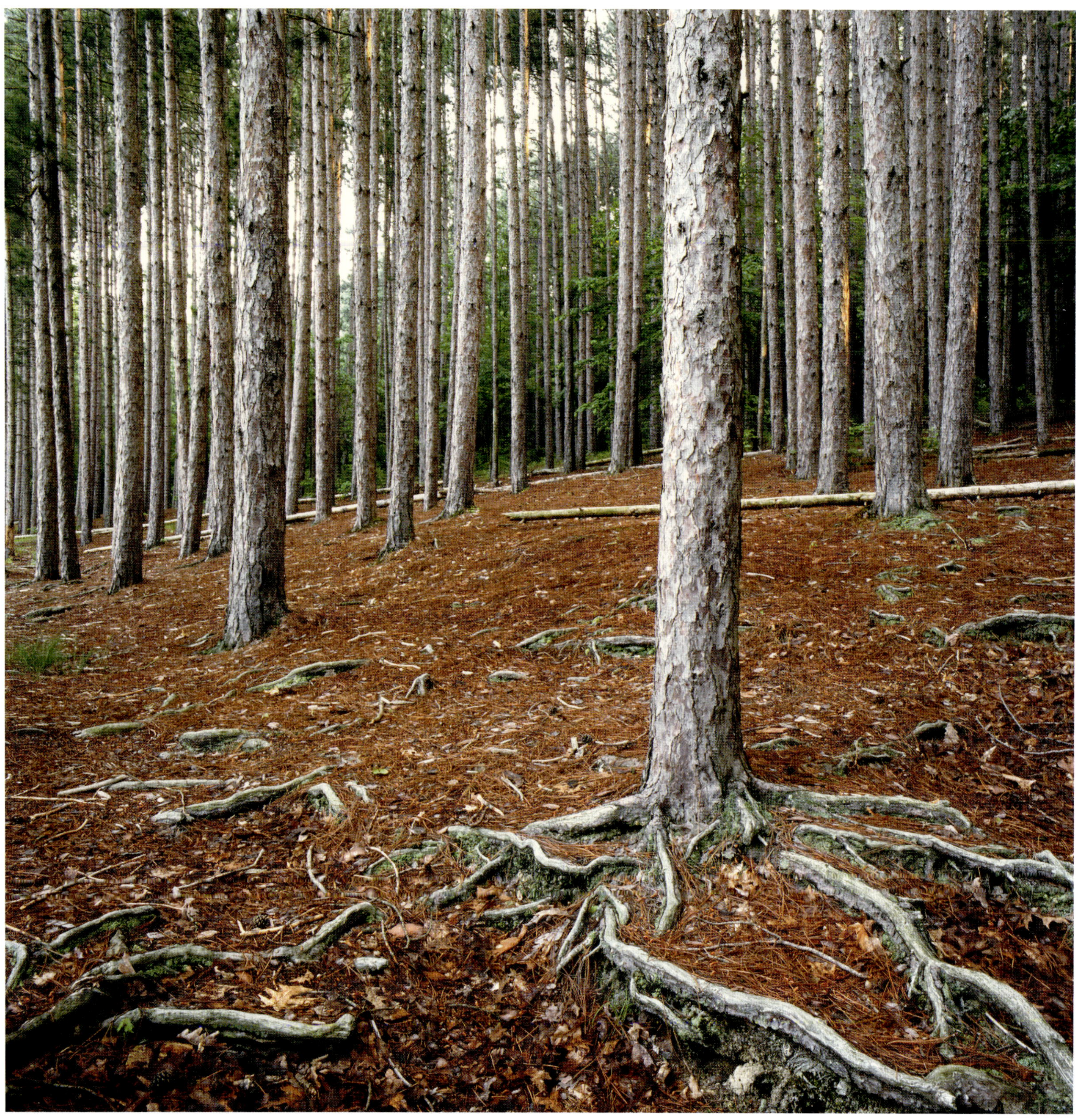

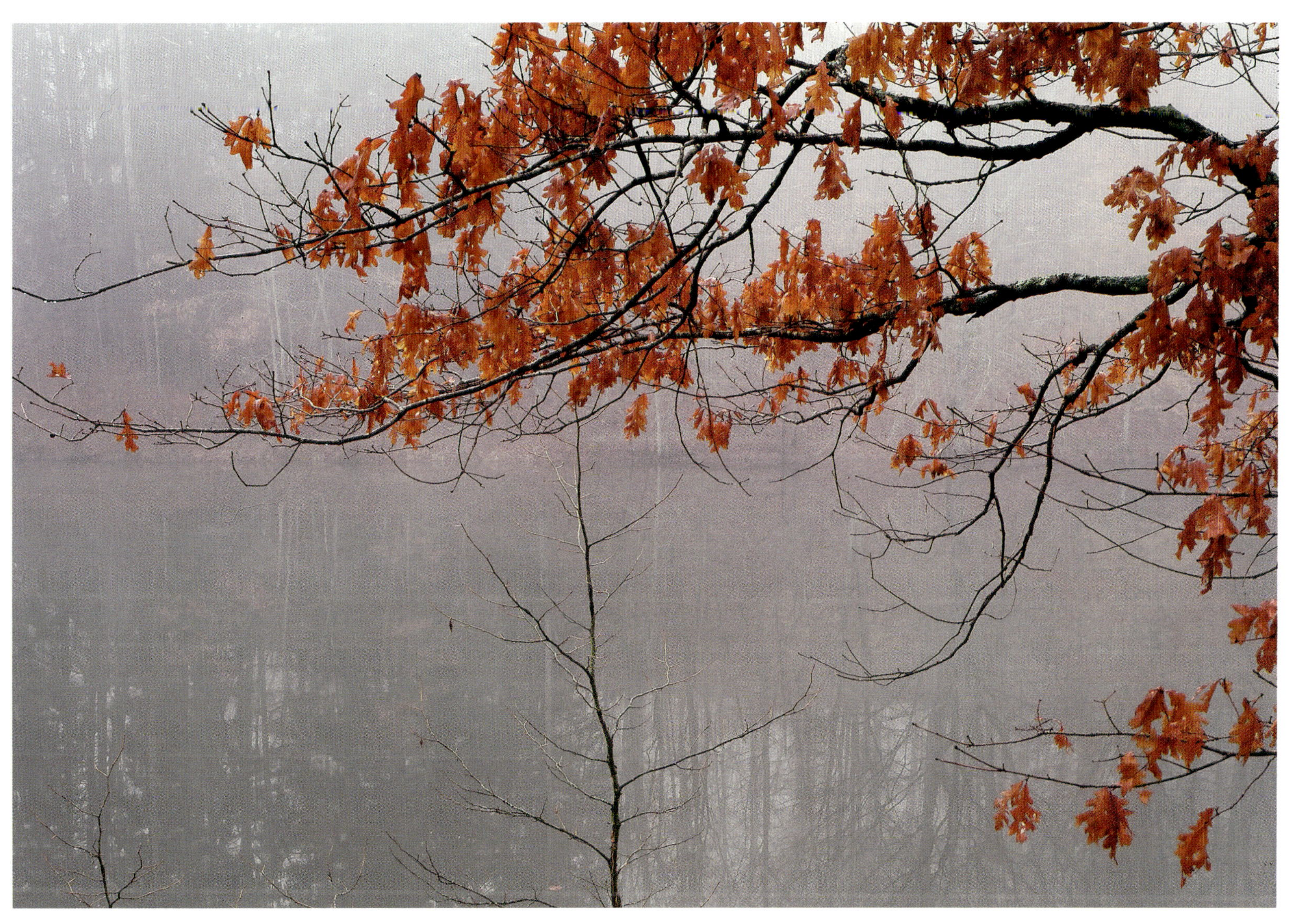

Near Strahl Lake in Brown County State Park.

Strahl Lake in Brown County. *Winter.*

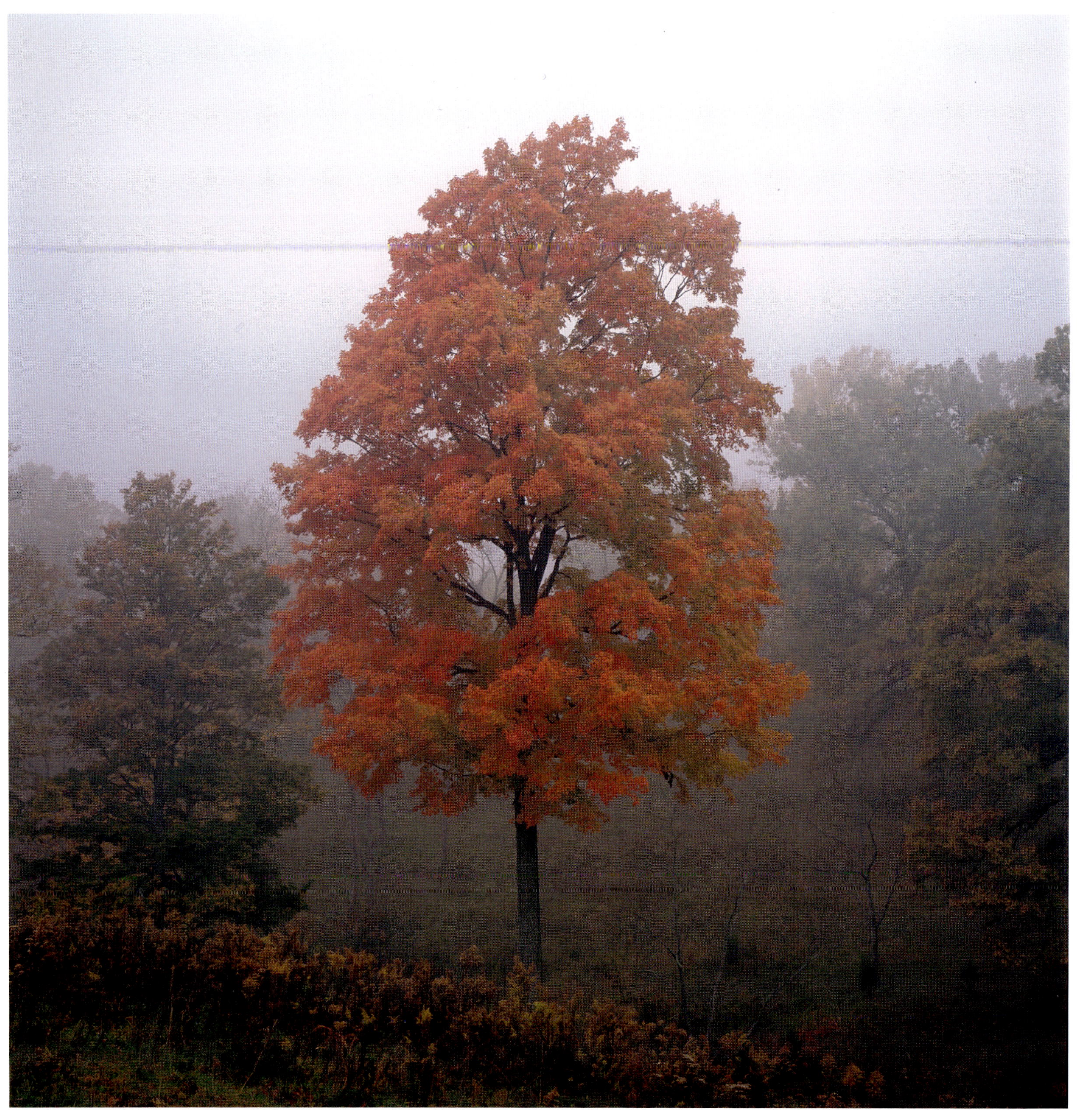

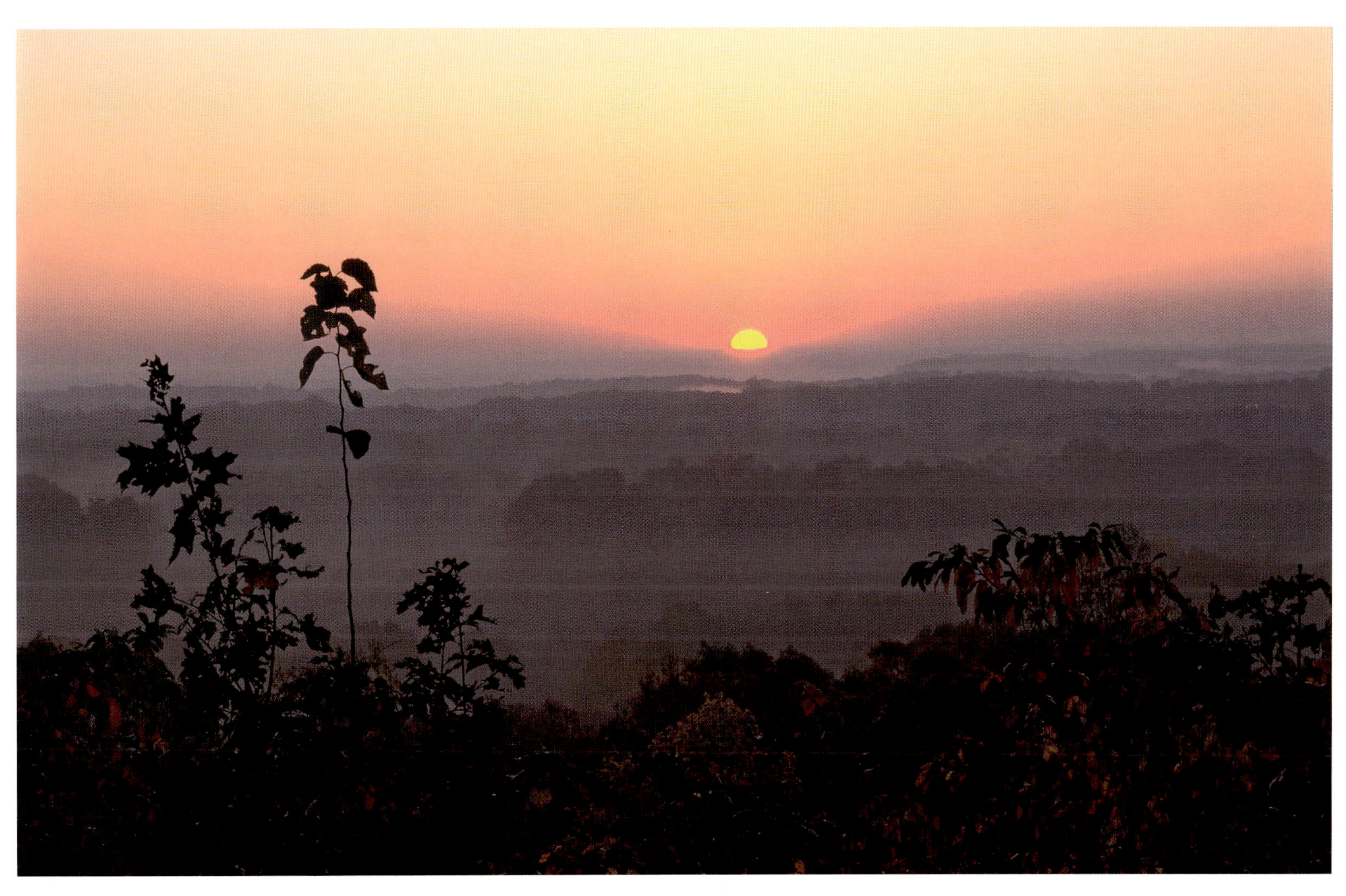

Private Property. *October.*

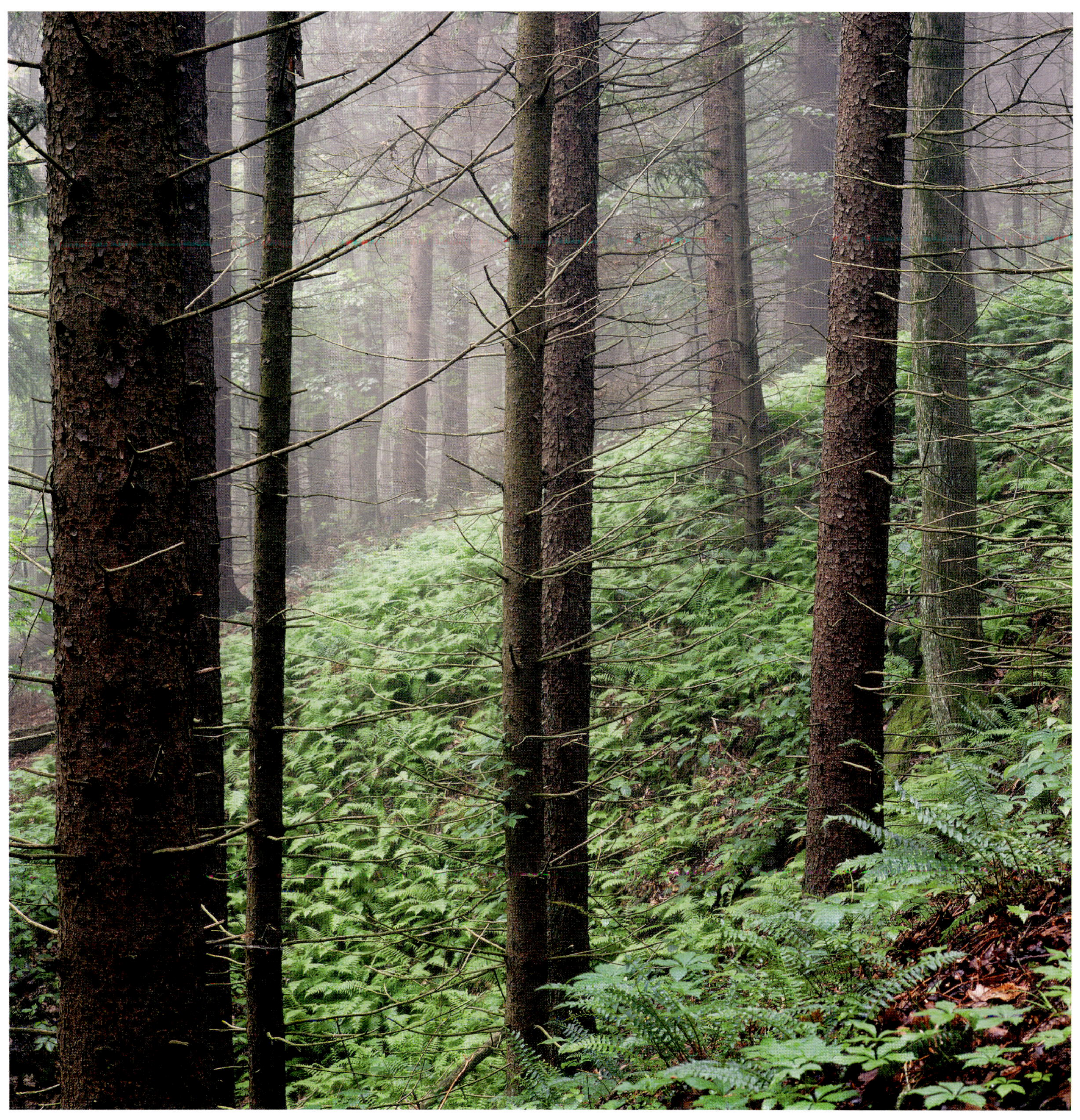

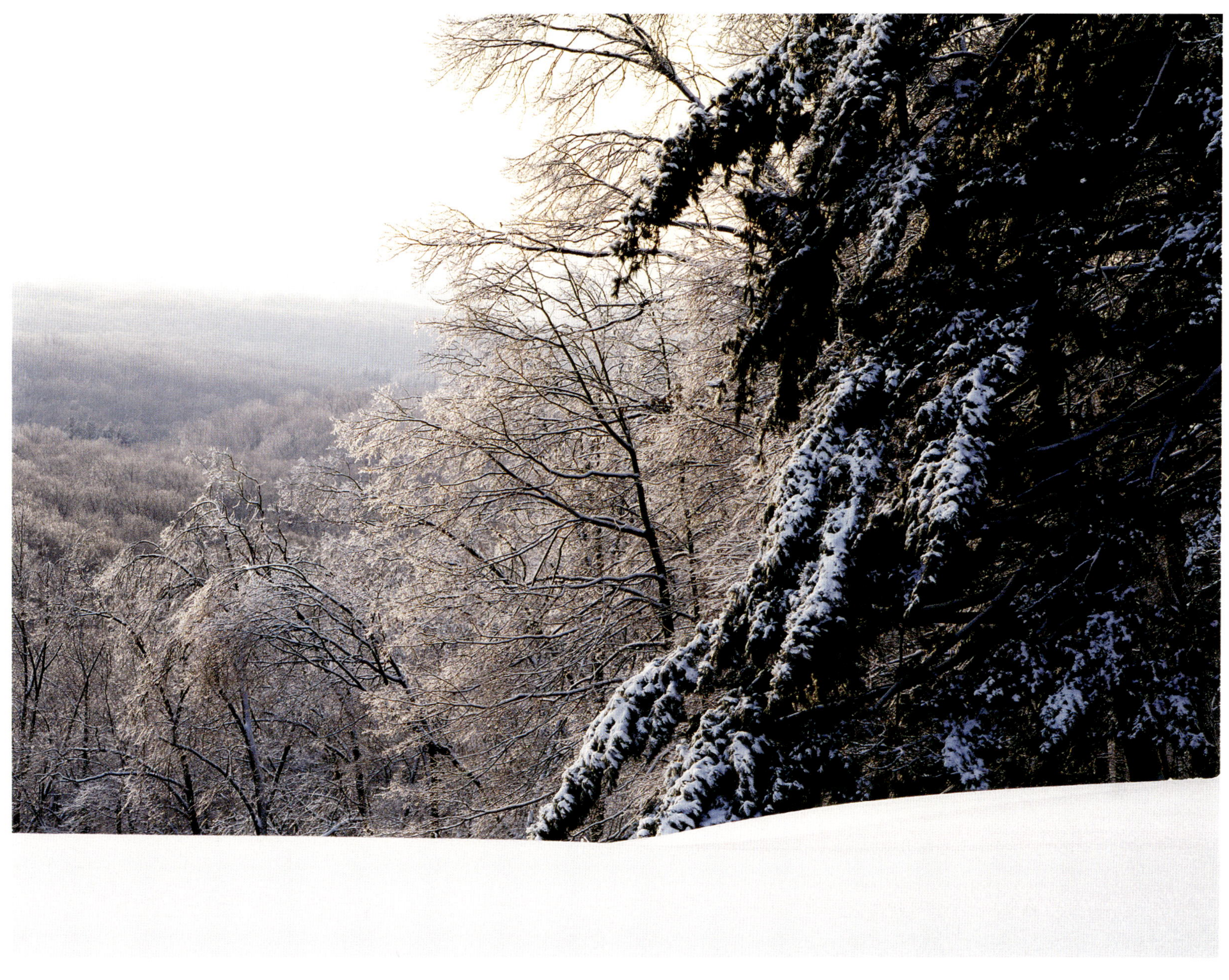

Brown County State Park.

Brown County State Park. *Winter.*

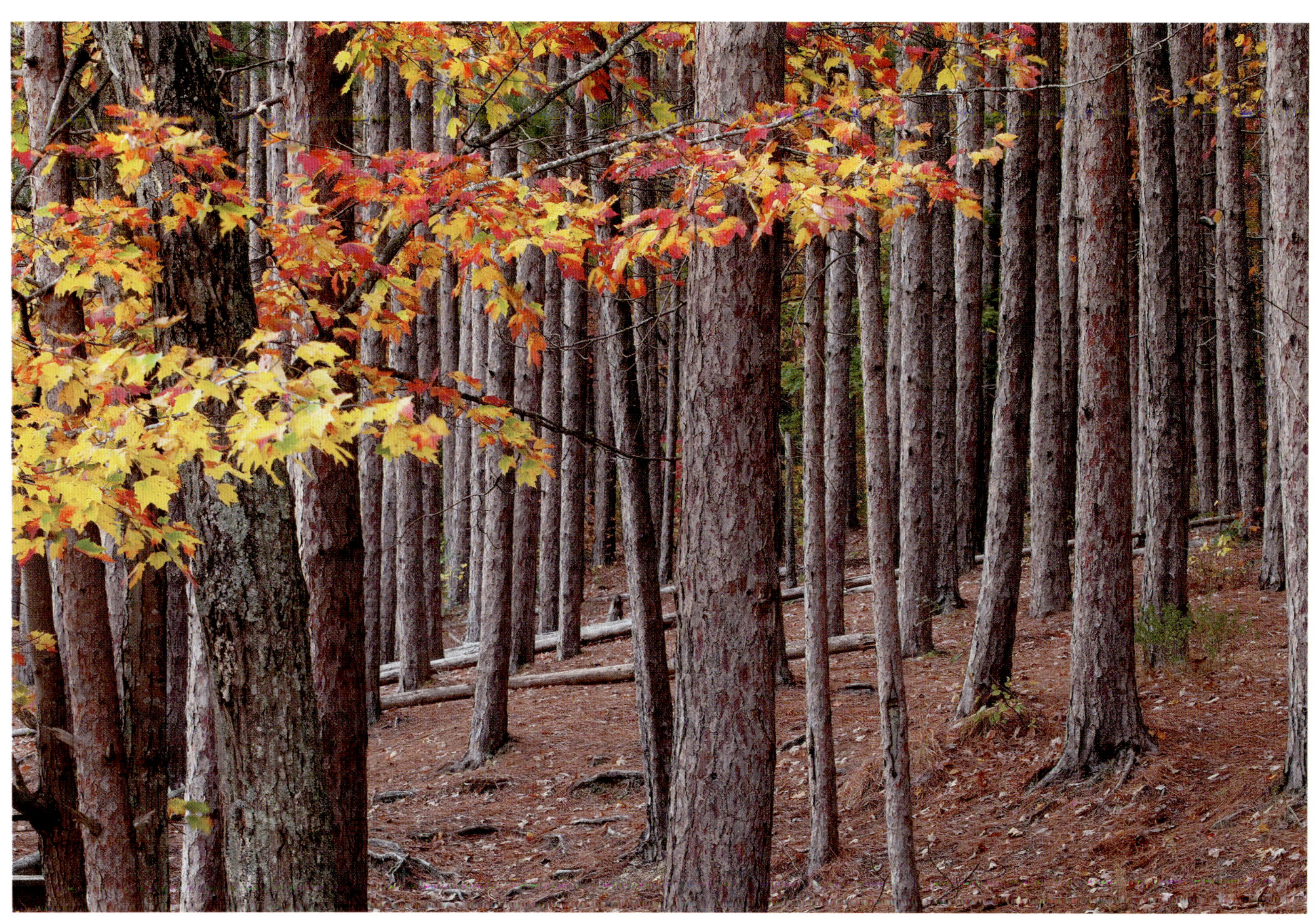

Near Strahl Lake in Brown County State Park. *October.*

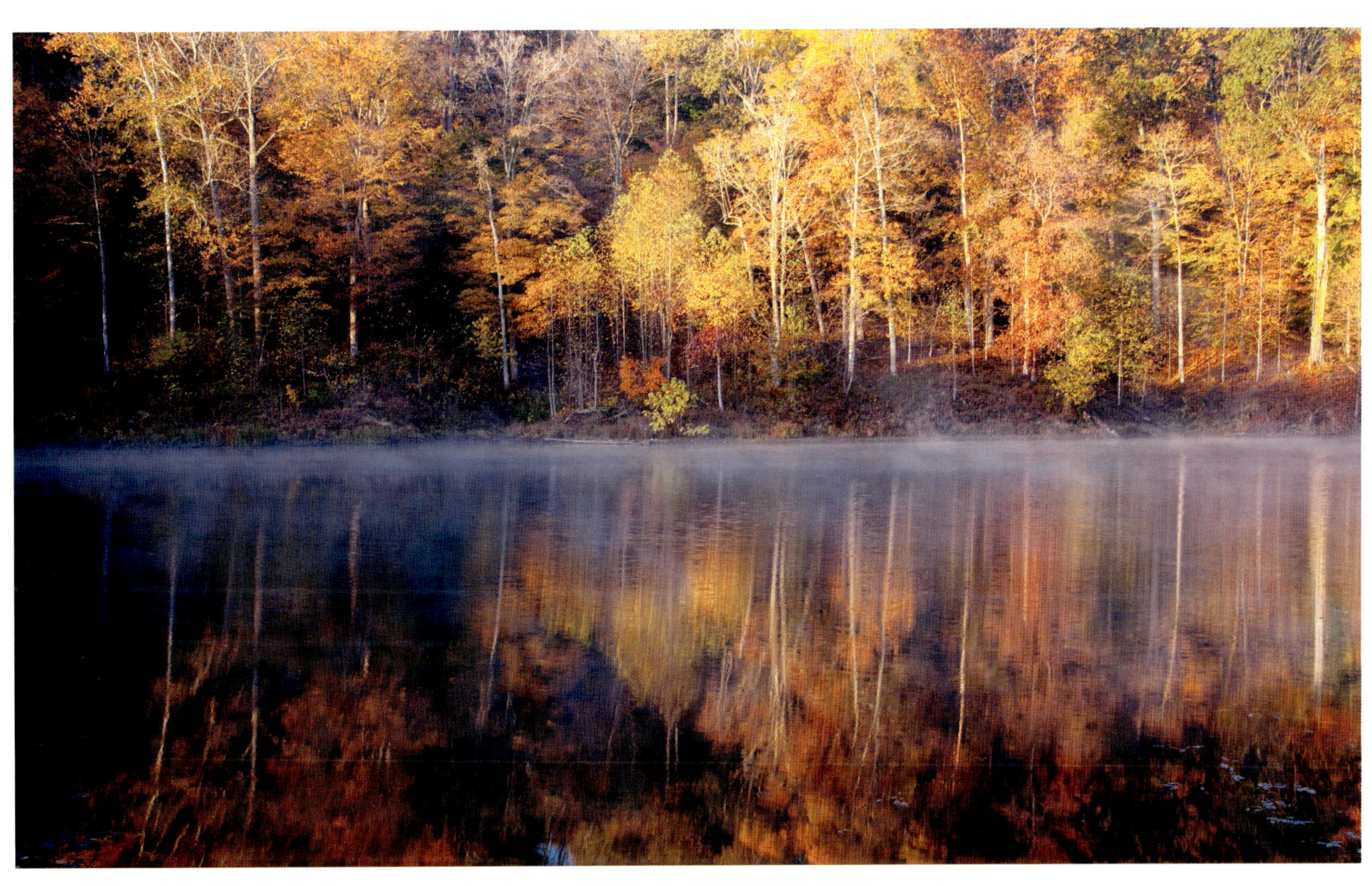

Bear Lake in Yellowwood State Forest. *October.*

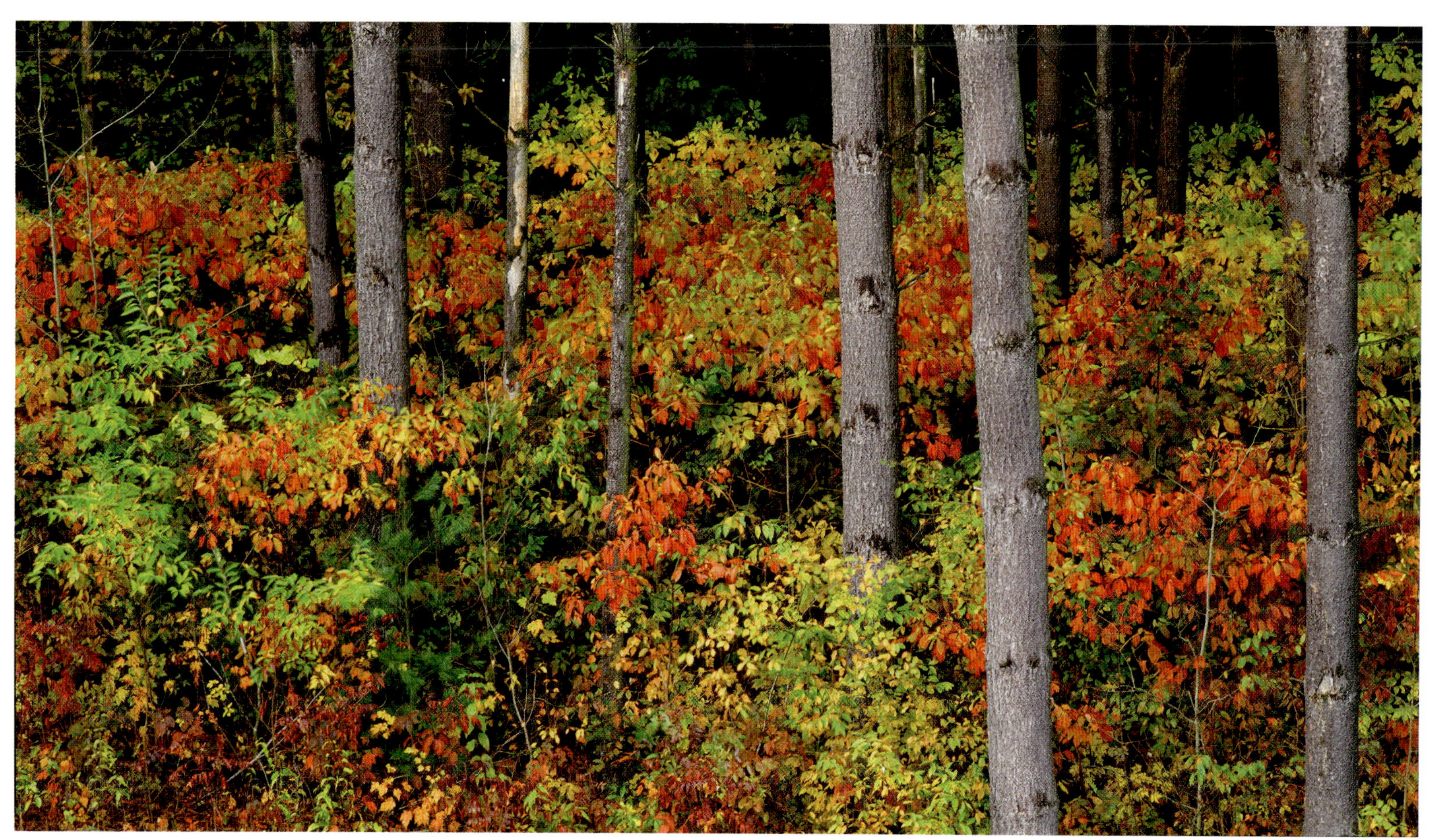

Hoosier National Forest. *October.*

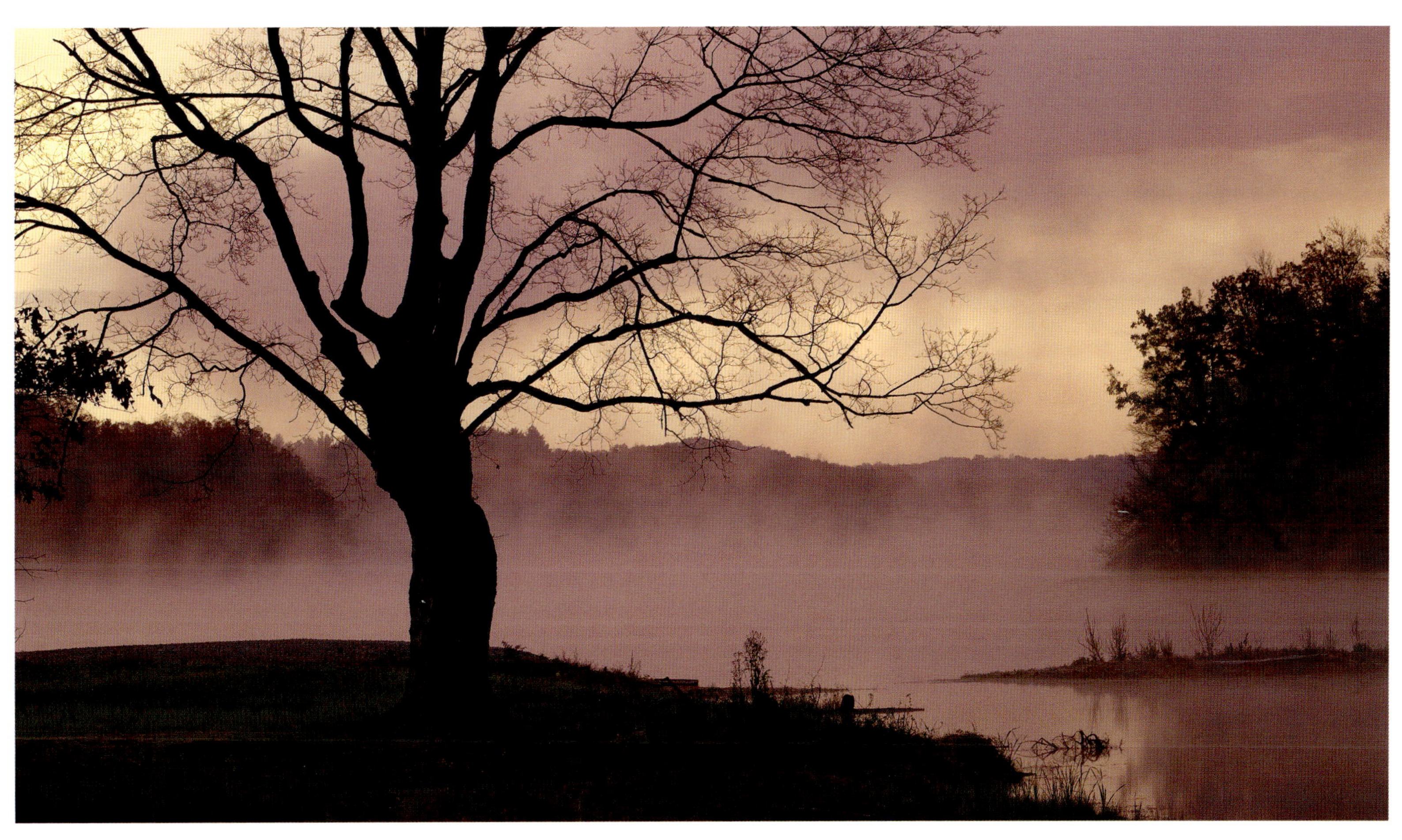

Yellowwood Lake in Yellowwood State Forest. *October.*

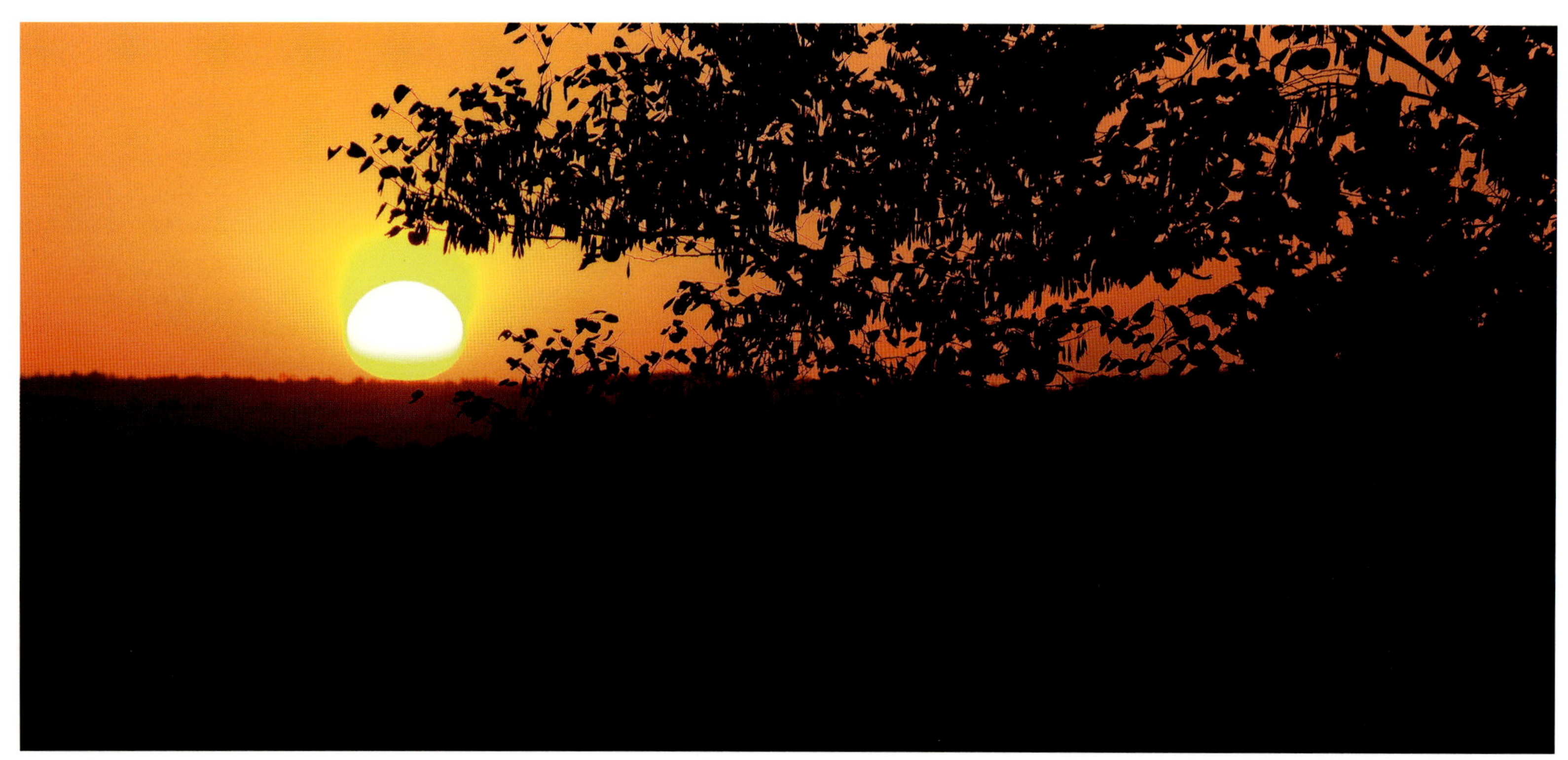

Brown County State Park. *October.*

Sundance Lake in Hoosier National Forest.

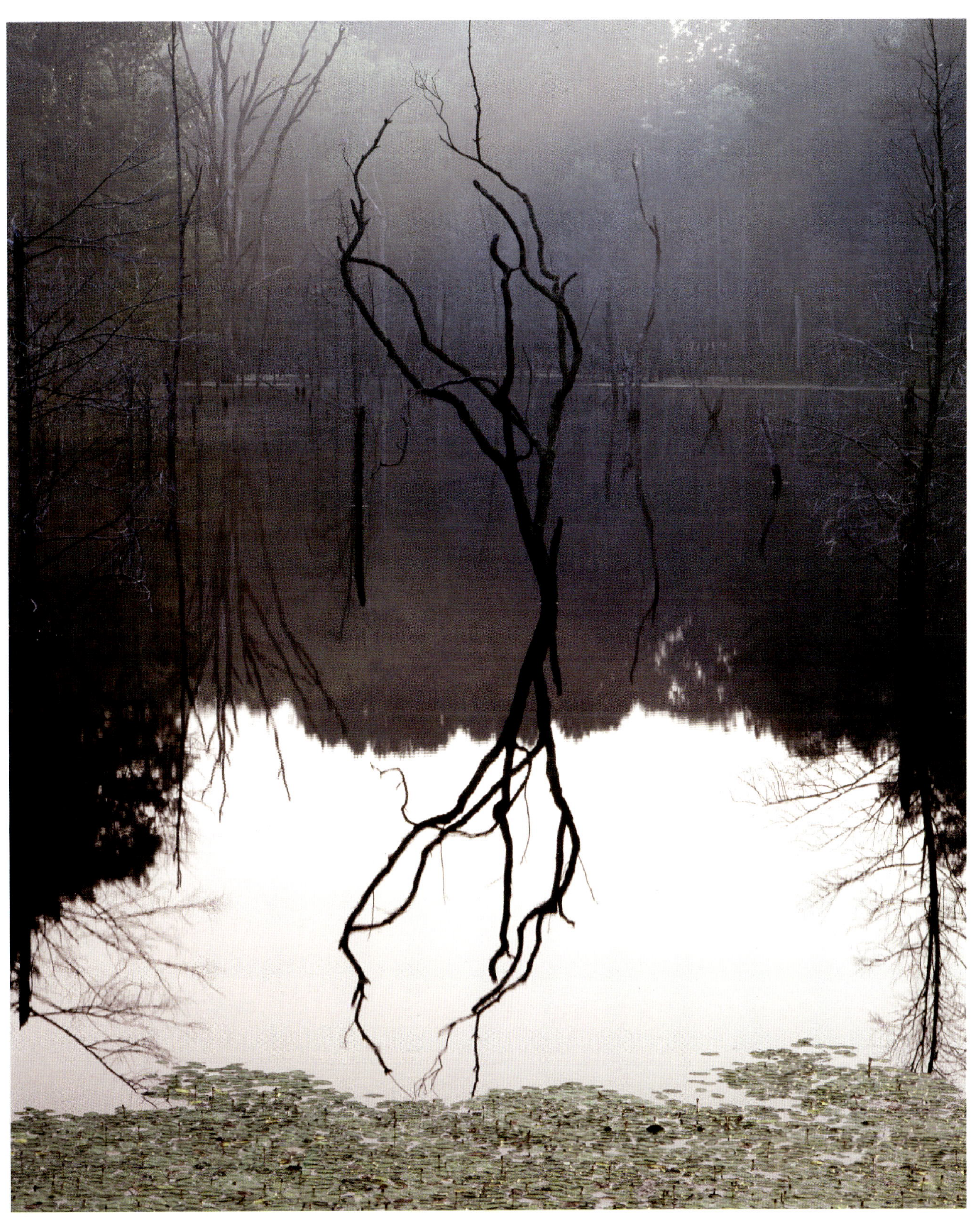

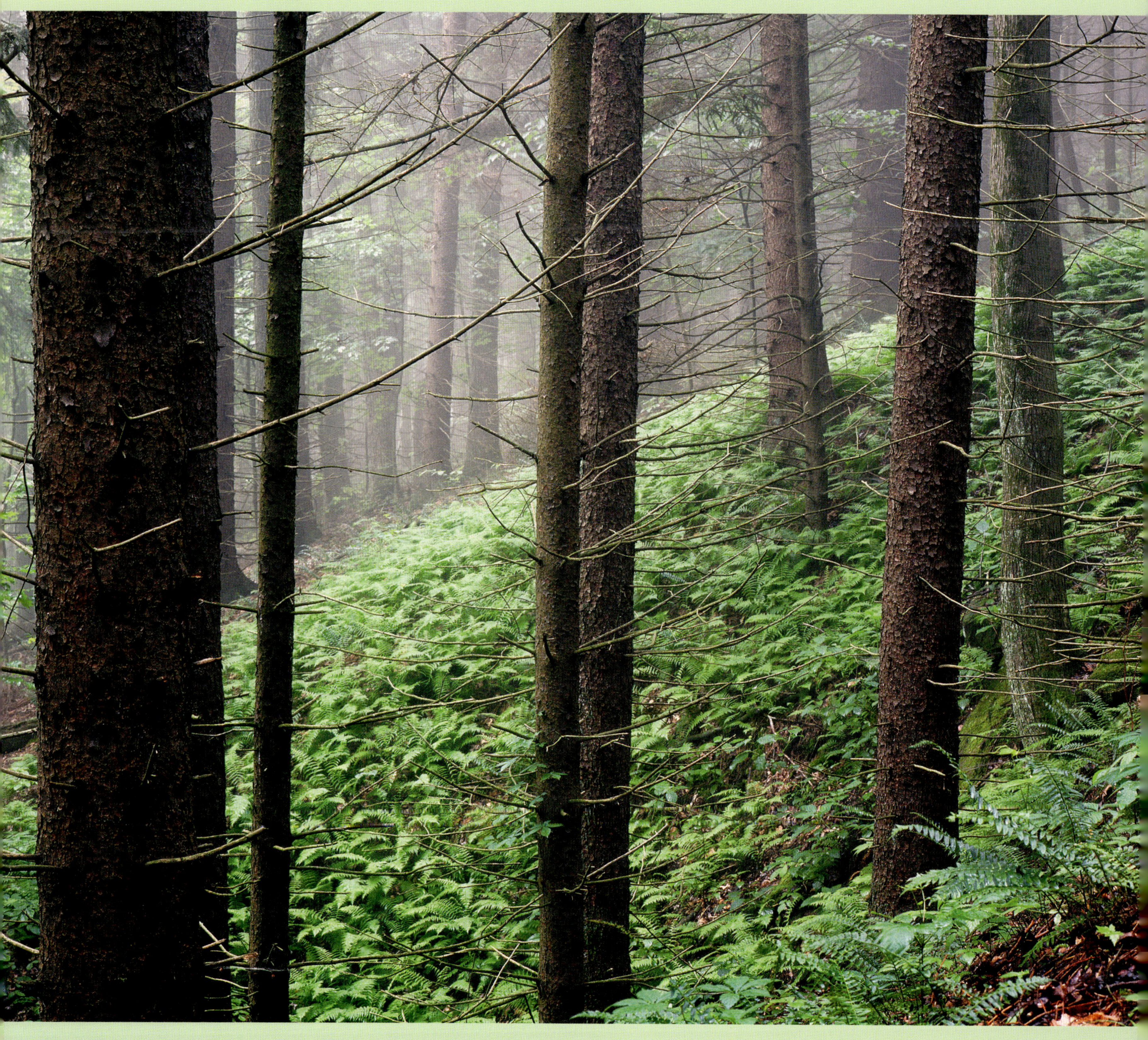

A FEW NOTES ON HOW TO APPROACH LANDSCAPE PHOTOGRAPHY

GREAT LANDSCAPE IMAGES

If you look at many books of landscape photography, calendars, postcards, etc., it soon becomes apparent that many of the beautiful photographs are of scenes in America's national parks of the Southwest. It's no wonder since the region is so blessed with outstanding natural features. Yet, creating a fresh image that doesn't closely resemble what has been produced by other photographers is hard to come by. If you are fortunate enough to spend a few days at the Grand Canyon or some other exotic location, consider yourself blessed if conditions make for a special landscape photograph that does more than prove you were there. You might think that at such a location you will come up with a spectacular image. Even at the Grand Canyon, which is an awesome sight to behold, the view alone will not do it! It really depends on the light, atmospheric conditions, etc. I find the following premise to be true and it is what drives my photography: When a photographer waits for the right light, stunning photographs can be made from landscapes that are not in themselves stunning, but rather commonplace. I hope the images here bear that out. I have been blessed with the opportunity to seek out, enjoy, and photograph some of the beauty in this tiny part of the world. I encourage you to get out there with your own camera and amaze yourself with beautiful images you record when the light is wonderful beyond description!

To get the most satisfaction from your interest in landscape photography, you should have access to a camera that allows you to manually control the aperture and shutter speed settings. Also, you will want a zoom lens that extends from wide angle to medium telephoto, or you can use interchangeable lenses if your camera allows for that. A tripod is also basic for your landscape photography since you will be shooting at slow shutter speeds much of

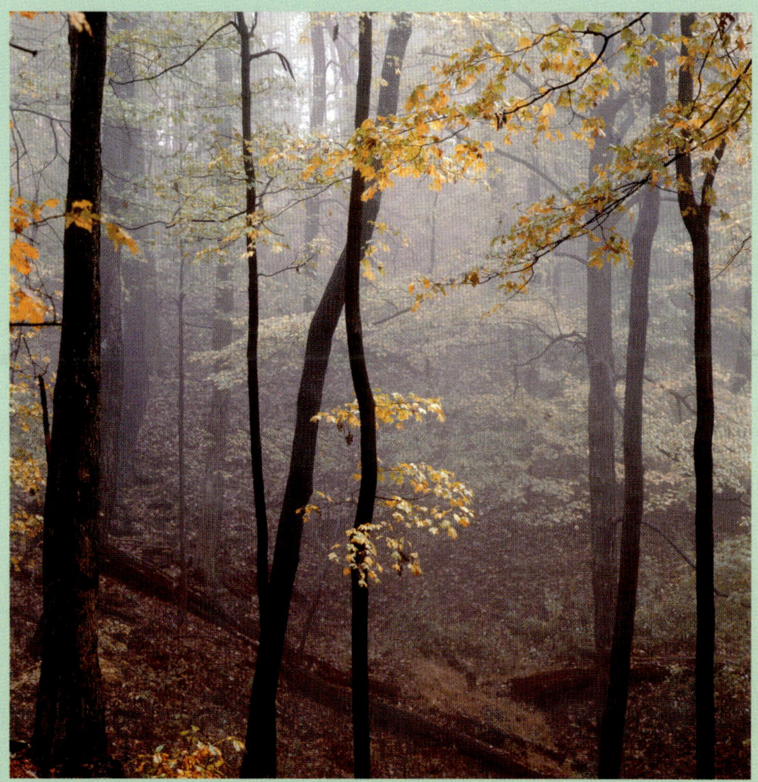

Brown County State Park. *Summer.*

the time. Using a tripod has the added benefit of making you take time to study your composition more closely than if the camera was handheld.

LIGHT

Light is the one thing that is necessary for all of photography. Every picture is dependent upon it. Galen Rowell (photographer and mountain climber) made the interesting statement in his book titled *Mountain Light* that "I am never photographing an object, but rather light itself." His comment is interesting to ponder as you look at a landscape. Light defines the scene as it plays on the contours, giving a sense of depth. Sometimes, the light is so transient, the way it changes can completely alter the scene you wish to capture. In fact, this makes it more fun, and a bit of a challenge, but mostly exciting! The change to the appearance of the landscape is noticeable as the sun breaks the horizon and continues to rise. Try this exercise to see the change: with the camera pointed at a landscape at 90 degrees to the sun, take one picture just after the sun breaks the horizon. Fifteen minutes later, adjust your aperture and shutter to provide an equivalent exposure of the same scene which is becoming brighter. Notice the change. Which is better? You decide which effect is more appealing to your taste. As the sun rises, the warm light will be replaced by cooler light.

Landscape photographers know the phrase "happy hour" or "magic hour" to generally mean the best times to shoot landscapes, one hour after sunrise or one hour before sunset. At these times of the day, the angle of the sunlight is low and warm and gives a very appealing effect. Cross light accentuates it even more. The combination of the warm light and long shadows leaves one with the sense that all is right with the world. What makes landscape photography interesting is the variety you get with different atmospheric conditions and the ways it can affect the lighting. The character of a scene can change dramatically based on whether there is drizzling rain, fog, steam hovering over water, a breeze, a misty morning, or cloudy weather which will reduce or eliminate shadows. I prefer foggy conditions. Fog simplifies the landscape by softening the view and reducing details. The viewer therefore focuses on the main subject.

WHAT DRIVES YOU TO SHOOT LANDSCAPES

Consider that we each have a God-given gift and that we have our own way of seeing (photographically, that is). We interpret what is before us in a way that is ours alone. I want my images to reflect my unique vision. Therefore, for the past sixteen years I have confined my landscape photography to the beauty in the picturesque hills of Brown County, Indiana. Measuring 16 × 20 miles, Brown County landscapes are typical of what you find in southern Indiana. I can identify very well with *National Geographic* photographer Bruce Dale's comment in *The Ultimate Field Guide to Landscape Photography,* "If you're not in the right frame of mind, pictures can pop up all around you, but you can't see them. You have to have a feeling for the place, to be open to it." By giving my time and attention to the small area of Brown County, I see more of its photographic possibilities. I want to shoot when the light is exceptional. I suggest that should be your goal as well. It's logical that by confining time and energy to one area you have opportunities to show it in the most desirable way and with greater variety. By living in one location, you see that area in all types of seasons, weather, and atmospheric conditions. More importantly, you are sensitive to the mood and light conditions. Time and time again, when I revisit a location I find something exciting to photograph that I missed before. I think to myself, "How did I not see that earlier?" Or, maybe the light has dramatically transformed the scene. As you view the transformation

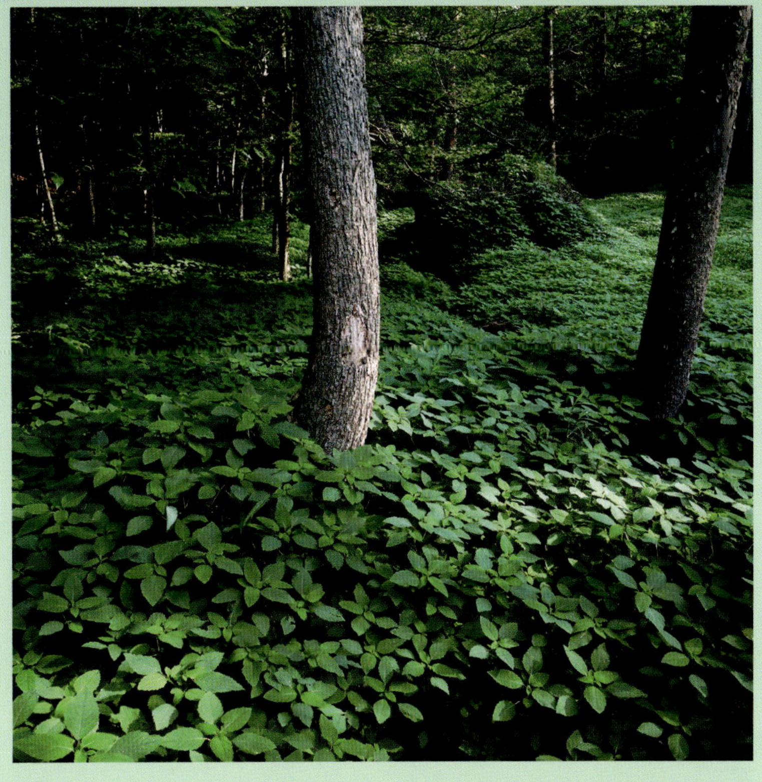

Brown County State Park. *April.*

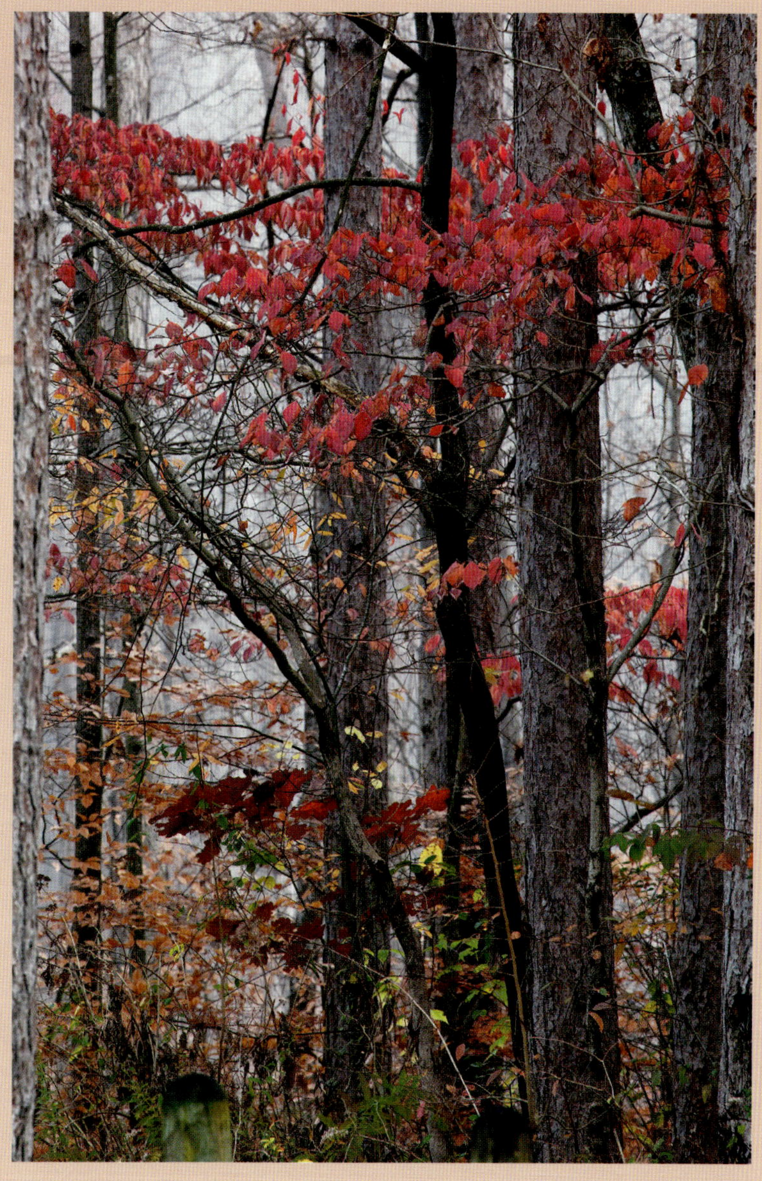

Yellowwood State Forest. *October.*

taking place, you may gain a greater appreciation for the natural beauty around you and be inspired to adapt your own creative way.

Although the Midwest has no mountains, deserts, or oceans, visually there is a lot to work with! You may find subjects such as a quiet lake to cast a lure, streams, hardwood forests, rolling hills, wetlands, and fields. Stands of pines sway in the breeze as they soar to the sky. Those of us who live in the Midwest are here to experience all the variety that the seasons bring. Renewal is announced each spring as prolific redbuds and dogwoods bloom, begging to be photographed, and streams meander along carrying pastel leaves. Oaks, maples, and tulip trees, to name a few, are bright with the green chlorophyll in early spring, and green seems to dominate the summer landscape. Autumn comes blazing to color the landscape with russets and gold while tourists descend on the small town of Nashville, Indiana. It's a great time to find colorful reflections on lakes and ponds. Winter arrives, and with it the land takes on a subdued look as colors retreat. If you feel as I do that it's rewarding to come up with great images that you haven't seen dozens of times before, then maybe you'll be motivated to seek out those special Midwest locations that are your own "find." As you scout around and find a location you want to shoot, be patient. Wait for the time when the light, the atmosphere, and all the elements come together to excite your creative instincts. It might mean waiting for an hour, for a day, or for a different season. Be willing to make repeat visits until you are satisfied with the image you get. Don't settle for ordinary images!

One might imagine that the ideal condition is a bright sunny day with no clouds in the sky, but that is not what makes for a good landscape photograph. A sky with no clouds and no color should be photographed with as little sky showing as possible, or at least some of the sky can be cropped out.

Famous landscape photographer Ansel Adams once said, "A good photograph is knowing where to stand." (Sometimes for Adams, that meant standing on a platform mounted on the roof of his car.) This is so true, and remember "where" includes standing next to your camera which is mounted on a good tripod. Some images suffer because you've tried to include too much. One of the first things to do if you don't like the composition is to simply include less in the image. Either move closer to eliminate objects around the edges or use a longer lens (i.e., medium telephoto). An easy way to make a picture better is to get rid of distracting elements.

Horizontal landscape photographs convey peacefulness and relaxation, while vertical ones imply more action. For example, imagine you are going to photograph a waterfall. A vertical image will give the sensation of water flowing down and emphasizes the flow. However, consider the possibilities if you shoot the waterfall using a horizontal format. Back away from the waterfall and determine what surrounds it that you want to include. Is there a nice tree or wildflowers off to the side? Can you show the stream flowing over rocks in the foreground as the waterfall is seen more distant? The horizontal approach can be a "scene setter" since some of the surroundings are included.

In relation to composition there is what is known as "the rule of thirds" which, according to Wikipedia, is defined as "a compositional rule of thumb in visual arts such as painting, photography, and design." The rule states that "an image should be imagined as divided into nine equal parts by two equally-spaced horizontal lines and two equally-spaced vertical lines, and that important compositional elements should be placed along these lines or their intersections."

Your composition will often look like this without consciously planning it that way. Remember that this

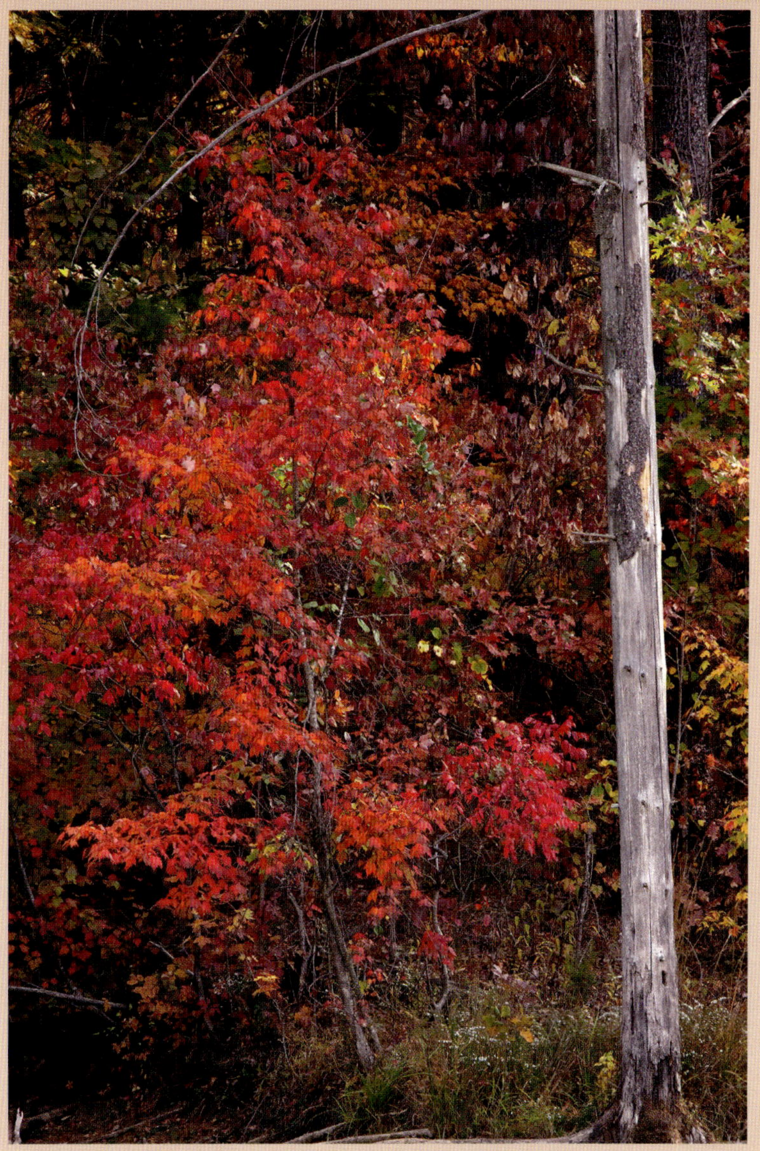

Hoosier National Forest. *October.*

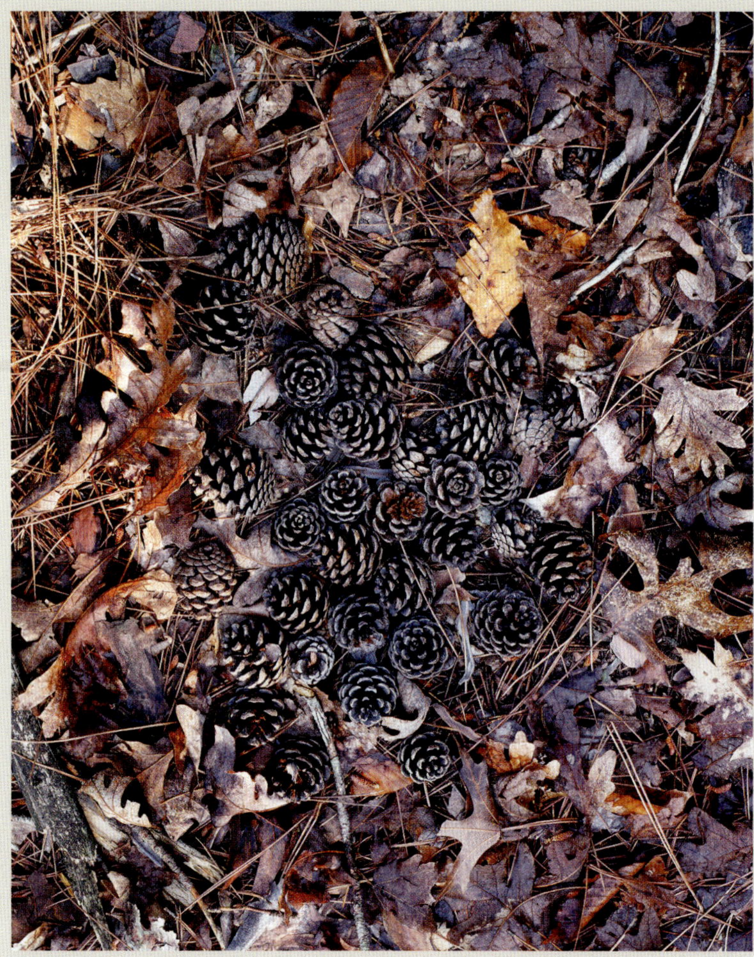

Yellowwood State Forest. *October.*

is a general guideline and not something that should restrict you in whatever way you want to be creative. A two-dimensional photograph gains a sense of depth if you include something of interest in the foreground by creating tension with what is beyond in the scene. Most pictures benefit if there is a center of interest referred to as a focal point. It's where your eye is drawn to as you first look at a picture, like the star of a film with the rest of the image being the supporting cast. Not every picture can be said to have a definite focal point, in which case the eye of the viewer takes in the scene as a whole. Eliminate any distractions that do not help keep the image simple. One thing to watch for that detracts from an image is bright areas that draw the eye of the viewer away from the center of interest. Also watch out for utility lines and those pesky jet trails in the sky. The view should not look cluttered. One time I was bold enough to ask a man sitting in his truck if he would mind moving it so that I could shoot a scene. He was kind enough to oblige.

Photographer Eliot Porter came up with the phrase "intimate landscape," which usually means the image does not include the sky or horizon. Examples might be a pattern of tree trunks or leaves in a stream. Pictures that do include the horizon are sometimes referred to as "grand scenics." Visualize a scene with something dominant in the foreground such as flowers, with a view of a lake and the sky beyond. That would be considered a grand scenic.

As you decide on how to compose your picture, what do you hope the picture will communicate? Do you want an image that includes trees, a lake or field in foreground with the horizon visible beyond (grand scenic) – like a picture which includes a sunrise – or will you be concentrating on a more intimate image that does not include the sky and horizon? Your creativity will help you decide what lens to use – normal, wide angle, short telephoto, or longer. If you are serious about landscape photography and have had the opportunity, you have probably already scouted out the area to see what vantage point (standing location) you prefer. Consider how the light falls on the landscape. Frontlighting flattens the image and is not as appealing. Sidelighting or backlighting are more interesting. Side-lighting and something in the foreground are important if you want the image to have a feeling of depth. Consider that you are attempting to give three-dimensionality to a flat piece of photographic paper. What you do is your choice and over time will develop into a style that becomes your own. As you compose your shot, consider these points:

1 If the horizon is to be part of the photograph it should be level.
2 If the sky is clear with no clouds, it is just dull and you should compose so only a small portion of sky is seen.
3 Large white areas draw the viewer's eye, and should not be at the edge of the picture.

It's easy to mistakenly overlook distractions in the foreground such as weeds or twigs. Normally, you want everything to be in focus, although there might be times when you want to blur out the background, like if you are concentrating on a detail shot of a flower. If you have picked out a scene and have your camera mounted on a tripod while waiting for the light, take a look around to see what other views look interesting. Some places have a lot to offer. I agree with the cliché that beauty is everywhere. I have seen places that are really beautiful, but finding a way to make an image portray how I feel about it sometimes just doesn't happen. It is a challenge worth pursuing.

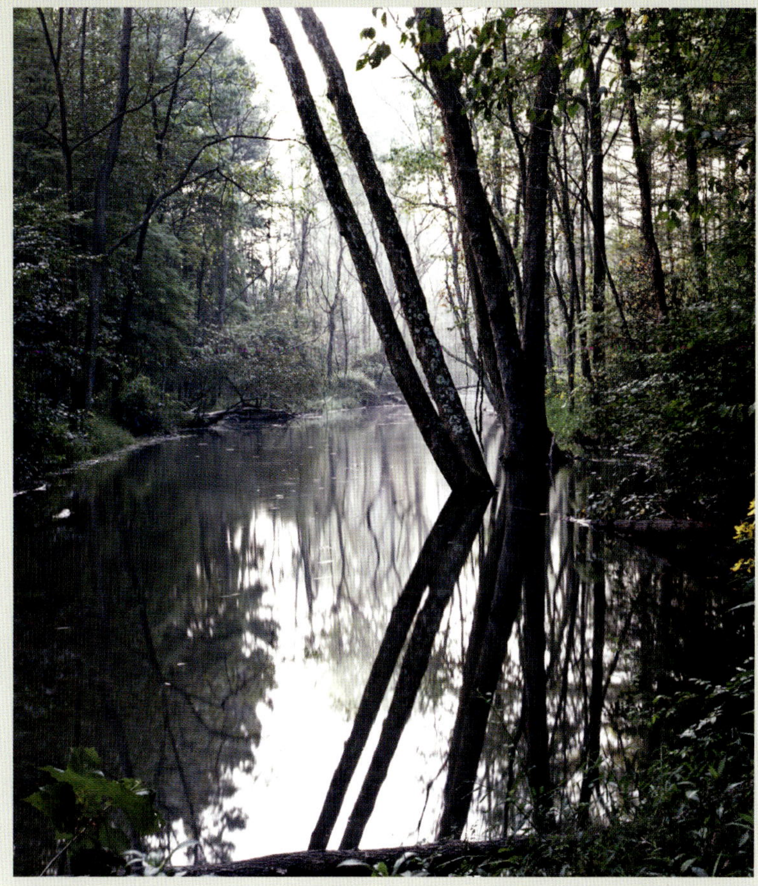

Jackson Creek in Yellowwood State Forest.

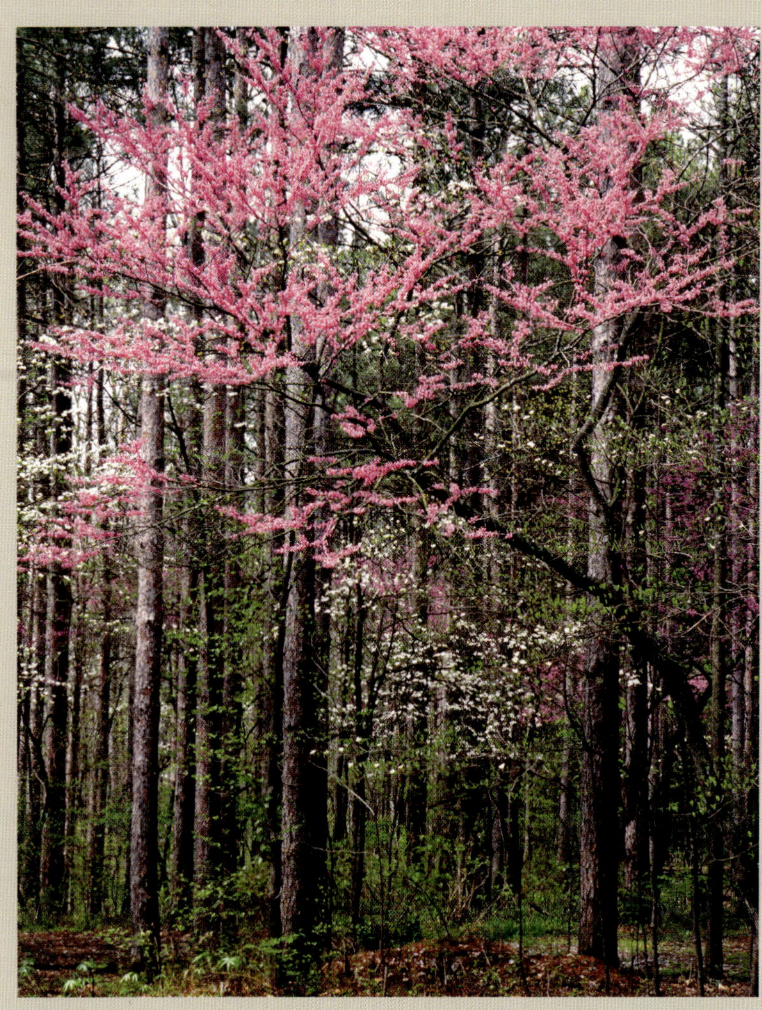

Yellowwood State Forest. *April.*

Rain and Fog

I find that unpleasant weather can be a time when there are interesting and unusual photographic opportunities. Damp and foggy conditions with drizzling rain are probably not what you imagine to be ingredients for an interesting landscape photograph, but it can be the opportunity to work toward a different effect. If you are out to shoot a scene with those conditions, have your camera mounted on a tripod with your camera and yourself protected. Of course, use common sense. No picture is worth risking being struck by lightning or other life-endangering situations. Shoot with a slow shutter speed (perhaps ¼ second or slower) and your camera will record a different effect than your eyes perceive. Take exposures using different slow shutter speeds to compare the effects. Your results might even resemble a painting because your camera is recording the scene viewed through the falling action of the rain. Imagine catching the wind-driven rain blowing almost horizontally across the scene. Experimenting with your camera will build on itself. With more experience and success you'll be encouraged to do it again. Be brave and try new things. As an example, the picture on page 82 was made when the conditions were combined snow, fog, and a drizzling rain. You don't have to show the images that don't make the grade, but one that "works" will make the effort well worth it and inspire you to experiment more. Experimenting costs nothing, but sometimes makes it worth the effort you made to be creative. You may scout out a location beforehand so that you think you have a pretty good idea what the picture you hope to shoot will look like, but there are an infinite variety of light conditions that cannot always be anticipated.

Fog brings simplicity to a scene because it seems to hide details and causes the viewer to dwell on what is most visible. It can also create a sense of intrigue. Realize that there will be times when you arrive at a place you know and plan to shoot it, but the shot just isn't there. That is part of the life of a landscape photographer. Other times, the same scene with other conditions will leave you standing there with your mouth open as you are awestruck at the beauty of it. If you had stayed in your comfortable bed, you would have missed the treat served up by the beautiful morning light!

The Sun

Do you want to make a landscape photograph that is really exciting? Include the sun! If you are shooting with film, one way to approximate a good exposure is to meter perhaps 45 degrees left or right of the sunrise. Set your shutter and aperture based on that reading. Then bracket especially on the side of underexposure. If you were to point your camera at the sun and take your light reading, you would get an underexposed image. An exposure meter is a valuable tool which many find hard to beat for determining correct exposure. With a single lense reflex (SLR) digital camera, you can check your histogram and see your result immediately. A histogram is a graph that can be used to determine if the image is over or under exposed. The camera's histogram can be more accurately used to judge the exposure, while the LCD screen allows the user to view the composition.

You can photograph the sun in several different ways. One way I like to include the sun is as a sun star. This means you let a tree or some other object block out part of the sun, but enough of the sun is visible to make a sun star. Try not to include so much of the sun that you get lens flare in the image, which is usually undesirable. When you try including the sun in the form of a sun star, you might be surprised at how fast the sun moves. It will

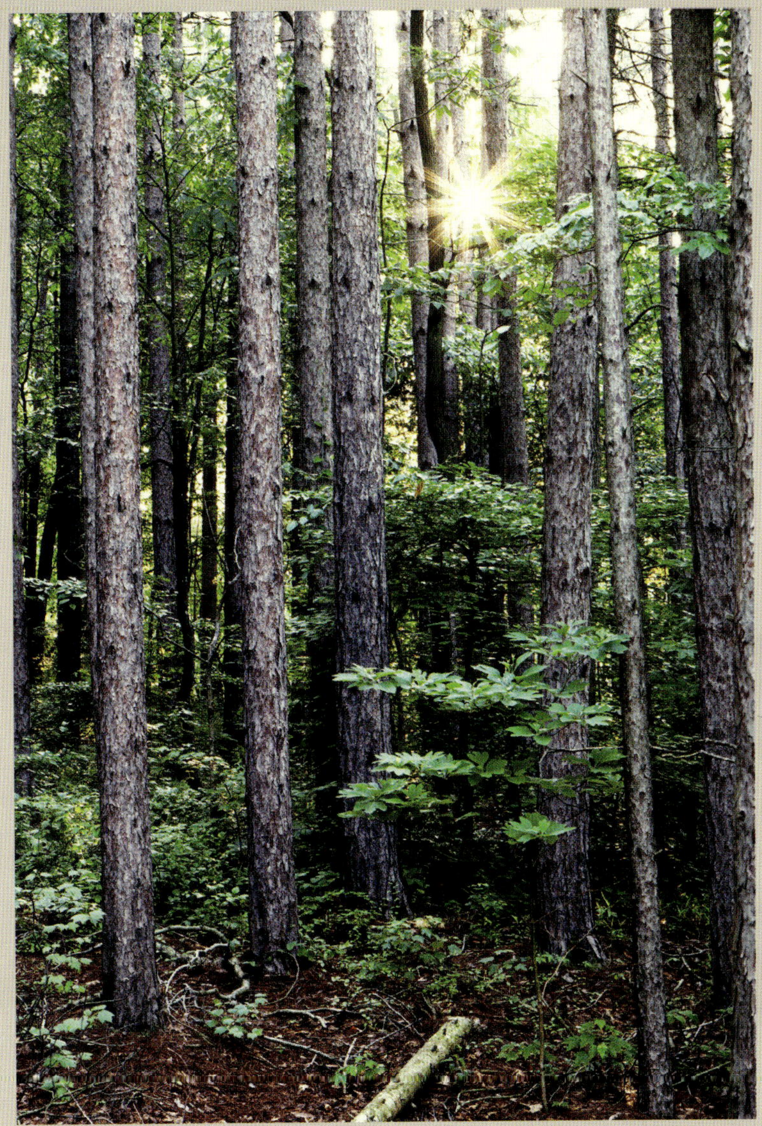

Brown County State Park.

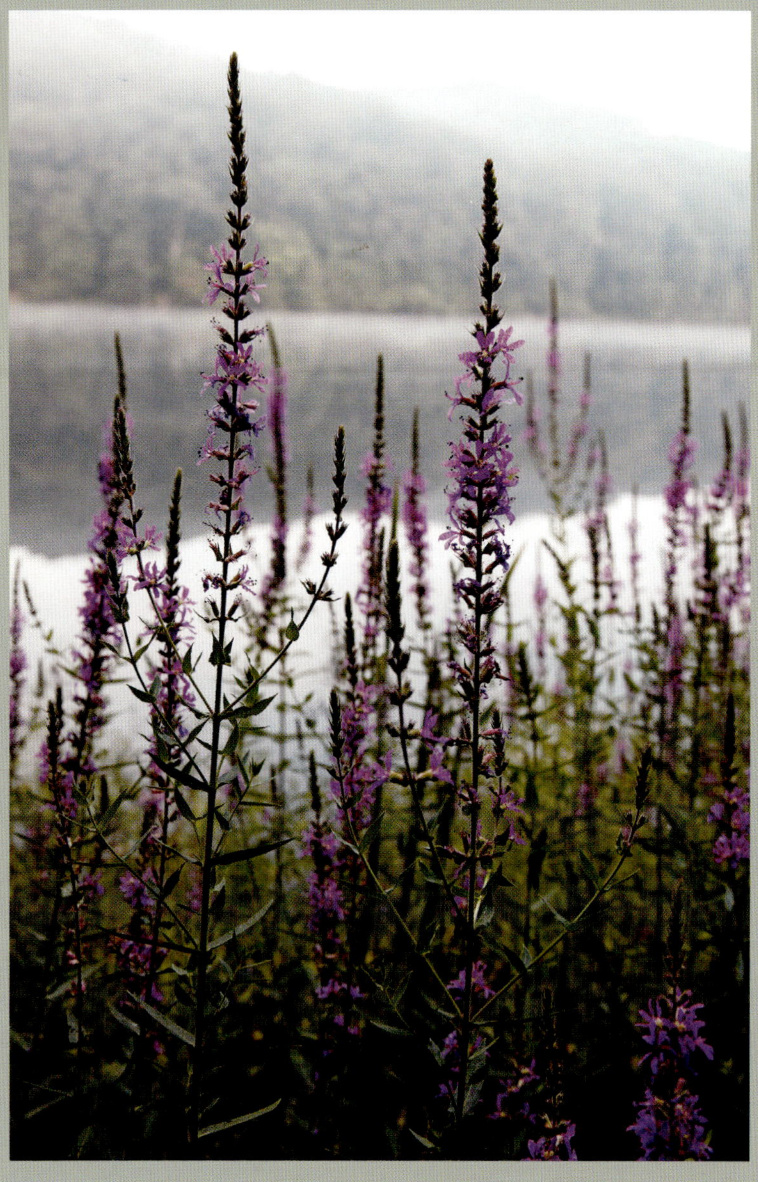

Yellowwood Lake in Yellowwood State Forest. *Summer.*

require that you keep moving the tripod every minute or less in order to block the sun to create your sun star.

Another possibility is shooting when there is enough atmospheric haze or dust to capture a nice image of the sun's disk shape shortly after sunrise. Note that the sun rises more quickly than you might think! Some mornings you might anticipate cloudy weather because no stars are visible while it is still dark, yet before sunrise the clouds might be lit by the sun below the horizon. The result can be breathtaking! Remember that sometimes your best opportunities in the mornings are before the sun breaks the horizon.

When photographing a stream, you have options with which to express your vision. If you want to show the flow of a stream, a slow shutter speed will give that impression. Remember, a slow shutter speed should be offset by setting your camera to a smaller aperture. Also, use a tripod to make everything that is not flowing appear sharp. The blur of flowing water is one of the few times when a portion of a scene is not rendered sharp. Normally you want everything sharp and in focus. If you prefer this style, use a fast shutter speed to "freeze" the action of the flowing water. However, some think this does not look as natural as the blur of water that you get with a slow shutter. If a pond or lake is part of the scene you want to shoot, keep in mind that the contrast between the water and its surroundings is lower before sunrise. The water will probably be calmer then, too. Calm water suggests quietness and solitude. When you are around a lake, look for reflections of trees, clouds, and other elements that beg to be photographed. This might be the time you want to freeze any motion on the water in order to make the most of the reflected image. Try using a shutter speed of 1/250 second.

For unique images, try looking straight up at the sky or straight down by your feet. What is the groundcover like? How do the trees look when your camera is pointed straight up? If the sun is not too high, a polarizing filter will darken a blue sky to make the leaves stand out more predominately.

Planning is a very helpful part of coming up with better landscape pictures. You should have your camera mounted in place on your tripod well before the time you plan to shoot. This assumes you're in a spot you have scouted out beforehand. Getting out early really pays off. Try to be there before fog burns off or steam disappears from the surface of a lake. Catching the sun at a low angle is highly desirable. Also, consider this fact as you try to make the most of your morning of shooting: higher elevations receive sunlight earlier than lower ones, which means you could begin the day shooting atop a hill or ridge. That could be followed by moving on to a valley or other location where you know of a scene you want to shoot as the sunlight arrives a bit later.

What about the details? Among the many facets of landscape photography, don't overlook the intricate handiwork that is tucked away in the details. It might help in finding nature's little gems if you switch your "big picture" perspective to what may be right at your feet. Having a close-up lens is very helpful in recording smaller things. Here again, simplicity reigns.

THE HUNT

As you seek fresh images in the county at places such as Brown County State Park, Yellowwood State Forest, and Hoosier National Forest, be a bit bold and check out places on private property as well. There are many private lakes and ponds to spark your interest, but finding them is the challenge. Be sure to always get permission before going on private property to take pictures.

Many owners prefer their privacy, but when I have been granted permission, it's a great opportunity to shoot a scene that most other photographers have not already shot, and I greatly appreciate the chance to do that. How

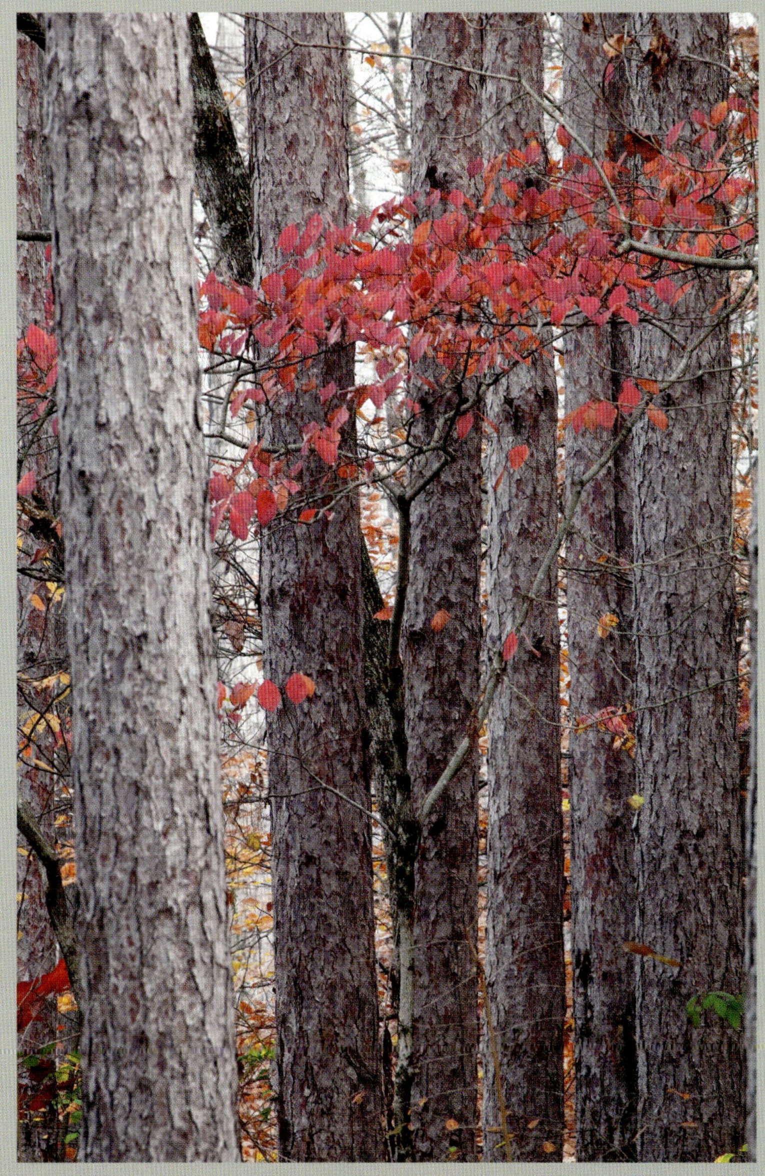

Yellowwood State Forest. *October.*

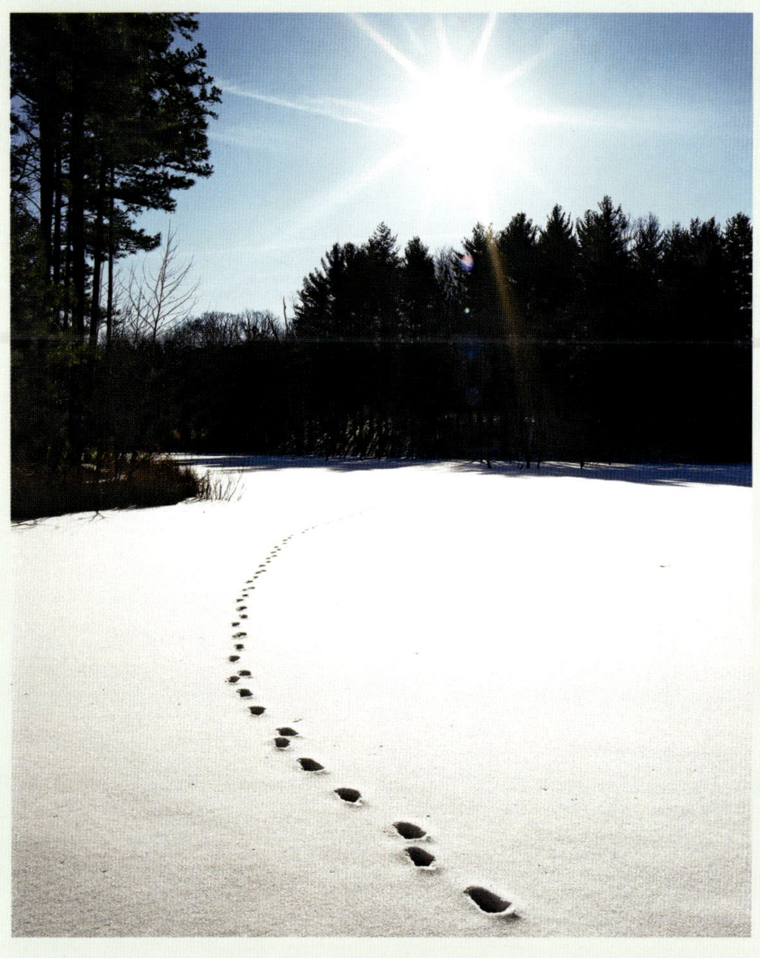

Sundance Pond in Hoosier National Forest. *January.*

do you find desirable scenes if they are not visible from the road? This is where your inquisitive nature will be put into practice. Find the property owner and show your sincerity by offering to provide a copy of a picture if allowed to shoot. I am always grateful to those owners who have allowed me onto their property. Take the time to revisit a location that interests you when atmospheric conditions have changed, or at different times of the year. The Midwest has all the variety that different seasons bring. Even after many visits to an area there are still new things to see. I've returned to some spots year after year, still finding new ways to get fresh images. I always find it interesting to see things I've missed on previous visits. So you can gain from going back again and again. See if there are other angles you had not come across the first time you were there. If you are set up and have to wait for the light, take a look around to see what you might be overlooking. Sometimes, I've found that the "other view" was more appealing than the one I had originally planned. Sometimes, you are just more alert and see the landscape differently than before. If you enjoy shooting landscapes, that means you like being outdoors, so returning to a place should be a delight for you.

YOUR PHOTOGRAPHIC STYLE

The landscape in some places may change over the years: houses spring up where large tracts of farmland are sold off; dredging of lakes changes landscapes (the Department of Natural Resources dredged Yellowwood Lake in 2008, changing the upper end of the lake); and gravel roads get paved. Brown County is a haven for those who want to get close to nature, seeking a respite from cities, expressways, shopping malls, and the hurried pace of life. It's also full of opportunities for exciting landscape photography.

Since light does its work silently, and clouds move into place with no announcement, it's important to watch for desirable changes that you'll want to capture. Many times when I'm out, I don't come up with a picture, but being out there makes a pleasant experience regardless. Keep your efforts in landscape photography on a level that allows you to enjoy it and don't feel you "have to produce." And, just as a writer does not include all that he writes in the final form, neither are you likely to include all the images you shoot in what you want to exhibit. Sometimes you use your camera to take visual notes so you can return at a later date. You need to experiment with your camera and offer only the best for others to see.

The more you do landscape photography, the more you will see that you are developing a style of your own. Some photographers work slowly and methodically while others seem to be haphazard in their method, but both get their image! If you have the gift of a "good eye," it will not be a contrived effort to have your own style, but you will feel at ease sometimes breaking the rules of composition and bringing your own approach to landscape photography. Let your creativity flow and don't adhere to a formula. Observe the light!

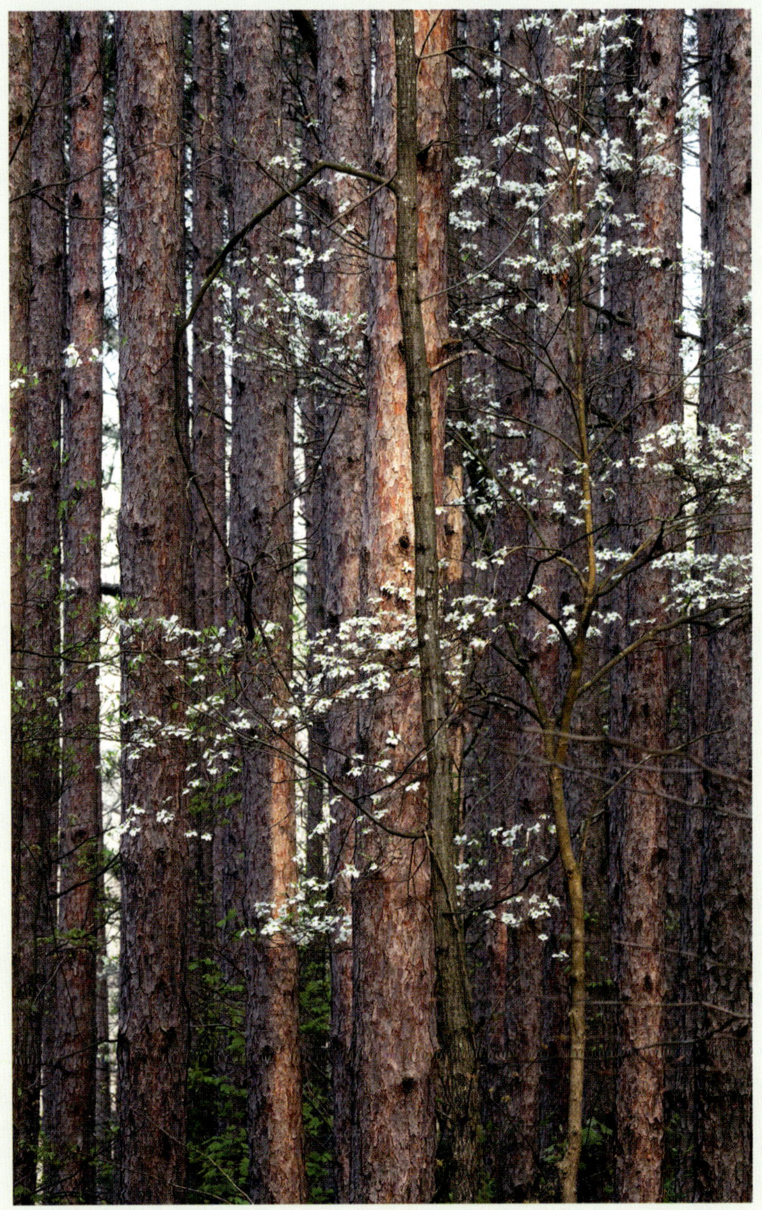

Yellowwood State Forest. *April.*

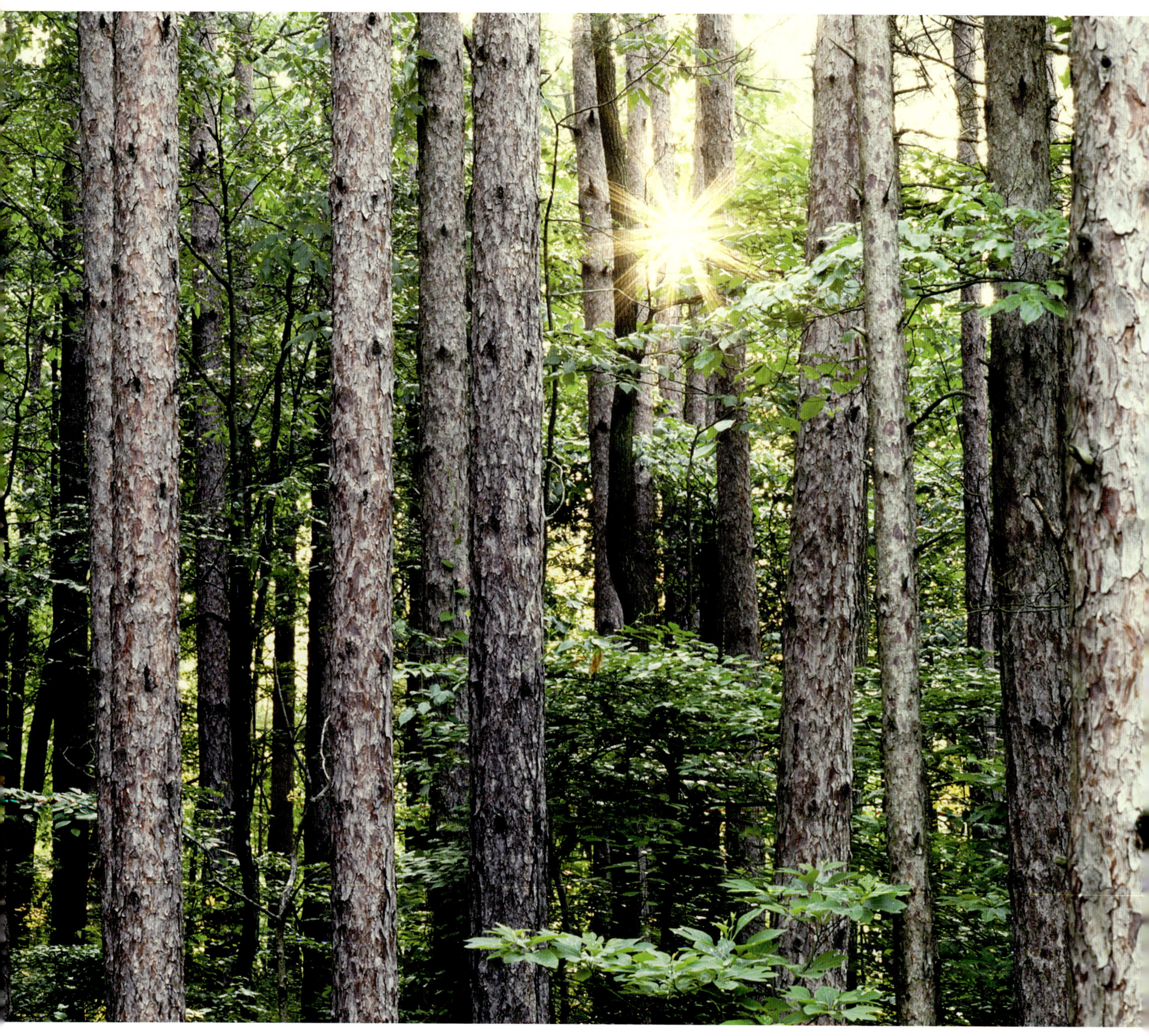

GARY MOORE earned his bachelor of fine arts degree at Ohio University with a major in photography. Moore enjoyed a long career as a staff photographer at *The Indianapolis Star and News* and retired in 2010. For several years, he has been blessed to "chase the light" in Brown County where he concentrates on photography of the landscape. Gary and his wife, Lynn, live in Indianapolis.

JAMES P. EAGLEMAN has been the naturalist at Brown County State Park for the past three decades. He has extensive knowledge of the Brown County landscape and its flora and fauna.

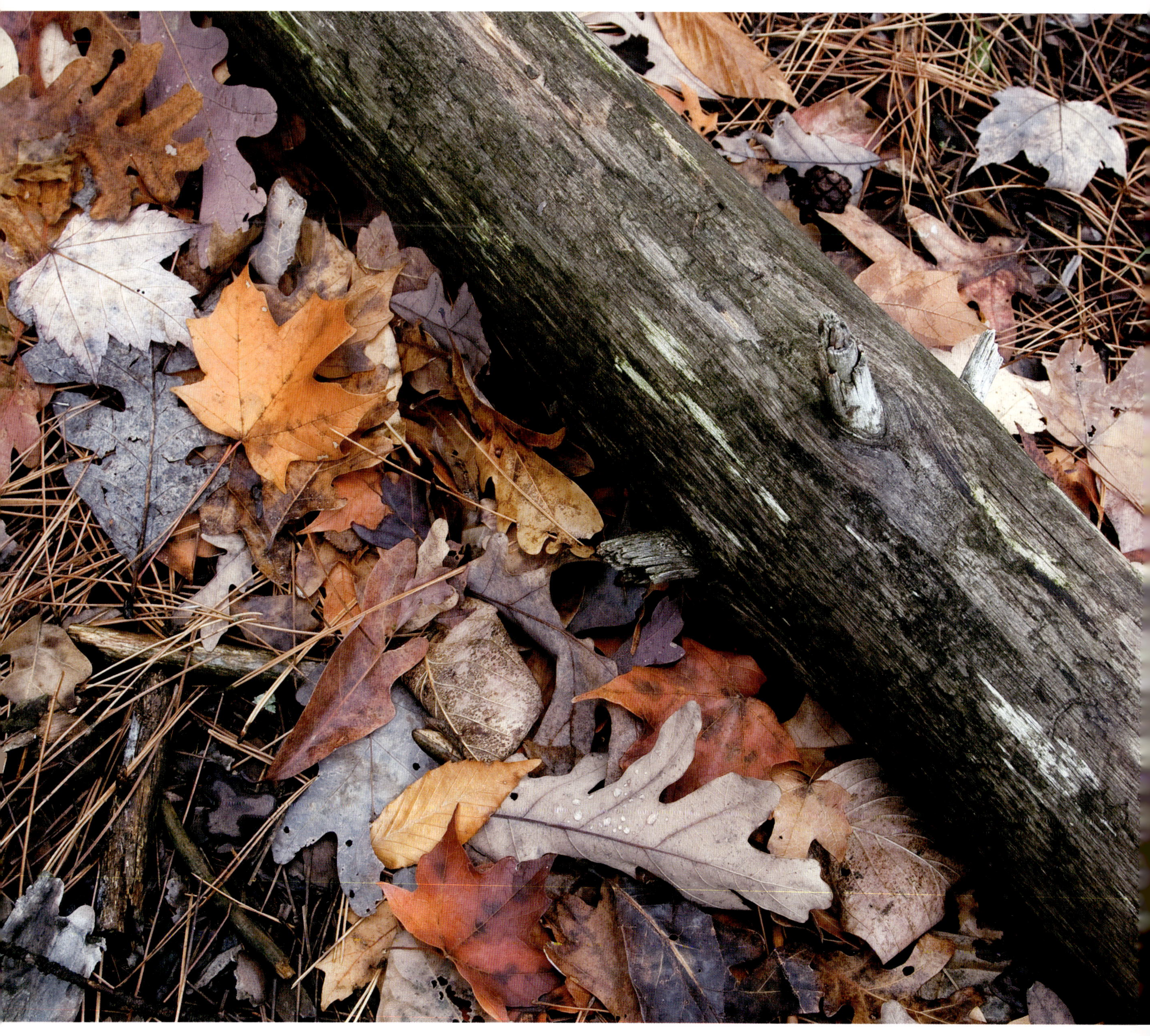

This book was designed and set in type by Jamison Cockerham at Indiana University Press, and printed by Four Color Imports, Ltd.

The font is Chaparral, designed by Carol Twombly in 2000, and issued by Adobe Systems.

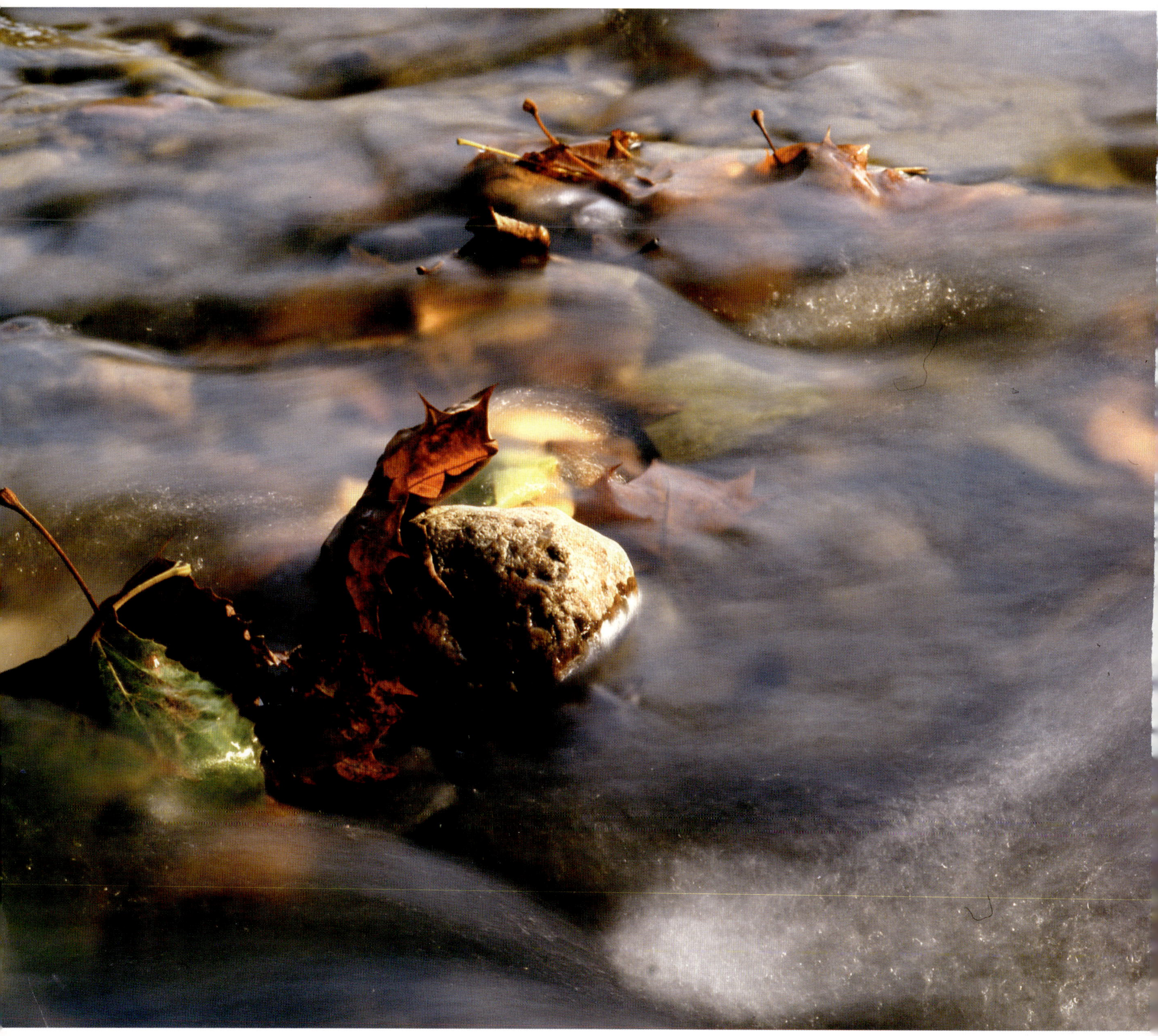